D0712503

MUSLIM BECOMING

MUSLIM BECOMING

ASPIRATION AND SKEPTICISM IN PAKISTAN

Naveeda Khan

Duke University Press Durham & London 2012

© 2012 Duke University Press
All rights reserved
Printed in the United States of
America on acid-free paper ∞
Designed by Amy Ruth Buchanan
Typeset in Quadraat by Keystone
Typesetting, Inc.
Library of Congress Cataloging-in-
Publication Data appear on the last
printed page of this book.

For Sophie

CONTENTS

ACKNOWLEDGMENTS

In the time it has taken to write this book on Pakistan, I have begun research and made swift progress toward a second, on Bangladesh. This discrepancy in the two temporalities of research and writing has me wondering if the difference lies in the fact that a first book takes longer to write than subsequent ones because one has never written a book before it. I don't think, however, that this fact alone is the reason, because I have come to understand that one's actions are not exclusively one's own, that they bear the impersonal impress of external forces. Pakistan underwent a sea change after I completed my doctoral research, with 9/11, participation in the United States' war against terrorism, and drastic rearrangements in its national politics, and this sea change, without a doubt, has left its mark in the temporality of this book, as I have had to return to Pakistan several times if only to absorb the shifting moods accompanying these changes. But I have also been slowed down by the overwhelming sense, at the completion of my dissertation in 2003, that while it was a more than adequate piece of writing I wanted to meditate further on Pakistan to be able to speak about it. While I wanted to critique its history and present, I wanted still to be affirmative. This was easier said than done, and the seven years that it has taken to complete this book have entailed considerable self-work, for me to be able to read widely and deeply into the literary and state archives and to visit and revisit friends and informants, some of whose fortunes have flailed and others flourished, while attempting to keep up with the changing political scene without falling into the apocalyptic mode that often creeps into discussions on Pakistan (remember Hillary Clinton describing the existential threat in Pakistan?). Along the way I was fortunate enough to be given the opportunity to edit a book on Pakistan, *Beyond Crisis: Re-evaluating Pakistan* (2010) whose each essay sustains me in its lively engagement with this place. To the generous contributors to that volume I owe an enormous debt.

This then is the place to acknowledge the importance of those who have helped forge my interests and, indeed, me. First, I thank Talal Asad and Kamala Visweswaran, who were at the New School for Social Research, for encouraging my interest in Islam in South Asia. I have also to thank Bill Roseberry and Rayna Rapp for their kind support. My deepest gratitude goes to my advisors at Columbia University, Brinkley Messick and Nick Dirks, and my undergraduate advisor, Hsi-Heuy Liang, from whom I learned my love of archives and texts. I wish to thank Partha Chatterjee and John Pemberton for their memorable classes, and Lisa Mitchell, Dard Neuman, and Fara Haniffa for their intellectual companionship and friendship in New York. At Johns Hopkins University, Veena Das and Bhrigupati Singh (now in Cambridge, Mass.) have been singular inspirations for the manner in which they think and the generosity with which they engage with others. They have been my intellectual beacons and indefatigable supporters in my long-drawn-out efforts to write the book I wanted. Both have spent innumerable hours reading and discussing each of my chapters with me. Others at Hopkins who have enriched the book include Richard Baxstrom (now in Edinburgh), William Connolly, Ranendra Das, Aaron Goodfellow, Jane Guyer, Sidharthan Maunaguru, Juan Obarrio, Anand Pandian, Sylvain Perdigon, and Deborah Poole. Graduate students who were kind enough to read and comment on various drafts include Caroline Block, Andrew Bush, and Bridget Kustin. Friends and colleagues who have given generously of their time in providing both critiques and intellectual nourishment include Asad Ali, Kamran Asdar Ali, Arjun Appadurai, Anna Bigelow, Iftikhar Dadi, Faisal Devji, Katherine Ewing, David Gilmartin, Shahnaz Hasan, Akbar Hyder, Matthew Hull, Humeira Iqtidar, Ruby Lal, Setrag Manoukian, Muhammad Khaled Masud, Stuart Mclean, Barbara Metcalf, Sameena Mulla, Gyan Pandey, Omar Qureshi, and Sharika Thiranagama. I thank Souleymane Bachir Diagne for his encouragement of my analysis of Muhammad Iqbal. The book is much improved by the suggestions of the three anonymous readers for Duke University Press and by my editors: the sage advice of Ken Wissoker and Leigh Barnwell's quick responses to my many queries. Max Bruce provided much appreciated help with transliteration.

The research for the book was funded by The International Dissertation Research Fellowship by the Social Science Research Council, Fulbright Hayes, the Dissertation Improvement Grant by the National Science Foundation, and the International Fellowship by the Wenner-Gren Foundation. The writing was funded by the Lindt Fellowship from Columbia University and the Jennings Randolph Peace Fellowship from the United States Institute of Peace. Follow-up research visits were sponsored by the Franklin Grant from the American Philosophical Association. I am also very thankful to the Department of Anthropology at Johns Hopkins University, particularly Jane Guyer, for giving me a semester off from teaching at the final stages of the book.

The support of friends and family has been very necessary for sustaining me. I thank Rosalba Cohen, who took beautiful care of my children when they were younger, Dina Hossain, Lopita Huq, Elizabeth Rice, Aleeze Sattar, Cissie Scoggin, Gabrielle Martino, Carolyn Norris, Bernadette Wegenstein, my two sisters Naureen Khan and Sabina Noor, and my brother Shahed Khan for their many kindnesses toward me. Friends in Pakistan who make me delight in returning include Salima and Shoaib Hashmi, Lubna Shah and Ahmed Kamal and their lovely family, who opened their homes and hearts to me, Razzaq and Mushtaque are my own terrific brothers, Junaid sahib and his family, and Rashid Rana, Quddus Mirza and Sohail Worraich. I was particularly happy to befriend Sikandar, Bina, Zara, Suroosh Irfani, Nadeem Omar, and Sadaf Aziz on my most recent visit. My parents, Munawar and Shafique, and my in-laws Bob and Darlene have been heroic in their efforts to support my efforts to complete this book, but none have been as heroic as my husband Bob and children Sophie and Sulayman, who have borne my long absences with fortitude and greeted my return with such joy that it made me forget the pain of separation. Long ago before Sulayman was born I promised the book to Sophie and later, much later, when I declared that I had finished my book, she asked what had become of the first. This book is dedicated to Sophie for her patience and love.

Some of the material presented in chapter 1 appeared in "Mosque Construction or the Violence of the Ordinary" in my edited book *Beyond Crisis: Reevaluating Pakistan* (2010). A section of chapter 3 appeared in "Trespasses of the State: Ministering the Copyright to Theological Dilemmas" in the *Bare Acts* issue of the Sarai Programme, while a section of chapter 5 appeared in "The Speech of Generals: Some Meditations on Pakistan," posted on the

SSRC Forum *Pakistan in Crisis* on January 2, 2008. In an earlier incarnation chapter 4 was "Children and Jinn: An Inquiry into an Unexpected Friendship During Uncertain Times" in *Cultural Anthropology*. I wish to thank the publishers and the journals for permitting me to reuse the material. I thank Sabir Nazar for permission to reproduce his cartoons in chapter 5.

In the Provincial Assembly Library

I arrived at the historic city of Lahore in Punjab to research neighborhood mosques built after the formation of Pakistan in 1947, intending to provide an empirical account of the integration of Islam into the state administration and the national imagination. Mosques became central to my study because, in earlier trips, I found people describing Pakistan, literally the Land of the Pure, as a mosque. Two days after my arrival in Lahore, General Pervez Musharraf declared martial law in the country. I expected at least a few dissenting voices and public protests. Instead, Musharraf's action was met by a calm that seemed to amount to acceptance or at least resignation toward the turn of events. This reaction was not entirely surprising, as Pakistan had already experienced three periods of military rule since its rocky formation. But it was not as if all conversations, debates, argumentation, or even dissent of the contemporary moment had ceased. For instance, while working in the library of the Provincial Assembly of Punjab studying records relating to the history of mosques in Pakistan, I came across four librarians, all Muslims, engaged in pious pursuits delineated by their individual pathways through Islam. It was in their reflections on what nature of Muslim they were and what kind of world they were living that I first found evaluations, even critiques, of this moment. Here is an account of an argument among the librarians in which I learned how everyday expressions of religiosity simultaneously impinge upon the local, the political, and the spiritual, in the temporal registers of possible pasts and futures. (In the interest of protecting my informants I have used pseudonyms for them and their neighborhoods and mosques except in the instances in which they requested that I not change their names.)

Of the four librarians I befriended in the Assembly Library, I identified one as a Shi'a (he was the most reticent of the four) and the rest as Sunnis. Among the latter three, one self-identified as Deobandi, the second as Ahl-e Hadis, and the third as Barelwi, the three major pathways (sing. *maslak*, pl. *masalik*) within Sunni Islam in South Asia. Akbar, the Ahl-e Hadis, prepared engaging *taqarir* (speeches) filled with vivid imagery that he gave in his capacity as a volunteer imam (prayer leader) in his neighborhood mosque. Naz, the Barelwi, spoke of his love for his *pir* (spiritual guide) whom he sought out whenever his days would allow and from whom he heard stories of the Prophet, his Companions, and the *waliullahs* (lit. friends of God, saints). Yaseen, the Deobandi, worked arduously to build the mosque in his neighborhood while his own house was only halfway complete. Each embodied his individual maslak almost to the point of stereotype. Akbar was strident, Naz was deferential, and Yaseen deferred knowledge to the proper religious authority. Riaz, the Shi'a, spoke the least about religious matters, agreeing with whatever was being discussed before quickly absenting himself. They knew well one another's positions on controversial topics and fell into playful hectoring and habituated responses. Their religious differences informed their relations but rarely disrupted their lives together, except in one incident, in which the high stakes of their differences from one another became clear to me.

Akbar, the Ahl-e Hadis librarian, arranged for me to speak to another member of the staff of the Provincial Assembly, someone he described in awestruck tones as very respected in his neighborhood mosque and in the space used by the Ahl-e Hadis in the Assembly building for saying their daily prayers (*namaz*). He would have a lot to teach me about mosques in Islam, Akbar said. We seated ourselves at a table in the library stacks and I settled into conversation with this person, a stern-faced man sporting a long, untrimmed beard in accordance with Ahl-e Hadis standards. As was typical in my interviews with such local authorities of Islam, I barely had to pose a question before he launched into a lengthy description of the importance of prayer in mosques. He spoke generally of the superiority of Ahl-e Hadis mosques as they allowed laymen to give sermons and encouraged women's participation in congregational prayer. In the midst of this speech he paused to mention that he had once gone on hajj (pilgrimage to Mecca). Sensing my opportunity to learn about his personal experience of mosques, I asked him if he would recount his memories of praying in the mosques in Mecca and Medina. He emitted a dismissive sound saying, "I did not pray at the Prophet's mosque in Medina."

Naz, the librarian of the Barelwi maslak, who usually sat in the stacks, looked over from his seat. He asked my interviewee how he could have denied himself such a pleasure. "It isn't a pleasure to pray at Medina, it is bid'a [unlawful innovation]." Seeing my confusion, since I had not heard anything against praying in the Prophet's mosque, the Ahl-e Hadis authority continued:

> It is commendable to pray at the Prophet's mosque, but it isn't necessary. Some among us have made it into a requirement by saying such things as, the Prophet is alive there, he can hear your prayers and he can grant you your wishes. Such claims are bid'a. One cannot pray there until such time as this bid'a has been vanquished, and there is not an iota of doubt that one prays there only out of respect for the early community of Muslims.

Two clean-shaven staff members dressed in Western clothes had joined us by this time. They sided with my interviewee while at the same time berating him for bringing up such issues in public since they caused dissension. An upset-looking Naz said in a challenging voice, "What would you say to the fact that I had *ziyarat* of the Prophet?" *Ziyarat* means going on a pilgrimage to a shrine housing the body of a Muslim saint. I knew Naz had not been to Medina. I took this to be his respectful way of saying that he had seen the Prophet. This claim took me by surprise because in all the time that I had been speaking with Naz he had never once mentioned seeing the Prophet, presumably in a dream. Such dreams were given great importance by my interlocutors. Even if no one knew what the Prophet looked like, it was understood that one would know that it was the Prophet that one had seen, for Satan could not impersonate him. Perhaps Naz's previous silence on the matter was explained by the fact that to speak about such an experience in contemporary Pakistan was to risk people's jealousy or suspicion that one was being a *munafiq* (hypocrite). But there was a further claim in Naz's statement. The fact of seeing the Prophet in one's dreams was premised upon his being alive in his grave in Medina. There was the subtlest suggestion on Naz's part that the Prophet could appear in people's dreams of his own volition and not solely at God's will (Kugle 2007). The Ahl-e Hadis authority snorted derisively at Naz's words, saying that this belief in a Prophet who willed his own appearance was similar to the Twelver Shi'a belief in the missing imam who was said to have occulted himself in order to re-appear one day (Arjomand 1996). The critical comparison to Shi'a belief obviously hurt Naz, who looked as if he would cry.

Akbar quickly came to Naz's defense. "Surely, you do not discount the possibility that the Prophet may appear in dreams. You know about different kinds of *wahy* [revelation]," he said respectfully yet forcefully to his Ahl-e Hadis acquaintance. By this I took Akbar to refer to the claim I have often heard that each dream bears a tiny fraction of revelation (Mittermiaer 2007). The two clean-shaven men kept escalating the palpable tension by saying such things as, "It is not a good thing to lie about seeing the Prophet." "You know that the Prophet is just a man. He always said so himself. So he must have turned to dust by now, just as any of us will."

Even though I had heard similar statements in the past, from Akbar no less, such utterances felt wrong to both Akbar and myself coming at this moment insofar as they were said in evident mockery of Naz, to impugn his love for the Prophet and make him out to be ignorant, even irrational. I plunged into the argument by asking the two men, "How can you be so sure? What about the body of the martyr?" It is said that the body of the martyr lived on in the same condition as it was at the moment it was struck down, so that on Judgment Day the martyr could bear testimony to the nature of his or her death (Cook 2008). This made the sites of fallen martyrs efficacious for whispering one's needs and desires for intercession with God, as with the burial sites of saints. The reason I did not make a comparison between the body of the Prophet and those of saints was that there was a regional history of reformist rebuke of such intercessionary practices as accretions of custom upon Islam (Metcalf 1987b). The bodies of martyrs were not as easy to dismiss, given that the newspapers daily reported on the many Pakistanis being "martyred" in causes abroad, from Kashmir to Chechnya.

My Ahl-e Hadis interviewee stood up abruptly saying, "This is a waste of my time," and left. Akbar dragged Naz away, while casting dark looks at me. The interview had clearly spun out of my control and become a heated argument about sensitive religious topics, such as the nature of the Prophet's body after his physical death. The two clean-shaven men who had joined our conversation sat waiting for me to explain my research to them so that they could correct any misunderstanding I might have. "These people are *jahil* [ignorant]," they said by way of explanation. Trembling as I left, I wondered just how close I had come that day to witnessing a physical fight and a possible accusation of blasphemy against the Prophet. The latter is a much-utilized charge enabled by the blasphemy law within the Penal Code of Pakistan bequeathed to the country by British colonial authorities (A. Ahmed 2006).

Time as Becoming

Such heated arguments on theological matters were not unusual, as I found over the course of my fieldwork, and they spoke to the relative freedom of religious speech even during times of martial law. But these arguments acquire a certain menacing quality in light of recent events unfolding in Pakistan, in which a non-Muslim woman was incarcerated on charges of defaming the Prophet in the course of a verbal fight with Muslim women, and one of the politicians who spoke up on her behalf was assassinated. On one hand, these events speak to a possible loss of tolerance for such theologically inflected conversations, as if no one but Muslims and only specific kinds of Muslims may speak of the Prophet. On the other, the very existence of such conversations may be read as a manifestation of a more deep-seated problem imputed to Pakistan. That problem has been analyzed as a lack of consensus on what Pakistan was to be among its various constituents at the time of its creation (Jalal 1994) or as an enduring contradiction within Pakistan's history and politics between a commitment to existing hierarchies and tribal ties and a universalistic religion whose vision of community transcended such ties (Gilmartin 1988). These important analyses question the simplistic association of Islam with Pakistan. But they have also been met by vigorous arguments that, although Muslims from different parts of colonial India did not necessarily share a single vision for Pakistan, the importance of Islam for Pakistan was taken for granted by all (Shaikh 2009). This reinstatement of the importance of Islam for Pakistan, however, still faults Pakistanis for their subsequent failure to achieve consensus on Islam, a failure that is claimed to have produced unending confusion in the political sphere. In other words, the argument in the Assembly Library remains proof of the failure of Pakistanis to develop a clear, consistent relation to Islam.

Rather than assume that such arguments manifest fault lines in Pakistan's relation to Islam, I suggest that by staying with this argument in the library we may see what other elements constitute it. For instance, the incident indicates the entrenched differences that inform maslak-based identities such as those between the Ahl-e Hadis and the Barelwi. It suggests a shared yet differentiated library of textual references within the *hadis* (sayings) of the Prophet. It increases the number of positions available to a pious self with respect to Islam, such as that of a Muslim who gives sermons in his mosque, or one who loves the friends of God, or one who builds mosques, to extrapolate a few such positions from the statements of my librarian friends.

What if we were to not focus on any of these elements individually but instead think of the potential lines of movement among entrenched differences, cited texts, and possible positions generated by selves encountering others in the world? From such a perspective one would not see the librarians' argument as the revelation of longstanding rifts in everyday life. Instead, one would see it as an encounter that made each of the participants align with tendencies such as the lure of thorny theological issues, the uptake of conversation, the unveiling of secrets about oneself in public, the deployment of risky arguments, the risking of the other's disbelief, even disparagement, the unexpectedness of someone crossing over from his entrenched place within a maslak to support a friend of another maslak in the midst of a heated exchange, and the distinct possibility of physical violence and legal retaliation.

On one hand, no hearts and minds were turned in the course of this argument and each person went away convinced of the superiority of his religious maslak and furious at the other. On the other, the argument displayed openness to such conversations, the intensities that burn within them, the unexpected gestures of incorporation, and the possibility of violent exclusions. In other words, this argument becomes an event constituted of movements not easily assimilated into the familiar argument of the lack of consensus over Islam in Pakistan.

Moreover, beyond informing the event as it unfolded, these movements and tendencies accompany the memory and narrative of the encounter and keep the unexpected and surprising quality of the event close to the stereotyped performance of religious differences, including the inevitable, seemingly disappointing denouement to the argument. By enfolding such movements and tendencies, time as becoming runs parallel to time oriented to specific ends and introduces becoming into the event and its afterlife. As Henri Bergson (1996) elucidates, in its first mode, time retains its capacity to surprise, to fork in ways that diverge from those expected; in its second, teleological mode, time's effects are fully anticipated or may be reconstructed in retrospect.

Time as becoming, as it plays out in the argument in the Assembly Library, informs the central ambition of this book. I aim to give an account of Pakistan that demonstrates its inheritance of an Islam with an open future and a tendency toward experimentation, alongside its much criticized historical record. In so doing, I pick an argument with those who would claim that Pakistan has not effected a unitary relation to Islam. Instead, I claim, time creates more movements, both actual and potential, than may be found within the historical records, and attention to time helps to draw a fairly consistent picture of Islam with an open future. Furthermore, I argue, experimentation entails the doing and the redoing of known forms (such as disputation) in a new spirit of striving, a notion that runs counter to the position that experimentation entails innovation in self-making, societal arrangements, and the form of the state. Disputation is a known form of interaction with much discussed risks and ill effects within the history of Islam, so to reveal the element of becoming within it means also attending to the risks courted by such becoming, notably the risk of alienation from one's world or the estrangement of others within it. Becoming means coming to terms with the trajectories and crystallizations of tendencies within the transcriptions of the state and in public culture. And it means excavating the resources that this way of being Muslim may give to itself to reflect upon, evaluate, and even renew its inheritance of Islam. To lay the foundations for my approach to Pakistan and Islam, I will now turn to some key terms and issues that I refer to in my analysis.

Aspiration in the Imagination of Pakistan

As historians have noted, the origins of Pakistan are mired in contradictions (Gilmartin 1988, Jalal 1994). Further literature suggests that Pakistan has not made itself into an exemplar of a pluralist Islamic state or Muslim nation (Rahman 1982, Cohen 2006). If anything, the historical records confirm that Pakistan may have deservedly earned itself the reputation of being intolerant of differences internal to Islam (Lau 1996). A much discussed instance of this is the state's treatment of the Ahmadiyya, who were declared non-Muslims by an act of constitution in 1974, following a long period of agitation against them from the 1950s onward. Given my interest in approaching this history from the perspective of plenitude rather than of lack, what would constitute plenitude within this archive of obscured ideological visions, lack of political cohesion, and state-sponsored persecution?

In his account of Pakistan in the years shortly after its formation, the theologian W. C. Smith gives us a possible line of becoming that moves through these historical records. Smith visited West Pakistan in 1948, a year after its formation. In *Islam in Modern History* (1957) he writes how almost every Pakistani spoke then of participating in something new, never before seen in the region, even in the history of Islam. When he inquired further into this newness of Pakistan, most were hard pressed to provide any specifics. What if we were to take seriously this original sense of inaugurating something new that Smith makes so palpable?

> We do not mean—and certainly the Pakistani devotees did not mean— that any independent state comprising Muslims is automatically Islamic. This is in fact not so. Egyptians, Turks, and other Muslims do not talk, do not feel, about their body politic as Pakistanis began excitedly to do about theirs. . . . Certainly Pakistanis themselves strongly felt their nation to be an Islamic state in a fashion unique in the modern world. Indeed, part of their enthusiasm was precisely for the point that they were doing something for Islam that other present-day Muslims were not doing: they were offering it a political existence that otherwise it has not had for centuries. Yet once again, their claim was not based on what their nation had accomplished; rather, on the spirit that it embodied. (Smith 1957: 217)

At first glance, Smith appears to say that Pakistan's newness hinged upon its claim to have given Islam a nation-state when he writes, "They were offering it a political existence that otherwise it has not had for centuries." This is how Pakistan's attempted contribution to Islam is usually understood. Consequently, we have a range of scholarly works analyzing and very effectively skewering the Islamic state forms that have devolved in theory and practice in Pakistan (Binder 1960, I. Ahmed 1988).

On closer scrutiny I find Smith claiming something a little different. He does not take the state form to be Pakistan's primary mandate. Rather, he takes the *aspiration* to the state form to be more important: "The Islamic state is the ideal to which Pakistan, it has been felt, should aspire. It is the aspiring that has been fundamental; not this or that pattern of the ideal" (1957: 240). Put differently, "not this or that pattern of the ideal" suggests that we should not assume that a particular Islamic state is the end point of Pakistan's aspiration. Smith writes further: "The demand that Pakistan should be an Islamic state has been a Muslim way of saying that Pakistan should build for itself a good society" (240). In other words, the demand for a state may be equally a demand for a society or a self.

Smith views the achievement of Pakistan to be, in his own words, the initiation of a *"process of becoming,"* "to achieve an Islamic state was to attain not a form but a process." Further on he writes, "an *actual* Islamic state is a state that its Muslim people are trying to make *ideally* Islamic" (italics in original). Consequently, even if an Islamic state were in place in Pakistan, efforts would continuously be under way to render it more perfect, to be led by the question of "what was to become of it" (1957: 219).

The ruminative words of a bystander give us an inkling of the upsurge of excitement accompanying the creation of Pakistan. They give expression to a tendency that Smith calls aspiration, which is not directed at achieving an ideal final form of an Islamic state, society, or self but rather at sustaining the striving toward one. Taking my cue from these writings, I ask what would it mean to look at Pakistan from the starting point that Smith provides? In other words, what would it mean to see Pakistan's historical record as shaped by the aspiration to strive as Muslims, while the question of what kind of Muslim one should be, and what kind of Islamic state or Muslim society one should strive for, remains obscure?

The aspiration to continual striving of which W. C. Smith speaks has little presence within the historical records of Pakistan or even within writings on contemporary Islam, in which the tendency has been to emphasize the increasing loss of originality and lack of vitality in modern Muslim thought (Al-Azmeh 1993, Lewis 2003). Perhaps this is because the aspiration to strive is only a tendency, rather than a social movement such as reform or piety with identifiable advocates and trajectories (see, for example, Metcalf 1987b, Devji 1993, Brown 1996). But its importance cannot be emphasized enough, for it provides a different perspective on Pakistan's historical records. From this perspective the contradictions, shortcomings, and failures in this history may be seen to arise not out of the lack of vision of what relationship Pakistan should bear to Islam but out of experimentation in seeking points of relatedness between the two. Thus, in this book rather than take Jinnah and factional politics as the start to Pakistan's history, my focus on aspiration finds its grounds in the intellectual inheritance of Pakistan, more specifically in the figure of Muhammad Iqbal, the poet, philosopher, and politician. Iqbal, who is considered the spiritual founder of Pakistan, provides the philosophical arguments for recasting Islam as an open religion with possible futures as yet uninstantiated. And he does this by means of a critical engagement with none other than Bergson, who was precisely preoccupied with time as becoming.

Religious Disputation and Its Spatial Extension

A trace of aspiration within mainstream Pakistani society is found in the classical disputation form, to which the argument that I witnessed in the Assembly Library bears kinship. A brief review of the place of disputation (*jadal*) within Islamic history and of such modern-day permutations as *bahas* (argument) and *munazara* (debate) will suggest how Muslim striving in Pakistan may rely not only upon a picture of Islam as open, but also upon the use of conventional forms such as debate and polemic, or even the building of mosques, in order to effect experimentation.

Whether we consider the Islamic disputation form to show the influence of *kalam* (theology) (Makdisi 1981) or *falsafa* (philosophy) (Miller 1984), it is clear that a tradition and ethics of debate and disputation was well entrenched among Muslim theologians and philosophers by the tenth century CE (Miller 1984, Lazarus-Yafeh et al. 1999). In fact it was considered an act of piety to engage in disputation, as it was in the service of the truth about the divine. However, unlearned use of the method came up for criticism by scholars who felt that it weakened faith by subjecting religious truisms to the force of logical argumentation (Al-Ghazali 1980). The continued attraction of scholars to theological disputation initiated a series of manuals directed at restraining wrongful behavior in the event of such encounters (Lazarus-Yafeh et al. 1999).

While Muslim disputation in South Asia incorporates this longer history, it came into greater visibility in the colonial era as the means by which Muslims tackled the onslaught of Christian proselytizing while continuing to spar with authorities of other Indian religions (Powell 1993). Given the fraught place of the Ahmadiyya in the region, it is noteworthy that they were actively involved in disputation both on behalf of all Muslims and against specific Muslims who protested their emergence (Lavan 1974, Friedmann 2003a). The study of these disputations show that while the *ulama* (religious scholars), as recognized authorities, were the ones who most often came face to face with one another, lay educated Muslims were increasingly involved in such confrontations (Powell 1992).

Anthropologists have shown that debate and discourse comprise important elements by which lay Muslims deliberate on what it is to be Muslim (Fischer and Abedi 1990, Bowen 1993). The almost formal qualities of the question and answer, the references to textual proofs and counterproofs, the attempt to bring about a defeat of one's opponent, or to read signs of defeat from the surface of these debates further hint at the classical form of disputation. At the same time, the conditions of possibility for debate and discourse in more contemporary contexts are quite distinct (Eickelman and Anderson 2003). Within this very changed historical moment, to what extent can one argue for the continued significance of age-old theological arguments, such as that of the status of the Prophet's body after his physical death, and the endurance of the classical form of disputation within contemporary arguments? And what relations do such continuities bear to Pakistan's aspiration to strive?

The concept of political theology provides us a strong orientation to the manner in which theology animates everyday conversations. The credit for revitalizing this concept in the early twentieth century is most often given to Carl Schmitt (2006), who is understood as claiming that politics discovers its modernity by repressing the theological foundations of its concepts and practices. A different reading of Schmitt has him saying that theology was always only about worldly politics. Hent de Vries (2006) offers this more nuanced reading of Schmitt's position. He suggests that we not attempt to decide once and for all whether Schmitt speaks on behalf of religious transcendence or worldly politics. The usefulness of the concept of political theology is that it allows the analysis to run in both directions, with the transcendental coming into play in some instances and worldly life in others. Put differently, de Vries makes an argument for both the transcendent vector and the immanent quality of political theology.

Bhrigupati Singh (2006) provides a further link between political theology and striving. He argues that instantiations of political theology (he takes Gandhi as his example) have to be understood as modalities of self-making and self-perfecting, what the moral philosopher Stanley Cavell calls moral perfectionism (2004). Bringing these perspectives on political theology to bear upon Pakistan, I posit that religious argumentation may be seen as expressive of ongoing striving. Furthermore, as I show, such argumentation finds its spatial extension in the building and fighting over neighborhood mosques such as those in Lahore. In other words, one works on oneself by revisiting and reinhabiting theological conundrums through words and practices.

Skepticism in Everyday Life, State Transcriptions, and Public Culture

Insofar as the rise and proliferation of disputation as a form has raised considerable concern within Islamic history, which continues into the present, it is important to consider the risks that the ulama and other commentators understand to accompany debate and discourse as a mode of lay striving. The major anxiety over disputation most often expressed in classical accounts is that indulgence in abstract thinking and theological questions stands to undermine the tenacity of individual faith and reduce the hold of the daily obligations of ritual worship (Al-Ghazali 1980, 2000). One also hears strains of this anxiety in contemporary discussions by the Pakistani ulama on the perceived eagerness for debate among lay Muslims. While the threats to faith and ritual obligation are the crucial concerns, an accompanying concern that religious scholars voice is that disputation may lead to a diminishing attachment to worldly life or stakes in the social (Ludhianvi n.d.). While Muslims are exhorted to treat this world as only a way station toward the otherworld, a refusal of worldly life and a turn away from it have never been authorized expressions of piety. And the annals of Islamic history depict consistent disapproval of this course of action (Bulliet 1995, Hodgson 1977).

One may productively bring this concern over disputation together with an anthropological line of analysis interested in the micropolitics of everyday religiosity. In a special issue on "Islam, Politics, Anthropology" of the *Journal of the Royal Anthropological Institute* (Oscella and Soares 2009), we find accounts of Muslim religiosity within changing political and economic realities. Several of the authors examine, for instance, the inconsistencies in observance that mark the lives of Muslim youth (Schielke 2009) and the influence of travel and play in inciting curiosity about religious learning (Marsden 2009). While these essays attend to the different arrangements of religion and politics at various levels, including that of the everyday, they don't sufficiently attend to the everyday as giving distinct contours to social life, for instance by introducing specific stresses and fissures into collective existence. In her anthropological attention to this dimension of social life, Veena Das (1998) draws upon Stanley Cavell to name the everyday forces tearing at social life as "skepticism." It is useful to draw out their understanding of skepticism as it resonates with the risks that religious scholars highlight as introduced by disputation into lay practices of religiosity. I should say at the outset that skepticism here is not the opposite of religious belief but rather a tendency within social and intersubjective relations.

According to Cavell (1982, 1988), skepticism is not limited to philosophical efforts at securing one's knowledge of the world unmediated by sense experience, as is classically understood. It is far more widespread as our human disappointment with our earthly condition of being distinct and separate from others and in our efforts to secure unmediated knowledge of others. Das gives historicity and ethnographic precision to this perspective by showing how skepticism serves to render others vulnerable to suspicion, unsettle social relations and produce the conditions of possibility for suffering and violence (Das 2006). Her understanding of everyday life invites us to consider how social relations are lived as much in the shadow of skepticism as in the grips of structural violence and political contingencies.

Bringing together Cavell's and Das's perspectives with those of the ulama, I suggest that in Pakistan disputation as striving perpetually runs the risk of destabilizing everyday life through its vulnerability to skepticism. Furthermore, skepticism within everyday life is necessarily conjoined with the striving immanent to this life. For instance, we sense skepticism's presence in two forms in the argument at the Assembly Library when Naz tentatively advances the claim to have seen the Prophet in a dream: in the suspicion he is met with and possible charges of hypocrisy and ignorance, and in the manner in which he is subsequently mocked.

What happens to the evanescent quality of skepticism and aspiration when they are transcribed, for instance, by the state? Since its formation Pakistan has identified itself as an ideological state, with its populace taught that its ideology is Islam or at least largely informed by the main tenets of Islam (Nelson 2006). At the same time the postcolonial state in Pakistan has inherited the colonial administrative structure and imperatives of government (Jalal 1991). If, as W. C. Smith highlights for us, Pakistan's claim upon Islam is more in the nature of an aspiration than a clear vision of the ends of such striving, we have to allow for the possibility that Pakistan's identification of itself as an ideological state enables some experimentation within its apparatuses. In other words, the articulation and dispersal of ideology in Pakistan is not linear or cumulative and flows in directions other than from the top down (Pasha 2001). At the same time, the colonial legacy of the state brings a particular inflection to Pakistan's claim upon Islam. As scholarship informs us, the British colonial state met its vexation over governing such a diverse and seemingly unruly place as India with widespread efforts to know its sub-jects (Cohn 1996). The effort was not only to acquire knowledge but also to conquer uncertainty and unpredictability, to ensure effective and economic government but also to produce the aura of an omniscient ruling power.

What we find in Pakistan, then, is a self-professedly ideological state and a colonial legatee, open to experimentation over what it is to be Muslim in Paki-stan and driven to ascertain and adjudicate its subjects' relation to Islam. Nowhere is this more evident than in the workings of its law involving the Ah-madiyya, as I explore in this book. The string of reports, constitutional amend-ments, and legal cases relating to the Ahmadiyya show that the state makes continuous efforts to fine-tune its understanding of what it is to be Muslim in Pakistan, with these efforts increasingly taking the form of determining the threats posed by the Ahmadiyya to Muslims. Over time, the legal transcripts of the state espouse a forcefulness in achieving certainty over who is or is not a Muslim that surpasses the capacity of the law. In other words, the state creates the conditions of possibility for experimentation on what it is to be Muslim as well as for skepticism with respect to those who strive.

If, as I have made the case earlier, we take skepticism to be a tendency within the social, then it is transformed from a shadow upon social relations and encounters into an impersonal force able to strike anyone or emerge anywhere through its transcription by the state. I further explore this disem-bodied aspect of skepticism in disparate discourses and genres in the public culture of Lahore that allude to the figures of deceiving Ahmadis and igno-rant mullas (a derogatory term for a religious scholars or prayer leaders) as threats internal to Islam. The self-other distinction is formulated differently in this instance insofar as these figures are seen to hide within the self, emerging unexpectedly within oneself, so as to make one's own self subject to skepticism. Consequently, while the stories of repugnant others are the grist of social tensions and collective violence (Appadurai 1998, Roth and Salas 2001), I consider how they may also give expression to individual anxieties about the impossibility of striving.

Spiritual Diagnostics and Dissent to the Present

Finally, how does one address these perceived disruptions to striving posed by an ungrounded skepticism from within this way of life? The persistence of a discourse of spiritual diagnostics, that is, the evaluation of one's spir-itual health by means of one's physiology, within this milieu raises the possibility that this may be one such address to obstructions to striving. If this is the case, then what relationship does this attentiveness to one's spiritual health and bodily processes bear to political critiques of the kind I sensed in my conversations with my librarian friends?

A hint of this attentiveness comes to me by means of my personal history. When my grandfather died at the age of ninety-three, I inherited a collection of books whose variety puzzled me as an nineteen-year-old insofar as it contained lofty philosophical and political tomes alongside pamphlet literature on subjects that clutter the self-help shelves of South Asian bookstores. This collection included writings by Iqbal and other Muslim modernist thinkers, but also the theological writings of Maulana Ashraf Ali Thanawi of Deobandi persuasion, considerably more traditional-minded than the others. Along with these volumes there were several well-worn booklets on the therapeutic uses of plants, yogic postures for better digestion, uses of fasting, and strings of prayers to fight physical and emotional ailments, to name a few. In retrospect I realize that what puzzled me was the coupling of the cerebral with the gratuitously bodily.

My grandfather was from East Pakistan (now Bangladesh) and chose to continue to live in West Pakistan (now Pakistan) after 1971 when East Pakistan won its independence after suffering a brutal civil war. He insisted on marrying his daughters to Bangladeshis, which is how I came to be born and raised in Bangladesh. In truth, his makeup was never distinctly Bengali or Pakistani. Instead he was a Muslim well known for his piety, one who held both progressive and retrograde views. And his continual efforts at bettering himself as a Muslim ran the gamut from spiritual to physiological exercises. I remember him purifying his body with bitter herbs "to clear his system," as often as I remember him reading the Qur'an, fasting, or giving charity, each in the service of "godliness," implying thereby that the physiological is an important gauge of one's spiritual health.

As my grandfather illustrates, spiritual diagnostics takes place through an evaluation of one's physiology. The importance of the physiological to contemporary criticism is one of the topics explored by Gilles Deleuze, whose attentiveness to this topic grows out of his commitment to health. In the case of ill health—which for Deleuze is never physical illness but rather the sickness of the soul or the spirit—he invokes symptomatology (1983, 1991). For him, symptomatology is the naming and treating of a condition and, consequently, a creative act insofar as it can bring about not only a change in health but also the affirmation of a way of life.

Deleuze relates striving to good health, and the blockage to striving to the sickness of the soul in need of symptomatology. Transposing this insight to Pakistan, it makes those who speak about their state of religiosity by gauging bodily actions and reactions both strivers and commentators on Muslim aspiration. In the pages ahead I show how Muslims reflect upon this bodily register within everyday life. Unsurprisingly, Iqbal is their hakim (physician), as his writings are shot through with attentiveness to the physiological as a means to gauge whether one's religiosity is on the right track. If Iqbal's concern for futurity within Islam comes by means of his engagement with Bergson, I show how his concern for the spiritual health of those who strive is forged in critical engagement with Friedrich Nietzsche. The German philosopher was himself a "physician of culture," of the diseases of nihilism and decadence that he diagnosed in Western society (Ahern 1995, Conway 1995). From him one learns how striving and self-diagnosis implicates the individual in the world such that one's efforts or failures at self-work may produce changes in the world for better or for worse (Connolly 2005).

Earlier, writing on theological arguments I mentioned the ulama who position themselves as critics of debate and discourse among lay Pakistani Muslims. As I show in the chapters that follow, their commentaries are filled with keen if sometimes unkind insights into the physiological effects of disputation. Perhaps their perspicacity derives from the fact that the ulama of this region have assimilated the Sufi tradition to the scholastic one (Rahman 1979). At the same time they are also heir to Iqbal's thinking insofar as they recognize lay debates and arguments to be informed by the quest to be better Muslims. And, finally, those Urdu literati who see a complicated relationship to Islam in Pakistan, with the Urdu writer Mumtaz Mufti specifically highlighted in this book, are keen observers of the condition of striving.

If we allow that both striving and spiritual diagnostics are potentially political acts (as understood by Deleuze and Nietzsche), do they constitute dissent to the present? After all, they do not take the form of civil disobedience, political activism, or even violence by which dissent is usually understood. If so, and the book considers this possibility, then work remains to be done before we can read this dissent back upon the way of life that produced it, to understand its value for illuminating, perhaps changing the present.

Let me illustrate what I mean by a more speculative analysis of the argument in the Assembly Library than those offered earlier. In line with my exposition above, I take this argument to be the scene of Muslim striving. But can it also be taken to comment upon, even enact a position toward its political present of a military regime? What if we were to consider the content of the argument, specifically the status of the Prophet's body after his physical death? If we take this claim seriously then we have to view how the next world is considered to be intermixed with this one, in which the next world retains its own ontology even under some duress, serves as an elsewhere from which to reflect upon this world, and functions as an imaginative horizon that folds into the present—with all three possibilities existing simultaneously. In other words, the argument in the library prompts the speculation that the workings of the state and the nature of the political present are addressed, critiqued, even reworked within everyday disputation, ulama fumings, and literary musing. But insofar as these are expressed in transaction with the future, the divine or the otherworldly, they may fall out of the usual purview of politics.

Research and Organization of This Book

My research was conducted between the late 1990s and the mid-2000s, although my historical frame goes back to the early 1900s. I carried out my fieldwork in Lahore, beginning with a ethnography of mosques in the city and in time incorporating the very sites to which I went to carry out archival research for the study, specifically libraries, state institutions and archives, religious bookstores, and record rooms of various madrasas. My growing familiarity with the family of my research guide also led me to incorporate them into my ethnography for not only did they get entangled in the stories I was writing with respect to individual mosques, but they were well placed with respect to the tendency toward striving and its ramifications that I was tracking.

While I carried out ethnographic field research, I also conducted research on written texts that attempt to inflect Muslim everyday life. These texts constitute the frame of reference for many of my interlocutors, many of whom engaged in conversation with these writings. They include Iqbal's philosophical works and poetry, state pronouncements on who is a Muslim, jokes, horror stories, and cartoons regarding the venal mulla that were in circulation in Lahore, ulama writings, and Urdu literature, specifically those of Mumtaz Mufti. While this is only a fragment of the texts within everyday life in Pakistan, I select them to show how texts may be productively studied alongside ethnography not only for their citation but also for the myriad ways in which they undergird everyday life, providing both an analytics of approach to such life and enabling actions, gestures, and affects within everyday life to be seen as extending the potential within texts.

My method of interweaving written texts with Muslim lives has three parts: (1) to locate traces of aspiration within everyday life and public culture, (2) to see how this tendency crystallizes at particular points, within particular persons or texts, and (3) to study how this crystallization comes to be overlaid or expressed through lived experiences to be productive of further movements of the tendency, countertendencies, or even its dissipation. With this method in mind, the chapters are organized by a series of inquiries into the nature of Muslim aspiration. In chapter 1, I explore if and how the tensions and conflicts I observed with respect to mosque construction and maintenance in select neighborhoods in Lahore give expression to the aspect of striving that W. C. Smith located in the origins of Pakistan. While such fighting may be viewed as a product of the failure to achieve a national consensus upon Islam (Shaikh 2009), I make the counterargument that they express Muslim striving through the spatialization of theological arguments. The tension to which I draw particular attention and claim as the shadow of skepticism upon striving is that between the desire to transcend the ordinariness of a given religious context to become better Muslims and the commitment to living together in a neighborhood.

In chapter 2, I inquire into the genealogy of Muslim aspiration evidenced in the argument in the Provincial Assembly Library and mosque-related struggles through a close study of Muhammad Iqbal's writings in the pre-Partition period in colonial India. Putting Iqbal in a series of conversations, with Bergson as his philosophical interlocutor; with Sir Sayyid Ahmed Khan and Maulana Ashraf Ali Thanawi as his intellectual predecessors; and with Muhammad Asad and Maulana Abul Ala Maududi as those with whom his ideas were to compete for attention in Pakistan, I attempt to draw out both the encompassing scope of Iqbal's thinking and its original contributions to Islamic thought, Muslim everyday life, and time as becoming. Through an analysis of the 1948 and 1954 debates of the Constituent Assembly established to write a constitution for the new nation state, I show the Pakistani state as seeking to inherit Iqbal's conception of Islam.

In chapter 3, I follow the trace of the Ahmadi within mosque-related conflicts to track Iqbal's troubled inheritance by the Pakistani state. In particular I examine how his analysis of the Ahmadiyya movement and the course of action he advocated with respect to them are folded into state efforts to delineate who is a Muslim through the workings of constitutional law. Of particular interest is the manner in which the state undertakes striving of its own by inserting itself into theological arguments and by arriving at some startlingly original reformulations of these arguments. At the same time I consider how the state's transcriptions circumscribe aspiration to specific Muslims and let loose the condition of skepticism from the bounds of social relations.

Chapter 4 returns us to neighborhoods in Lahore through an inquiry into the manner in which a single worshiper absorbs the tensions inhering in mosques within his domestic life as so many competing expressions of striving. I show how his choice of striving, which is to rely unusually upon a jinn for guidance on better ways to be Muslim, is informed by a shared library of references, evident in his consideration of theological debates on the Prophet and evocation of Iqbal encircled by the state's own pronouncements on the Prophet and the now dreaded figure of the Ahmadi. To continue my study of the entwined relations of aspiration and skepticism, I examine the ways in which striving puts everyday life, specifically that of living together as a family, under some jeopardy.

Chapter 5 reaches beyond the neighborhoods and domestic arrangements that house mosque-related conflicts to consider how the mosque circulates in the public culture of Lahore through the figure of the mulla. I examine how media representations of the mulla, the popular genres of jokes, stories, and cartoons of the mulla, and Urdu literary writings capture both a sense of the growing unfamiliarity of Pakistani society and one's estrangement from oneself. While earlier chapters (1 and 4) locate skepticism within actual social relations, these genres provide a sense of how a disembedded skepticism works more widely upon a milieu and individuals.

With chapter 6, I return to Iqbal to show how his Nietzsche-inflected writings, in conjunction with ulama evaluations of the excesses of lay disputation and Mumtaz Mufti's writings on the disappointment of being a Muslim in Pakistan, help to diagnose skepticism in its specificity, as a tendency within the social, and as depersonalized, institutionalized, and made rife by the state and society. Insofar as the writings of the ulama address the populace and those of the Urdu literati address the state, I argue that we may consider spiritual diagnostics as a mode of political commentary, even dissent.

My epilogue draws out more explicitly what constitutes becoming in my fieldwork sites and the texts I studied. It follows more closely the elements of surprise that becoming introduces into established common sense about Pakistan but also into settled positions within social theory. The epilogue leaves us to consider the threats and possibilities of becoming for the present moment in Pakistan.

Chapter One

SCENES OF MUSLIM ASPIRATION

NEIGHBORHOOD MOSQUES AND THEIR QABZA

Pakistan as a Mosque

"Why study mosques? They are only shells for prayer." Statements such as these greeted me on a daily basis as I made my way around neighborhoods of Lahore with my Urdu teacher and research guide Farooq *sahib* to do a preliminary reconnoiter of mosques before settling into the long-term study of a few. There was truth to this observation since mosques of the present were not like mosques of old, part of famous complexes devoted to learning, dispensing justice, channeling charity and serving as *sarais* (hostels for travelers) (Frishman and Khan 1994). They were also not like mosques that were once part of *darbars*, complexes housing the shrines of saints to which pilgrims flocked (Troll 2004). They now stood singly, as monumental structures built by the state, convenient sites of prayer close to office buildings or places for Friday prayer in residential neighborhoods. Oleg Graber (2002) claims that the historical diminution of the mosque's functions translated into a stronger focus on prayer and a heightened sense of the mosque as sacralized space.[1] Nowhere is this transformation from a place of prayer to sacralized space more apparent than in the case of the mosque in Ayodhya, India, which was destroyed by Hindu fundamentalists in 1992 and which produced region-wide Hindu-Muslim conflicts.[2]

I was drawn to the study of mosques because of the oft-repeated statement that Pakistan was a mosque (Pakistan *masjid hai*), to see what purchase this formulation gave us in understanding what it meant to be Muslim in Pakistan. Given the historical transformations of the mosque as institution, this statement could be taken to mean that Pakistan was a place of assembly for Muslims or that it was a sacred place and should be treated as such. Certainly, those who exclaimed that Pakistan was a *mojiza* (miracle) viewed the nation as sacralized (Rozehnal 2010). But there was something more to this statement. As I had learned from my conversations with Lahoris about everyday sites and practices of religiosity, I needed to begin with books on mosques. This was an early instance of how texts facilitated my entry and navigation of this milieu. In the bookstores of the crowded Urdu Bazaar I found no fewer than twenty books and booklets that promised to provide the definitive history of mosques. With titles such as *Masjid Allah ka Ghar* (The Mosque Is Allah's Abode, by Badrul Qadri, 1999), *Islami Mu'ashare men Masjid ka Maqam* (The Position of Mosques in Islamic Society, by Ajmal Khan, 1993), *The Role of Mosque in Islam* (M. S. Qureshi, 1989), *Masjid ka Maqam* (The Position of the Mosque, by Quasar Niazi, 1976), these books were primarily concerned with correct comportment within mosques. Starting as a rudimentary structure abutting the Prophet's house in Medina, the mosque had not only undergone transformation, even monumentalization, as a built form, but an etiquette had also evolved on how to behave in them. Over time, spitting, gossiping, and hawking wares had been firmly proscribed and new admonitions added: removing one's shoes before entering the mosque, greeting everyone, reciting a formula to oneself, and sitting quietly in place until the congregational prayers began. These books invariably traced the trajectory of mosques from the imposing ones in Mecca and Medina to the humblest in Pakistan. This was undoubtedly to provide a respectable lineage for contemporary mosques (considered daughters of the Great Mosque in Mecca, in one formulation) but they also provided the sense that one had to learn to inhabit a mosque and that such learning was continual. There was clear evidence of this effort to teach proper behavior in the mosques I visited, with signs requesting that people not spit or urinate on the walls outside the mosque, others issuing warnings to those who stole the shoes of assembled worshipers, and cupboards with doors ajar holding prayer caps and copies of the Qu'ran draped in sumptuous fabric inviting those sitting around.

The most enduring example of learning to inhabit a mosque appears in the many efforts taken to apportion the space and prayer times of a mosque so that competing groups could be accommodated. The books listed above tell how the Prophet himself, learned, over time, how best to allow non-Muslim traveling contingents egress to the Medina mosque for their worship. The books mentioned this as a concern also for Muslim rulers who had to accommodate different interpretations of the Prophet's commandments with respect to prayer times and modalities. Colonial archives show that British authorities too had to adjudicate among competing Muslim groups, newly ascendant in the colonial era, over claims of ownership of mosques (Fyzee 1999). Since land was usually given in endowment in perpetuity (*waqf*) for mosques or became an endowment through an uninterrupted period of prayer, the question of the ownership of mosques posed a problem for British authorities deciding these cases under the rubric of Muslim personal law (Kozlowski 1985). As I came to learn through my own study of mosques in residential neighborhoods in Lahore, the competition over mosques and the Pakistani state's refusal to adjudicate on questions of their ownership meant that learning to inhabit a mosque with other groups was a continuing concern.

Transposing these perspectives on mosques onto Pakistan, one might take the statement that Pakistan was a mosque as a way of saying that one had to learn to inhabit this place, to acquire the right etiquette in sharing it with others with differing perspectives on how to be Muslim. This formulation captures the ongoing aspect of the striving to be Muslim that oriented Pakistan's origins, which I described in my introduction. But there is a qualifying clause to this statement. Most of my informants who said that Pakistan was a mosque were equally quick to complain that it had undergone violent seizure or *qabza*: "Pakistan masjid hai jis par qabza kiya gaya hai" (Pakistan is a mosque that has undergone forcible possession). Depending on whom I spoke with, Pakistan as a mosque was under seizure by the state, venal religious figures, unscrupulous lay Muslims, or sectarian groups. Moreover, the description of Pakistan as a mosque under qabza seemed to draw upon actual events of qabza, because almost all the mosques that I studied in Lahore had either undergone seizure or their administration feared that they might.

The colonial archives show evidence of conflicts over mosques (Freitag 1989). In fact the very same groups, the Shi'is, Barelwis, Deobandis, Ahl-e Hadis, and Ahmadis, of whom I spoke in my introduction, who engaged in theological disputation and religious arguments with one another, also fell into disputes over one another's mosques in their neighborhoods. One could say that religious disputation and arguments had their spatial counterpart in the building and struggles over mosques (Bowen 1993). And these conflicts carried over into the Pakistani context, where they acquired sectarian inflections insofar as religious differences were institutionalized by state administration and national politics and empowered by modern weapons (Malik 1990, Zaman 1998, Nasr 2001).

What is notably different in the postcolonial context, however, is the affect with which these experiences of forceful possession were recounted. The stories of mosque construction and their subsequent qabza were told with deep disappointment, even shock, that Muslims could behave this way with one another. It is my claim that such narratives of loss speak to an additional investment in mosques in Pakistan beyond their being a place of prayer or a sacralized space that demanded proper comportment. These narratives speak of investments in self-betterment and bettering one's community, tying moral and spiritual development to the progress of the nation-state. Moreover, the qabza of mosques could not thwart all such efforts at striving for everybody. In fact, in some instances, it extended striving by accentuating disputation, thereby producing the conditions of possibility for the unexpected becomings I outlined in my introduction when speaking of the argument in the Provincial Assembly Library in Lahore. Consequently, rather than detracting from the idea of Pakistan as a mosque, the qabza of mosques turns out to be important in illuminating the aspect of striving that informs Pakistan.

The emergence of independent mosques within residential neighborhoods point to the simultaneous emergence of new property arrangements, administrative bodies, and sources of funding, which have been studied to understand the growth of civil institutions within modern Muslim societies (Salvatore and Eickelman 2006, Clark 2004) and diasporic Muslims (Bartello and de Jong 2007). The persistence of qabza with respect to such mosques in Pakistan made it such that it was not so much the civility of these institutions that struck one as contributing to our knowledge of Muslimness in Pakistan but their incivility or the violence attendant upon them. Here I am drawing upon Matthew Hull's formulation that the city bureaucracy of Islamabad has produced what he calls "uncivil politics" rather than a civil society, but which he affirms as politics nonetheless (2010). His affirmation of uncivil politics as politics is in contrast to Robert Hefner's claim (2000) that civil society and state requires a politics of civility without which politics can get unrestrainedly violent, putting the political into question.

In this chapter I first locate mosques and their qabza within the changing urban landscape of Lahore. I explore the semantic range of the term *qabza*, which incorporates both physical seizure and the more intangible condition of being bound. This wider meaning supports my claim that the qabza of a mosque can shed light on the experiential state of striving and its closures within Pakistan, most specifically within everyday life. Next I present the stories of three mosques in three distinct neighborhoods in Lahore and their equally distinct experiences of qabza. These stories illuminate how qabza makes explicit the wide scope of striving to be Muslim within the milieu of neighborhoods infused by religious differences of the kind I describe in the introduction, which often acquired violent sectarian inflections. Within these neighborhoods, qabza is the obstacle thrown up in the path of striving, but which may paradoxically serve as the opportunity to expand the scope of one's initial efforts at striving. In my concluding section I draw out the threads of aspiration within these stories while considering other tendencies that emerge as well, such as those of skepticism and the commitment to neighborliness.

Mosques in the Lahori Landscape

Lahore is a metropolis of over six million people (Qadeer 2006). Instead of dissolving the past in the hypermodern, Lahore's urban fabric retains the feeling of a palimpsest of different eras of history, political leadership, social composition, aesthetic styles, and modalities of social engineering (Glover 2008). Perhaps this is because it has grown out of the Walled City, the historical center, by accretion rather than by the strict application of modern town planning principles. As William Glover has noted in *Making Lahore Modern* (2008), British colonial authorities, although not averse to large-scale demolition to produce more sanitary and secure Indian cities, did not attempt to recast Lahore in such a thoroughgoing manner. They reoutfitted many existing buildings for administrative purposes, and when they built their civil lines they did so with some sensitivity to existing settlements. Subsequently new housing and suburbs sprang up amid the more historical parts of the city at the same time as they extended out to the surrounding countryside. At the time of Partition, Lahore experienced a large influx of refugees (Talbot 2007). In absorbing them, the city acquired another layer of change upon its existing built form as its social composition changed from merchant-class Hindus and Sikhs to Muslim agriculturalists. And the sense of a palimpsest continues into the present.

My interest in studying mosque construction in Lahore was informed by David Gilmartin's insight that the city provided the best instantiation of religious institutions and politics in the province of Punjab, the hegemon within Pakistan (Gilmartin 1988). While Gilmartin was speaking of the late colonial and early postcolonial eras, Lahore remains the best site for research in the postcolonial period if not more so, given the upsurge of organized sectarian politics in Punjab in the 1980s and 1990s (Ali 2002, Zahab 2002). Given my interest in studying mosques built in urban neighborhoods in different eras of Pakistan's history, I decided to focus on a neighborhood close to the historical part of the city, constructed shortly before Partition but emptied of its original inhabitants and filled by refugees in 1947. I refer to this neighborhood as a muhalla to indicate its pre-Partition origins. My second site was a new neighborhood built within the city in the 1970s, which I call a suburb to indicate its Western-style planning. And my third site was an outlying neighborhood still very much under formation at the time I was there in the late 1990s, which I call a colony to indicate its preponderance of apartment-style housing earmarked for specific sections of the city population, such as government employees.

Although it was not difficult to decide on the neighborhoods to work on, deciding on mosques proved to be more of a challenge, given the large numbers of them in each neighborhood. My final choice of mosques was shaped by the opportunities that came my way to access mosques in the neighborhoods I had selected: a fortuitous break in a trip by my research assistant, my residence in a particular neighborhood, or my chance encounter with a bureaucrat whose husband was deeply engaged in local mosque related politics. These were only a few of the plethora of mosques in the city, many of which I visited or learned about through other sources. By the end of my stay I had become familiar with the reputations of most of the larger mosques in the city, having examined twenty in different sites and undertaken detailed studies of three. Before I speak of these three mosques it is necessary to embed them further within the landscape of Lahore.

With demographic change, population growth, and the strengthening of sectarian polities, mosques were the most commonly constructed buildings in Lahore, as elsewhere in Pakistan. The state has had a troubled history with this growth industry. After Partition, the state enacted urban planning, which rendered previously built mosques "illegal." While some had been "regularized," that is, their presence had been accepted within the planning maps or, in some cases, their physical form had been altered to match their surroundings, others continued as "illegal." Moreover, people continued to build mosques flouting urban planning principles and zoning regulations. This was particularly true in squatter settlements on government land, for instance, along railways or highways, where the presence of a mosque helped secure tenuous claims on land.

On the other hand, town planning had also encouraged a new kind of illegality. Once maps of new settlements were published, they were distributed to real estate agencies to sell circumscribed plots of land to customers. These maps indicated the area put aside for "civic amenities," such as mosques, parks, schools, and so on. Once these maps were in circulation, people laid claim to empty plots earmarked for mosques or parks by building mosques there with the confidence that the government would not be able to remove them, as such buildings were considered mosques for perpetuity. In a sense these mosques were "legally illegal," that is, they were illegal structures on land legally put aside for this purpose.

The arrival of mosque committees, neighborhood-based mosque maintenance groups, date to at least the early nineteenth century in South Asia, inaugurating the presence of the bureaucrat within mosques (Freitag 1989).[3] These bureaucrats, usually employed at various levels of government, were active in legalizing those mosques with which they were affiliated through the production of official documents. Most mosques, whether legal or illegal, were now able to present fat files of documents asserting their legality as, theoretically, the state only recognized mosques whose land documents and design plans had been registered with the proper authorities by mosque committees, which had to be registered as well. Veena Das and Deborah Poole (2004) have shown the importance of such documents in securing the authority of the state in those areas outside of its direct concern, which they consider the margins of the state. At the same time, as we shall see in the case of the mosque in Gulshan, such documents were deployed by their holders to make claims upon a state largely indifferent to their situation. These documents also mimicked the state's mode of administration and government as if re-creating an ideal state by means of the mosque.

The building of mosques being standard, I was told that urban dwellers, reluctant to trust advertisements for new housing developments, could be coaxed into buying empty plots if the property developers built mosques on the grounds, thus conveying the genuineness of their intention to build further. While mosques were considered necessary for initiating or completing a neighborhood, they were also the sites of the most violent struggles within the neighborhood. Most often these struggles over mosques took the shape of their seizure, attempted seizure, or counterseizure by competing groups within the neighborhood. Such events catapulted to the fore simmering tensions in the locality, while translating the spectacular nature of sectarian violence on the national stage into a cut and thrust of a less spectacular nature.

Sometimes, the fact that a qabza had taken place was indicated by the mere change of a prayer leader or, if it was an ongoing process, by the progressive increase or decrease in sound levels within the mosque around prayer times. So, for instance, if a mosque was being taken over by a Barelwi-dominated group, then one would notice an appreciable increase in sounds due to the introduction of loud zikr (formulas chanted in remembrance of Allah) and regular na't (songs in praise of the Prophet) sessions. Or if a mosque was taken over by the Ahl-e Hadis, then these practices would be slowly disallowed and the extraneous decorations on the mosque stripped off.

Oftentimes such seizures entangled the state. The reams of document kept in files indicated that the arrival of the state in the figure of the police or the law was always imminent. Yet upon their arrival at a possible event of a qabza there was little the police could do, as they considered the mosque to be of an inviolable sacred nature, with God as its owner. Consequently, these struggles toward possession did not even have the status of an accepted legal transgression in the state's ideological register. More often than not, the police attempted to protect the mosque from competing groups and their conflicting practices by placing a padlock upon it. As I mentioned earlier, the legal courts did not adjudicate on multiple claims of ownership if they could help it, that is, unless the state was implicated through writ petitions or there was egregious violence. Most judges I spoke with considered these conflicts best resolved at the local level.

Looking across the city of Lahore, one would see mosques of all different scales and sizes: grand mosques of considerable antiquity; mosques of modernist design, most often in commercial centers and in a few upscale residential areas; mosques patterned on the Prophet's mosque in Medina, that is, with a green pointed dome and tall minarets in various states of construction almost everywhere in the city; or humble prayer structures, a few with only a platform and thatched roof over them. Many of the doors of these mosques would be open, with a few worshipers assembled during prayer times, and Friday prayers seeing the fullest occupation of most of these mosques. At such prayer times a few women might slip in through side doors to pray in the area designated for them. At other times, men would be seen sitting and talking within mosques or laid out in rest and repose. And then there would be the ones with an air of disuse about them, with big padlocks on their doors, as in the instance of qabza.

The Semantic Field of Qabza

The term *qabza* (lit. grasp, clutch, seizure, confiscation, occupancy) has both a neutral and a negative connotation. A few older people associated with Masjid Noor, one of the mosques I discuss, used the word *qabza* in a neutral manner to speak of their laying claim to land and properties left by fleeing Hindu and Sikh families at the time of Partition. They saw their action as a necessary and common means by which to stake a claim upon Pakistan (Zamindar 2008). In its negative connotation, *qabza* was most often used to mean the illegal occupation of land, a distinction being maintained between professional land grabbers, referred to as qabza groups, and those who were landless and had of necessity settled upon land other than their own, most often state-owned land.

The qabza I studied was specifically that of neighborhood mosques. Qabza applied to a mosque in two senses, both negative. A mosque might be known as a qabza mosque because it was built on land that had been illegally occupied. This association with illegal occupation gave the mosque a vague air of disrepute to those who knew this fact. Some tried to avoid praying there, so as not to have to worry if the prayer performed in such a site was acceptable to God or not. Others felt that a mosque was a mosque regardless of how it had come into being. They felt that the more prayers were held at such mosques, the greater their chances of being cleansed of such associations. Alternatively, a qabza mosque might have been built by a group of people of a particular maslak or, in a few cases, of a particular *firqa* (Shi'a or Sunni), and had subsequently been seized by those of a different maslak or firqa.

Furthermore, the term *qabza* was also used to describe the sensation of being forcibly bound up. For instance, again in the case of Masjid Noor, a mother and a daughter with whom I spoke complained about the mosque's imam (prayer leader), who was a different maslak from them and liberal in his abuse of this family, that "he has done qabza on us." They explained that they felt silenced by him. In this particular use, *qabza* referred to the denial of their voice. This semantic range of the word *qabza*, running from violent seizure to the violent usurpation of voice, suggests that the study of mosque-related qabza has the potential to shed light on the ways in which people bind each other up in the context of attempting to undertake a collective project, or the entropy that shadows such projects. In other words, it has the potential to teach about the state of striving and the obstacles to it within everyday life in Pakistan.

Ganeshgar was a neighborhood named after the Hindu god Ganesh, re-named Momin Town or the Town of Believers in the 1970s. Masjid Noor was built shortly after 1947 by Muslim refugees to Pakistan who found themselves in Ganeshgar, in the environs of government institutions in downtown Lahore. Thus, in addition to meeting the needs of this migrant population, the mosque was built to stake a claim upon a new nation and begin the work of writing over the physical traces of its previous inhabitants.

By the time I began fieldwork in this area, the neighborhood had undergone another change, from being a mixed Shi'a-Sunni neighborhood to being a largely Shi'a-dominated one. This change was attributed to the presence of a large Shi'a *imambargah* (congregational hall) in Ganeshgar and the presumed desire of Shi'as to live close to their sites of worship and assembly in the face of widespread anti-Shi'a violence in Punjab in the late 1980s and early 1990s. The anxiety precipitated by the increased numbers of Shi'a neighbors led a friend who had lived her thirty-five years in this neighborhood to say, "Naveeda, these Shi'as cry fat tears. I am not always sure that they are genuine."

In an interview, the imam of the mosque, Imam Aziz, a frail man in his seventies, described to me that in 1952 some of the people of the locality literally grabbed him, then a young *maulwi* (religious scholar) and a newcomer himself to Pakistan. They placed him on a bare patch of land on which they had done qabza and bid him begin *namaz ba jama'at* (congregational prayer). And so he continued while the mosque came up in fits and starts around him, as the monetary donations from local residents would allow. Other than those mosques that predate Partition and may fall under the auspices of the provincial Auqaf (Religious Endowment) Department, such as the monumental Badshahi Masjid or the Wazir Khan mosque in Lahore; or those built and maintained by the state, such as the Shah Faisal mosque in Islamabad or the many mosques and prayer rooms within government institutions, the majority of mosques in Pakistan were built out of neighborhood initiative. While in some instances the state might make grants of land, in most instances government land was simply appropriated. The head of the Lahore Development Authority once said to me that he thought that 90 percent of all mosques in Lahore were built on illegally seized land (or at least land whose transfer had not been completed to satisfaction to meet the bureaucratic criteria of legality). These mosques were built and maintained by mosque committees through monthly donations collected from the residents of the neighborhood. In a few cases, a prominent resident might fully support a mosque. In an even fewer number of cases mosques were supported by *waqf* (religious endowment) or sponsored by foreign funds or political parties based outside the neighborhood.[4] More recently urban neighborhoods developed through private initiatives came with mosques already built and fully operational, as part of the services provided by the developer. In sum, it is fair to say that there existed an unwieldy patchwork of financial sources and strategies, largely unconnected to and undocumented by the state, underwriting the building and management of mosques. This structure of mosque administration made it susceptible to tensions among the manager of the waqf, the members of the mosque committee, and the prayer leader of the mosque, for although the prayer leader was most likely employed by the waqf administration or the mosque committee, he yielded authority in the daily workings of the mosque. Yet Imam Aziz had stayed the imam of Masjid Noor for over forty years and claimed himself aptly rewarded for his services by the enduring love and respect of those who prayed in his mosque.

In support of what I had heard from the head of the Lahore Development Authority, members of the committee of Masjid Noor told me that they did not think it necessary to wait for any permission to build a mosque. The government was preoccupied with bigger concerns in those early days, they said. Their need for a place of prayer being urgent, they simply laid claim to an unoccupied space for prayer and a future mosque. Yet the shadow of the state lay upon their efforts. In anticipation that the state officials might come to inquire into their mosque, they had subsequently secured all the necessary paperwork. The minimal bureaucratic requirement that a mosque had to meet was to have its mosque committee registered as a society under the Societies Registration Act.[5] Even papers showing the legal acquisition of land on which mosques were to be built were not deemed absolutely necessary to commence construction. Moreover, such papers may be acquired legally (through state transfer of the land to the society) or illegally (through payment to *patwaris* [land record keepers] to insert the name of one's mosque into the records) after the fact of the mosque being built. While the state on occasion made noises about centralizing mosque construction and management, this was not its priority. The state shared with the average Pakistani Muslim the sense that mosques were necessary, yet unremarkable aspects of being Muslim and, as such, residents should take the initiative as the need arose. Seen in another light, residents saw it as their implicit right as Muslims to build mosques as they saw necessary. It was not uncommon to find three or four mosques, each of a different maslak, close together in a small neighborhood.

Masjid Noor bears traces of the changing fortunes of its worshipers, largely storekeepers, local businessmen, and civil servants who worked in the nearby government offices. In its early years it was no more than a platform upon which the men in the neighborhood congregated for Friday prayers. As monthly collections became regularized, a concrete structure went up, consisting of a covered central hall, a courtyard outside of it with an area for toilet facilities and ablution at the back of the courtyard.[6] The mosque committee struggled to provide basic services, such as electricity to run the fans, those that hung over worshipers standing in the courtyard being the most important. Running water was a luxury, so in keeping with the traditional emphasis on running water as the purest means by which to perform ablutions, tanks of water were placed just above the ground to generate water flows from the taps that ringed the bottom of the tank. More recently, a generous worshiper replaced the rotting jute carpet lining the hall and the courtyard with a presumably indestructible plastic one.

The most recent additions to the mosque are the aesthetic flourishes added to the façade of the building. A cement cutout of a dome with a little minaret on each side adorns the doorway leading into the central hall. A black-and-white marble sign bearing the name of the mosque hangs by the doorway. Underneath the name of the mosque are the words that this mosque followed the tenets of the Ahl-e Sunnat wa Jama'at (People of the Prophet's Tradition and Congregation, a title usually claimed by the Barelwi). The head of the mosque committee explained to me that those words had been added to the sign very recently to discourage anyone other than those of the Barelwi maslak from entering the mosque.

When I met him, Imam Aziz was very ill. His breath was labored. Yet his quivery voice held forth in a diatribe from a body that was doubled in pain. In an interview he spoke about the new addition to the signage, done at his behest because he no longer felt that it was possible for those of the Deobandi maslak to pray alongside Barelwis. Before Partition he had found much to recommend in Maulana Muhammad Ilyas's Tablighi Jama'at and had steadfastly supported the presence of Tablighis in Masjid Noor over the years.[7] He had allowed them to pray, give *dars* (lessons), stay overnight while on *chilla* (forty-day trips), and do *gasht* in his neighborhood (call the men of the household to pray in the mosque). But the Tablighi Jama'atis had betrayed the philosophy of the founder of their movement, that is, to reconvert lapsed Muslims to Islam, and were no longer welcome at Masjid Noor.

I was not surprised to learn that the Tablighi Jama'atis used Masjid Noor as a place in which to do their *dawa* (missionary) work. As the Tablighis traveled far and near to do their work and do not always find Deodandi-affiliated mosques in these places, they often relied upon sympathetic mosques to host them. What interested me was that this disinheritance of the Tablighis should occur within the context of the emergence of the Barelwi dawa group Dawat-ul Islam, first established in 1981. Adeeb, eldest son of my Urdu teacher Farooq, and a young Tablighi himself, who worked as my research assistant, told me that this later group mimicked the structure and work of the Tablighi Jama'atis. They were formed to rival the Tablighis, just as new Barelwi-inflected jihadi groups with fancy names, such as Al-Buraaq (a reference to the horse on which the Prophet Muhammad went on *mihraj*, ascension to God), were emerging hell bent on making an entry into international jihad, notably in Kashmir. Up until this point the field of jihadi politics was primarily monopolized by groups associated with the Ahl-e Hadis and the Deobandis (Jaffrelot 2002).

What surprised me was that despite expelling the Deobandis from Masjid Noor, Imam Aziz continued to have a bad reputation among Barelwis outside of his congregation. In early 2000 I heard a young *maulwi* (religious scholar) refer to Masjid Noor as Masjid Zarar while I was sitting in another Barelwi mosque in Momin Town. (Masjid Zarar was the name of the mosque built by hypocrites at the time of the Prophet Muhammad and which he was commanded to destroy by Allah.) I became acquainted with this term in legal judgments involving the Ahmadiyya. In these judgments Ahmaddiya places of worship were referred to as Masjid Zarar for attempting to pass themselves off as Muslim mosques [N. Khan 2008]. Clearly the term was not free of a certain damning judgment, informed equally by theological precedents and the workings of the law. When I pressed the young man on his use of the derogatory name he explained that Imam Aziz's past close association with Tablighi Jama'atis made the mosque not quite what it claimed to be, that is, a Barelwi mosque. The imam kept things close to his chest despite the young man's repeated efforts to learn the real maslak of the mosque and recruit the imam into Barelwi-influenced party politics, specifically that of the Jamiat-ul Ulama-e Pakistan party. I took his words as indication that Masjid Noor was under some pressure to make clear its Barelwi affiliations, to which Imam

Aziz may have conceded by expelling the Tablighis from the mosque, but not to the extent of making the mosque available for other arrangements.

However, I never did learn the specific instance of Deobandi betrayal to which Imam Aziz referred in our conversation. There were dark hints from members of the mosque committee to the effect that some among the Tablighis had tried to seize the mosque. But from what I could gather afterward from the local police, who were surprisingly loose-lipped about mosque politics in their jurisdiction, and from Tablighi Jama'atis, who were long-term residents of the neighborhood and still prayed at Masjid Noor, this story had been invented to impose police restraint upon Tablighi gatherings in the mosque.

The view from the other side, from the perspective of the Tablighis, was not much clearer. It was Adeeb who had first taken me along to Masjid Noor to confirm for himself that it was the Barelwis, and not the Tablighis, who had done qabza on the mosque. After he made more inquiries and I had met and spoken with the imam and various members of the mosque committee, I was told by him that the largely Barelwi worshipers were holding Imam Aziz captive. That is, in exchange for letting him continue on as an imam in the mosque in his frail state, they had imposed this new restriction on the Tablighi Jama'atis. Meanwhile, the Tablighis had been tagged as qabza agents, making them the object of local suspicion and fear.

Nor was the imam's reputation spotless among the Tablighis. I was told that he had given sermons in several Shi'a imambargahs during the month of Muharram, the Islamic month in which the Shi'a mourn the tragedy of Karbala. This led to him being coded as a Shi'a sympathizer. He was drifting toward those Barelwi practices which most showed the influence of Shi'ism and were frowned upon by the Deobandis for being in excess of obligatory duties (weekly na't sessions in praise of the Prophet broadcast over the loud-speaker; giarwi or monthly lavish distributions of food among gathered worshipers in the name of the Baghdadi saint Shaikh Abd al-Qadir al-Jilani, who had a large following among the Barelwis; yearly celebrations of the Prophet's birthday, Milad un-Nabi; commemorations of the death of Hazrat Hussain in the battle of Karbala during Muharram, and so on).

As mentioned earlier, Shi'a-Sunni violence was at its zenith in the Punjab in the 1980s and 1990s. However, by the time I started this fieldwork, most of this violence had abated to the occasional event in a mosque or during Muharram. Yet, listening to Adeeb excoriate not only the Barelwis for their Shi'a-inflected practices, but also the Ahl-e Hadis, perhaps the most stringent of the three masalik in terms of religious obligations, I realized that that earlier period of conflict had recast animosities among Sunnis in its terms. A possible Shi'a stood behind every Sunni other than a Deobandi, for Adeeb and his companions. And every Sunni was vulnerable to shading into Shi'ism. I began to understand better my friend's fears about the Shi'a propensity to cry, as it spoke to her fears about whether her own tears were perceived as genuine by others.

Despite my efforts, I could not fully grasp what had happened in Masjid Noor to occasion the expulsion of Talighi Jama'atis. Just the hint of the possibility of a qabza had had a volley effect on rumors, almost all of them about Imam Aziz, setting contradictory ones off in different directions simultaneously. And I was being absorbed into the rumor mill. Imams in mosques in other parts of Momin Town demanded to know of my interest in Masjid Noor. Adeeb, at all times nonjudgmental toward my research despite his Tablighi leanings and circumspect in making inquiries for us, was becoming deeply involved in uncovering more and more gossip on Imam Aziz, leaving me worried about how I might be contributing to the tense situation. On one occasion the muezzin of Masjid Noor, a blind old man, called me an American spy to my face. Consequently, after three months of work in the neighborhood, which took me through the local police station, markets, various households, and mosques, I decided to abandon my research on Masjid Noor.

On a return trip to Pakistan, I serendipitously found myself in a house in Momin Town belonging to a family of Ahl-e Hadis persuasion. In the course of my conversations with the mother and the daughter of the family, it dawned on me that I was sitting at the back of Masjid Noor and that the imam they were complaining about was none other than Imam Aziz. It turned out that Imam Aziz had welcomed them to the neighborhood some ten years earlier with a shrill announcement over the loudspeaker that "wahabis" had moved in. Ahl-e Hadis were commonly referred to as wahabis in Pakistan because of their perceived ideological closeness to the Saudi Wahabis. It was also understood that Ahl-e Hadis political parties, research institutions, mosques, and seminaries received funding from Saudi Arabia. Feeling their difference in a largely Barelwi neighborhood, the family assiduously avoided their neighbors, forgoing attendance at Masjid Noor and attending instead a neighboring Ahl-e Hadis mosque.

At the same time the family had gained some intimacy with Imam Aziz over the years by being barraged by his daily announcements over the loudspeaker. The mother and the daughter clucked to indicate their disapproval at his speech, in which he often lapsed into unsavory details of how women ought to clean themselves after menstruation, how men and women ought to undertake ablution after sex, and so on. Often, the mother said, she had to cover her daughter's ears with her hands as her own ears burned red. It was also in the course of my long acquaintance with this Ahl-e Hadis family that I observed how disoriented they were during the time that Imam Aziz, now somewhat recovered, undertook a month-long trip to India to do pilgrimage at an important saint's shrine in old Delhi. They would stop in the middle of a conversation with me to say that the imam's substitute recited the Qur'an very poorly and that they missed Imam Aziz's melodious voice. They even acknowledged that on occasion they had learned important things from his announcements, for instance, what du'a (prayer) to say before trying for a visa to travel overseas. With the aid of the prayer the son of the family had indeed secured a visa to London after repeated failures at the visa office. Through Imam Aziz's daily announcements they had come to imagine they understood what preoccupied him at the moment, thus gaining unexpected insight into the inner workings of a quixotic man.

For all that, the mother and the daughter felt deeply resentful toward Imam Aziz. "He has done qabza on us," they said forcefully. They used the term qabza to mean the erasure of an individual's singular words and gestures arising from her embodiment of her maslak. They had been forced into a passive reception of his hateful speech. They felt that his poisonous words about them had alienated their neighbors from them. And they steered clear of the mosque for fear of being publicly ostracized for the different style of prayer they adopted as Ahl-e Hadis.

The events that unfolded around Masjid Noor in the late 1990s and rippled across time substantiate the insights of Roma Chatterjee and Deepak Mehta (2007) on Hindu-Muslim riots in Bombay in the early 1990s. It is their contention that one should not think that Hindu-Muslim tensions at the level of the neighborhood are straightforward reflections of politics at the national level. Instead the dynamics of the neighborhood are crucial to giving to communalism, or sectarianism in the case of Pakistan, specific discursive forms and strategies, like the ones we saw worked out on the site of Masjid Noor between Barelwis and Deobandis. But Masjid Noor in Momin Town wasn't only a story of how sectarian difference came to be folded within or unfolded from everyday life. At the center of the story was the figure of Imam Aziz, the focus of Muslim desire for a place of worship in a new country, and the means by which to lay claims upon its land. An educated maulwi would have been a rare find among the many who migrated to Lahore and found themselves dispersed among makeshift shelters, houses that would not belong to them and neighborhoods that still bore the strong presence of their last occupants. Yet Imam Aziz was also a man who produced tensions and controversies. He effectively isolated a family from the sociality of the neighborhood and he repeatedly left uncomfortable both Barelwis and Deobandis.

Eventually the mosque committee intervened to have their way, to act to dispel the shroud of ambiguity upon their mosque. An attempted qabza of their mosque, whose veracity was hard to confirm, gave them the opportunity to act to expel Deobandis from their mosque. In that act they effectively pulled the rug from under Imam Aziz's feet. The events that followed suggested consort between the material qabza of a mosque and the condition of finding that one's words were not one's own. Words were no sooner uttered that they were wrenched from one's mouth to take on life of their own or, conversely, they were silenced.[8] They revealed that one's vulnerability to being taken over by the words of another was an imminent threat within the everyday life of neighborhoods. And Imam Aziz was not free of this threat. He was a man who slighted and silenced but who also became the object of rumors about whom anything could be said and believed.

At the time of the qabza a few wondered out loud if Imam Aziz would live much longer, given the intensified pressures on his frail health. A year later found him still going strong over the loudspeaker. And in the mother and the daughter's resigned acceptance of his speech, an instance of the vulnerability to be bound by the words of another, there was also a hint of how he would likely remain a part of their lives for some time yet. They had even begun to send food on occasion to the blind muezzin in the mosque and to offer Qur'anic lessons to neighborhood girls. It paradoxically appeared that Imam Aziz had a future with them.

A Planned Mosque for a Planned Neighborhood and Its Planned Qabza

The mosque in Gulshan was unnamed. As the only mosque that had been allowed to be built in the neighborhood by its residents it went by the name of "the mosque in Gulshan." Gulshan was a typical upper-middle-class planned urban neighborhood, constructed by the Lahore Development Authority after Partition. Its residential plots were scaled to wealth. It boasted many public amenities, such as a central marketplace, post office, police station, mosque, schools, and a public park. These were located on an identifiable grid, which also accommodated natural topography and surviving historical landmarks (Qadeer 1983). In the 1970s the colonial city jail, from which the main road through the neighborhood received its name, Jail Road, was cleared and moved to the outskirts of the city. The colonial mental asylum stayed, though its walls were raised to mark it off from the rest of the area. The area that was newly cleared of the jail was divided into generous plots of land that were sold at subsidized rates to top-ranking civil servants, such as retired judges, ministers, and engineers. Some built their homes there. Others preferred to sell their properties at a high profit to Lahori businessmen seeking to move out of the Walled City. The Walled City was where most of the commercial wealth of the city and the families associated with it were once concentrated, but these families now sought to live in the more fashionable and better-serviced residential areas of the city (Weiss 2002).

Civil servants cultivating a modernist cosmopolitan air and their educated, well-traveled, nuclear families now lived cheek by jowl with Lahori businessmen, who more readily espoused a Punjabi ethos in their way of life, living and entertaining on a lavish scale within joint family networks thickened by intermarriage. It was these two subcultures that clashed over the construction and maintenance of the mosque in Gulshan, although, as I shall show, there were other divisive forces at work as well.

As in similar suburban neighborhoods, land had been allocated for a mosque in the design plans for Gulshan. Those who settled in the area in the early years of 1970s busied themselves constituting and registering a mosque committee and applying for a transfer of the land from the state to the committee at a nominal rate. A retired judge of the High Court of Lahore took most of the initiative in planning for the mosque, going to each house in the neighborhood every month to secure donations to help buy the land and begin construction. Each donor was given a receipt for his/her donation to keep financial flows into the coffers of the mosque committee legitimate and transparent. The judge also called monthly meetings of the committee, often in his own home, keeping meticulous records of attendance and decisions taken at these meetings. The committee was to run itself as a public-minded society, attempting to be representative of the neighborhood, securing the consensus of its members and maintaining proper records to be accountable at all times. A constitution was written for the society, along with an eight-page document of rules and regulations guiding all aspects of the society and the mosque.

The engineer put in charge of the construction plans for the mosque was similarly infused with public spirit. Like many in the 1970s for whom restrictions upon travel to the Middle East for work and pilgrimage had eased (Lefevbre 1999), he had been to Mecca and Medina several times and been impressed by the Prophet's mosque in Medina. He wanted to build a mosque to resemble it. But most important, the engineer wanted to refound the spirit of the mosque from the era of the Prophet. Built within the compound of the Prophet's own residence, the Prophet's mosque was famous for its openness to all, Muslims and non-Muslims. It was a place of public congregation, communal exchange, learning, and contemplation. Toward these ends, the engineer sought to have a large mosque compound with numerous doors to encourage the flow of people in and out of it. Raised pathways smoothly separated movement through the mosque of those who had undertaken ablution from those who were as yet unpurified. There were lavish provisions for ablution and toilet, different ones for those who came for daily worship and those who stopped overnight or came for longer study trips. A balance was sought between the built form and the natural environment, with gardens surrounding the mosque and the courtyard (left deliberately grassy) to take the overflow of worshipers from the central prayer hall. Looking into the mosque from any of the doors, one saw an alluring blend of architecture and greenery.

The mosque committee envisioned a thoroughgoing reform of mosques in Pakistan through the example of their own. They sought to hire religious scholars to run the mosque through a competitive process, advertising and interviewing candidates to seek out those who combined religious education with secular knowledge, demonstrated an interest in educating others and tremendous prowess in communication, and showed the capacity to care for the worshipers above and beyond their ritual needs. Such widespread care of the community was unusual, inasmuch as the tasks of mosque employees were quite circumscribed (see below). It suggested an attempt to bring *Bildung* or education (Bleicher 2006), or more likely the tradition of self-formation associated with *adab* (Metcalf 1984), within the purview of mosques. The employees would be provided housing with their families within the mosque compound, regular salaries that they would not need to supplement by taking in students or going out to provide tuition, insurances and pensions to provide for their future, and whatever else was needed to raise them to the stature of community leaders in equal standing with all. As the engineer once told me, "I wanted to transform maulwis into pastors in the Christian sense."

Additional land was bought alongside the land for the mosque so that these community leaders would in the near future be able to build residential schools to raise and educate poor children in the shadow of the mosque. This land included enough acreage to provide for a playground for the children. The society also planned to apply for grants from the Auqaf Department, Child Welfare Department, Department of Health, and others to pay for an open library and a medical dispensary within the compound.

Customarily, a mosque has at minimum two employees, an imam (the person who leads the five obligatory prayers in the day except perhaps for the Friday prayer) and a muezzin (the person who gives the call to prayer). In addition, a mosque may hire on a full-time or part-time basis a khatib, the person who gives sermons during Friday prayers, that is, who has received more Arabic and Islamic education than an imam to better equip him to give a fluent sermon in Arabic (usually excerpts from the Qur'an and hadis). Among those usually hired on a part-time basis was the qari, one who has received at least enough training to render a proper recitation of the Qur'an and is usually entrusted with teaching neighborhood children on how to read and recite the Qur'an properly. The hierarchy of these religious posts is pegged to the level of religious education, with the post of the khatib at the top followed by that of the imam and the qari, with the muezzin at the bottom of the hierarchy. Sometimes the muezzin is also responsible for cleaning the mosque. The wealth of a mosque or the strength of its support by its worshipers is suggested by the number of employees it has. For instance, Masjid Noor was well off enough to pay for a full time imam and muezzin, with a qari coming by several times a week. But the mosque in Gulshan was much better off than Masjid Noor, as indicated by the fact that it could afford a khatib, an imam, and a muezzin to stay at its premises, supplemented by a part-time qari who came daily.

Given that the mosque committee of Gulshan had such a strong reformist agenda and that they had erected an extensive hierarchy of employees in the mosque, it was not surprising that some tensions would develop between the mosque committee and the employees, if one can even think of either as a unified group. One prominent form this tension took was class tension. When I arrived on the scene in late 1999 I saw committee members grit their teeth in frustration that the current khatib and imam were getting ahead of themselves by inviting people to attend lessons in the mosque, letting Tablighis stay in the mosque, and daring to invite religious political figures to give talks in the mosque. Yet the khatib and imam, who did not necessarily see eye to eye despite being of the Deobandi maslak, both felt that the committee members regularly belittled them. Their salaries had been frozen for years. There was an unrealistic cap on how much the committee would pay toward monthly electricity and water charges. And if this was not humiliation enough, these two employees were expected to stand for hours outside the gate of the committee member in charge of paying them their salaries. Since their salaries were so low, both had stopped going to collect them, preferring to seek employment outside. One taught Islamiat (Islam as a school subject) at a local school and another worked as a qari at a posh school for boys in Lahore, where he was also the cricket coach. Even so, the imam remained quite deferential to the mosque committee. Committee members spoke approvingly of his loyalty, although some read his deference as a cover for his tenacious hold on his position. The khatib was more openly dismissive of the committee.

These prefatory details about the mosque in Gulshan are necessary to understand the dynamics underlying its qabza, which spread out over a number of years in the early 1980s. However, the wealth of information I had about this mosque did not offer a clearer narrative of qabza than in the case of Masjid Noor presented earlier. This was because the event of qabza amplified the dissonances within the social fabric of the suburb of Gulshan, specifically the clash of the subcultures of parochial Lahori businessmen and cosmopolitan civil servants, and class tensions between them and their employees at the mosque, which were not easily resolved.

In what follows, to draw out the story of the qabza, I move between the records maintained by the retired judge between the years of 1975 and 1995, and conversations I had in 1999 with members of the mosque committee, employees, worshipers, and neighbors, in which they spoke of those earlier years. These records, written in the recognizable genre of official memos with neutral wording, gave little evidence of the crisis that embroiled everyone relating to this mosque. In the case of Masjid Noor, the mosque's registration documents shored up the authority of the state by serving as a constant reminder that a visit by a state official was imminent. In the case of the Gulshan mosque, the range of documents held by the mosque committee, from its constitution to these records, reproduced the administrative structure and unemotional persona of the state. The documents needed oral narratives and evident expressions of anguish to animate them, to become, that is, written texts that enfold the speech, gestures, and affects of everyday life.

The Gulshan mosque records, no more than a half-page typed report for each meeting of the mosque committee, made note of the rise of several aberrant practices within the mosque in 1979. People had begun to say na't and durud sharif loudly in the mosque. The mosque committee met to discuss these practices and all, except for one dissenting member, decided to disallow them. In 1999 I found out from members of the mosque committee that the dissenting member was a Lahori businessman from the Walled City now living in the neighborhood. I was told he was intent in introducing his *rasm-o rawaj* (cultural practices) into the mosque. Soon the committee became upset that these practices continued despite the fact that they had been officially disallowed.

By 1980, the committee contemplated filing a civil suit against certain unnamed neighborhood residents who were not a part of the mosque committee but were seen to be interfering with the administration of the mosque by continuing banned practices. In 1999, the judge's sons and daughters-in-law informed me that by this point in the mosque's history, the businessman from the Walled City, now identified by the committee members as being Barelwi, had made an unsuccessful bid of qabza on the mosque. He encouraged the imam of the mosque to force everyone coming to pray to abide by Barelwi practices. Opponents to this change were forced out of the mosque.

In 1981, the records note that the committee had sought the resignation of all employees of the mosque after affiliating itself with Jamia Ashrafia, the highly reputed Deobandi madrasa (seminary) in Lahore. The report stated that this affiliation had been sought to secure help in finding dependable employees. In 1999, I learned from the judge and his family that when members of the mosque committee found themselves barred from the mosque under threat of physical harm, help from the police had not been forthcoming. Instead they approached the madrasa for help, having now identified Deobandis as the natural opponents of Barelwis. They claimed not to have known anything about such religious groups within Sunni Islam and the infighting among them prior to the qabza of the mosque. The rector of the madrasa advised them against pursuing a civil case, as it was unclear what constituted help from the government on such matters. Instead, he helped mastermind a counterqabza of the mosque. He arranged for a truck to pull up in front of the mosque. It was filled with young men carrying weapons, who forced their way into the mosque, ejected its imam, presumably loyal to the Lahori businessman, and replaced him with a Pathan imam. The choice of a Pathan imam was motivated by the rector's advise that they would do well to place a person known for his loyalty in such a position.[9] The records meanwhile simply relate that the previous imam tendered his resignation and that Jamia Ashrafia found a suitable replacement.

While the records make no mention of a legal case, in 1999 I was told that the committee decided to file a civil suit after all. This was met by a counter-suit against the new employees of the mosque by the defendants in the civil suit. The police came and put the mosque under lock and key and later released it to the Lahori businessman, who, I was told by members of the committee was favored by the district commissioner of the time. The committee, strong in legal expertise as it was made up of judges and lawyers, responded by filing a writ petition against the Provincial Government, naming the police and the defendants of the civil suit. The judge's son, himself a judge, told me that the government upheld the petition and returned the mosque to the care of the committee.

This narrative provides the bare bones of the actual events of qabza between the years of 1979 and 1981 from the records of that period and oral narratives of the late 1990s. The narrative spoke of qabza as an ongoing event, most clearly expressed in the growing sense of the mosque committee that it had lost control of its mosque and misplaced its spirit of reform. In the 1980s, the records described new struggles, this time between the mosque committee and the Pathan imam. Each complaint from the committee to the rector of Jamia Ashrafia had him begging and pleading the case of the imam, promising to remove him as soon as new arrangements could be made. Meanwhile the new khatib, also provided by Jamia Ashrafia, started to give trouble. He had begun to give long political speeches during Friday prayers despite being asked to stick to the khutba. After repeated incidents, the committee members decided to throw out all its employees in 1985, and the rector of the madrasa once again interceded. He helped to draw up rules of conduct for the employees, asking them to refrain from party and factional politics, misusing mosque property, and soliciting donations. This was the memorandum of understanding in effect when I was there in 1999, although I heard that the khatib had again begun to disturb the committee with his broadening alliances with sectarian politics.

With the history of the mosque and the details of its qabza in mind, we see that its construction was the expression of a broad ambition to found a new religious space that would extend beyond the daily needs of worship to forge the model Muslim community. The physical plan of the mosque, the newly imagined role for its employees, and the inclusion of education, play, and contemplation, was not only expressive of a desire to modernize an Islamic institution. It may be seen to reproduce the state in Islamic form and to attend to the fullest needs of the Muslim individual, to give every aspect of his or her life sustained attention. But this striving for an Islamic form of the state and better expression of the Muslim was hampered by a certain fealty to the bureaucratic form. I am not speaking here of the insistence upon a constitution for the mosque, the eight-page-long guidelines on the rules and obligations tying one to the mosque, nor the records or account-keeping of the committee. These legal exercises and bureaucratic forms are intrinsic to Pakistan's mode of experimentation in being Muslim. Rather, it is the reliance on injunctions, rules, and suits to have one's way with others and the necessity for an memorandum of understanding to enable civil relations. These means suggest an inability to countenance the full sweep of changes that reforms had set in action, which were met by the recourse to rule-making to enforce the status quo.

At the center of this conundrum between desiring a sea change and being revolted by it was the judge, the original mover behind the mosque in Gulshan. Now very old and frail, he no longer attended the mosque. He could barely speak about the mosque without getting teary-eyed and upset. At one point in our conversation it seemed as if he cried for the mosque. He could not fathom the humiliation forced on the mosque and, therefore, on Allah by that padlock placed on its doors by the police. His son, himself a judge who had earlier served as the liaison between the mosque committee and its employees, and who was the one who made them wait at his gates, no longer prayed there. The Lahori businessman had also moved to a Barelwi mosque at the edge of the neighborhood, one that had been partially demolished under instructions of the governor of Punjab during the widening of Jail Road. He had tried unsuccessfully to build a Barelwi mosque in the neighborhood after the mosque in Gulshan came under Deobandi control. The committee had managed to block his efforts to do so, even if they could not withstand the overt Deobandi influence in the mosque. The only person from the original committee who prayed there any longer was the engineer. Now very frail, he was driven to the mosque every day by a member of his family; in his weak state he used a chair to pray and had it set in the middle of the grassy courtyard if it was sunny or else in the prayer hall. When I asked him why he continued to go to the mosque he said, "I am not going to neglect my prayer, nor am I going to neglect the mosque."

A third neighborhood, Gauhar Town, was a more recently planned settlement in the outlying areas of Lahore in which land allocations were not yet complete in the late 1990s. The area had a scattering of houses and apartment buildings intermixed with empty plots of land. Built to accommodate the bureaucrats in Pakistan's civil service, it catered to people at different rungs of the official hierarchy from peons (office attendants) to officers. As such it was a locality still under construction and heavy negotiation over the sociality yet to be expressed through its final built form.

On one of my trips to the Lahore Development Authority I met the patwari of Gauhar Town.[10] I was told it was established in 1984 for low- to middle-income people. Like all such developments, the land was allotted in four ways: one portion was given to those individuals whose land was taken from them to develop the scheme, a second to individuals whose names were picked through lottery, a third was sold through public auction that brought in most of the Development Authority's revenues, and the final portion, comprising 3 percent of the total land stock, was given to the chief minister of the state to give away as he saw fit.[11] In addition, the patwari claimed, there was a concerted effort to distribute the land among people of different occupations (although it was unclear to me how either lottery and public auction allowed for such careful demographic distribution), including defense and High Court and Supreme Court workers, government servants, lawyers, artists, media persons, journalists, sportsmen, ulama, authors, scholars, poets, engineers, doctors, businessmen, executives, and industrial laborers.

However, the patwari confessed, very few plots reached those for whom it was meant. After all, a recent newspaper article named Gauhar Town as one of several new schemes with the most corrupt land allotment. In 1990, Nawaz Sharif, then chief minister of Punjab, gave away 399 plots as political bribes, of which 264 were located in Gauhar Town alone. Furthermore, as the patwari showed me in a tour of the area, most mosques in this locality were built without the proper permission of the necessary authorities, of either the district commissioner or the Development Authority, and sometimes even without the knowledge and support of the residents of the various neighborhoods. At one disputed mosque in Gauhar Town, whose file I examined in the district commissioner's office, the residents complained that worshipers were bused in from other parts of the city to fill the space and give the impression of wide public support of the mosque. I witnessed what the residents were referring to; judging by their uniform look, the bused-in worshipers were students from madrasas. This was quite unusual, as the mosques I presented earlier were all built through local efforts even if these did not extend to acquiring the land legally or garnering the correct permits from the state. In other words it was rarely the case that Muslim authority figures and worshipers associated with mosques in Lahore were outsiders who infiltrated the neighborhoods, as widely portrayed in the media; Here my finding is in line with Salwa Ismail's studies on Muslim politics in urban neighborhoods in Cairo (2000) in which he shows that Islam was only one element of a complex weave of politics involving local leadership and emergent communities of dissent and activism against an indifferent state. However, Gauhar Town did exhibit a degree of outside religious and political influence on new urban settlements that was unprecedented in Lahore.

A tour of the mosques in Gauhar Town could only be described as a journey through a regime of illegality. A few mosques were fully legal in that they were built on plots allotted for this purpose with the necessary authorization. The patwari showed me a few more that were partially legal in that they were on allotted plots but built illegally. One in particular stood out as so basic as to call attention to its illegality. It comprised an uneven platform with a single light bulb hanging by a string from a temporary thatched roof covering it. The patwari pointed out these features of illegality knowledgeably, cheerfully telling me the story of an illegal mosque that had been erected overnight on a friend's plot in Gauhar Town. When the friend turned to him for help, the patwari showed up at the "two-brick" (do int) mosque with the development plans of the Gauhar Town scheme. He opened up the map, pointed out the legally allotted space for a mosque to the mulla responsible for the illegal mosque and, after heavy negotiations, helped him "transfer" his mosque to that site.

In my attempts to understand how legality, or the lack there of, was perceived by Lahoris, I went to the district commissioner's office to find out whether residents of such places as Gauhar Town ever complain about these illegal mosques, their sudden appearance, their activities, or even the sounds emanating from the loudspeakers affixed to these mosques. I was given to understand that although mosque-related conflicts are common, people approach the commissioner's office only when their appeal to local police does not yield results or when they feel that the local conditions are so compromised as to make any appeal to the police a superfluous gesture. So conflict over mosques is deliberately kept a local matter. This is also partly why so few such cases actually show up in the courts. Another reason why courts see few cases is that it is very hard to represent a mosque since it belongs to all and none. Even its management committee cannot claim back a mosque after the fact of its seizure by another group because the committee has no rights of ownership over it. Cases made either on grounds of adverse possession or prevention of entry are hard to argue in court. In most cases people accept the instance of qabza and either continue attending the mosque or shift alliances to another mosque, even building another one if possible.

The standard mode of approach to the district commissioner was in stock bureaucratic language complaining that certain mosques were disturbing "law and order" and "public peace," and expressing concerns of harm to recognizably beleaguered social types, such as, "the sick," "the working tired" or "students." They were very like the standard letters people wrote to newspapers and were more of the nature of flagging a social problem than filing a complaint. Yet a few such letters did express grave concerns over the threat to personal safety posed by mosques, more specifically, by those who ran these mosques. Furthermore, I noticed that a large number of complaints to the commissioner's office were anonymous, simply pointing to offending mosques. People were clearly concerned not to identify themselves.

While investigating the effects of affixing loudspeakers to mosques at the local office of the Environment Protection Department, Punjab, I befriended an environmental expert, who told me that if I wanted to see a qabza in action I ought to speak to her husband. This was how I came to be introduced to Dr. Khan, a scientist who worked for the government and was deeply interested, if not implicated, in a qabza situation in their local mosque in a neighborhood none other than Gauhar Town. That is how I came to study his mosque in Gauhar Town, one built legally but which was undergoing qabza the entire time I was in Lahore for my fieldwork.

In what follows I provide an account of qabza solely from the perspective of Dr. Khan as the situation was too delicate to warrant my conducting fieldwork on site. Dr. Khan, a short excitable man, rattled off the story of how he had come to be in Gauhar Town. He and his wife were no longer young but had been delayed in entering government service due to the time it took them to get their doctoral degrees. They had no children of their own and had legally adopted a daughter, a very unusual move within the South

Asian context, suggesting a modern couple with commitments to the nuclear family. Dr. Khan calculated that if he had to wait for the seniority necessary to be offered a subsidized plot of land within an urban scheme, whose size and subsidy would be commensurate to his position within the state bureaucracy, then he and his wife would not be able to start their lives as an independent family until much later. Consequently, in the early 1990s they bought someone else's plot in a private scheme in Gauhar Town.

To explain this briefly, when plots of land of a newly developed settlement are sold in public auctions, a private developer might buy up a number of them, put a wall around them, and a gate to regulate access to what was now a colony with its own administration that negotiated with the government to secure electricity, gas, sewage, and water. Although this private scheme went by the name of Punjab Government Employees Welfare Society and was probably composed of plots to be allotted by the government to its own employees, the government had sold the whole series of plots to private developers. This may have been done to accelerate readiness of the area for habitation, as sectors of the government are notoriously slow in providing public services to new settlement, as well as to generate funds for the government up front rather than the piecemeal way in which monies would have trickled in if they had sold the plots individually. In keeping with its mandate to provide houses to its employees, the government required the private developer to give first choice of the plots with subsidies to government employees, with the employees free to do with the plots what they wished after buying them.

The person from whom the Khans bought a plot was lower in rank in government service than they were. Consequently, their plot was small. But the Khans calculated that this was the most they could afford as they were forced to buy the land at market rate, rather than the subsidized rate at which the owner had acquired it. Although this put them among a class of people with whom they did not commonly associate, they wagered that others like them would buy into the private colony and that the final neighborhood was be more diverse than originally planned.

As the colony became more inhabited, people needed a place to pray. As Dr. Khan explained it, the administration of the Government Employees Welfare Society colony had allotted a plot of land for a mosque and had collected considerable funds through monthly donations from its residents. When requested by the residents, the Society, as the colony administration was called, took it upon itself to build the mosque. As this was a private development, the Society had access to engineers and an extensive labor force. But it also meant that the Society was not made up of residents. Here Dr. Khan broke off from his narrative of the qabza of the colony's mosque to say ruefully that it was through his efforts, in his capacity as an educated person of high professional status held in high esteem by all, that the Society was convinced to hold elections to put together a mosque management committee more representative of the colony's inhabitants. It was this action of his that produced the conditions of possibility for people to enter the committee to try to seize the mosque, to impose their ways upon it. At some point the management of the mosque had taken such violent turns that the Society had to step in to disband the committee. Now a single engineer unassociated with the colony sat in a small office in the side of the mosque overseeing the daily running of the mosque. One had to go to him to ask to have even a bulb replaced where once this mosque had run itself, complained Dr. Khan. However, rumbles continued within the mosque over which maslak style should be adopted within it.

The qabza was undertaken by none other than the chairman of the committee, a seemingly simple and pious old man, with whom Dr. Khan had had good relations prior to the construction of the mosque. This qabza mosque took the form of gradually introduced changes and then the experience of a perceptible shift in the atmosphere of the mosque and the inclinations of its committee members. It was these slow encroachments to which Dr. Khan was attentive and which he attempted to stave off.

The pious old man whom Dr. Khan once respected and whom he had asked many times to lead prayers before the actual selection of a permanent imam, began to introduce "unsavory practices" into the mosque shortly after his appointment as head of the mosque committee. The practices that Dr. Khan claimed to have never seen before included "decorating" the azan with prayers to the Prophet, "dressing up" the mosque with lights, and hosting na't sessions after prayers, as well as celebrating Milad-un Nabi, to which prominent Barelwi politicians were invited. Although Dr. Khan was not of any of the masalik within Sunni Islam in Pakistan, he knew of their existence. Ultimately maslak affiliation was irrelevant to him, just as the fact that he knew a member of the mosque committee was an Ahmadi, which was illegal according to the law of the land and a punishable act. It never crossed Dr. Khan's mind that such things should be made public and he had reassured the Ahmadi member of the mosque committee that he would not divulge his secret. Upon encountering these highly visible Barelwi practices he found them to be very distasteful. They seemed to him as *jahil* (uncultivated, ignorant).

It was at one such public occasion within the mosque that Dr. Khan ripped up a poster among those liberally plastered on its walls and threw it into the waste bin. He told me that it was no more than an advertisement for a public lecture by a religious scholar and politician, Dr. Tahir-ul-Qadri. However, relations among the worshipers had deteriorated to such a point that someone in the committee charged him with blasphemy claiming that the poster had Qur'anic script on it. By throwing the poster into the wastebasket, Dr. Khan had effectively disrespected the Qur'an. It was at this point that Dr. Khan, a man of science, with progressive views on democracy and representative government, confident of his social status, and trustful of his own instincts and analysis, felt the ground fall from beneath his feet.

First, he described, the crowds brayed at his gates. "I couldn't tell if they were humans or monsters. What kind of neighbors turn on you in this way?" He picked up the phone to call the police but found the line continually busy. He was certain that the police was in on a conspiracy against him or else why would their urgent line be busy? This suspicion was promptly confirmed when the police came to arrest him. Was he going to rot in a jail somewhere? He had written an anonymous letter to the district commissioner reporting the activities in the mosque in a scandalized tone. Would they use that letter against him now? But how would they know the letter was his?

Dr. Khan was able to convince the police officers of his innocence. As he recounted, his education and good breeding, manifest in his reasoning powers and sober manner, put into sharp contrast the *jahalat* (ignorance) of those who had filed a complaint against him. Jahalat was not class-coded for Dr. Khan, as he was not particularly well off, while there were many among the worshipers in his mosque who were very rich and politically powerful. Rather, his was a case of the educated battling the resentment of the uneducated. Despite his success in persuading the police to let him go, Dr. Khan remained anxious that he would not be able to convince them the next time he was wrongfully accused.

At a point when most people I knew who had experienced similar seizures of their mosque would have withdrawn, Dr. Khan threw himself into the struggle for the mosque. He asked the Society, which had taken over management of the mosque, that an imam be installed who was acceptable to everyone. He took to reading the religious books cited by Barelwis, reading further and further into Islamic theology to be able to engage in polemics with his opponents. They were no longer simply enemies of the mosque; they were also his enemies. As he showed me the impressive book collection that he had amassed, he told me that he was actually quite thankful for this terrible experience because it had brought him closer to the richness of Islamic thought.

Each time I contacted Dr. Khan, I found him further and further entrenched in the struggle. Once he told me that a whole group of Barelwi maulwis had gathered in the mosque one evening apparently to take it over. By this time he had renewed his university association with the political party Jama'at-e Islami. His political contacts sent over a few young Jama'ati boys with guns who came and "sorted out those mullas once and for all."

What interested me the most in this account of qabza was Dr. Khan himself. Dr. Khan's involvement in the ongoing qabza of the mosque, after all what made his bid to regain control of the mosque any less of a qabza, brought about vertigo in himself. However, Dr. Khan attempted to weigh things down, to put them in perspective, so as not to be swept away. His faith in common sense, education, and good breeding seemed to prevail in each turn. Nonetheless, a thread of being subsumed by the moment also ran through Dr. Khan's account, suggesting the darker undercurrents of everyday life.

Just before I left Pakistan, I called Dr. Khan to say goodbye. He said that he was sorry I was leaving because the "drama" was only just beginning. A case had been filed and the fight was going public. He would not tell me more over the phone. Meanwhile I kept wondering how his wife and his adopted daughter were faring. A long time ago Mrs. Khan had shrugged her shoulder when I had asked her opinion of all this, as if to say she couldn't care less. She was much more preoccupied with playing with her adopted daughter, a beautiful two-year-old when I last saw her. The daughter had a male caretaker, another unusual practice in this family. Young and sweet, he was very tender toward both the mother and daughter. It was as if a surrogate family was taking form in the blind spot in Dr. Khan's growing surveillance of the mosque.

Qabza as the Scene of Muslim Aspiration

Through each of the above instances of qabza—whether rumored, as in the case of Masjid Noor; engineered, as in the mosque in Gulshan; or unfolding, as in the mosque in the Punjab Government Employees Welfare Society colony—we catch a glimpse of the specificity of neighborhoods in Lahore, differentiated by their individual efforts at striving, the modalities of violent seizure, the tensions that inform these seizures, and the work of crafting and maintaining a fragile sociality within neighborhoods. Insofar as qabza made explicit the arc of continuous struggle to be Muslim in each of these neighborhoods, it served as the scene of aspiration and possibly the site of its closure.

Through the events in Masjid Noor, we see the necessity felt for the transparency of religious affiliations in Momin Town in the midst of its becoming a Shi'a stronghold. While Imam Aziz helped to mark out insiders and outsiders, particularly with respect to the Ahl-e Hadis family he publicly impugned, he introduced as much ambiguity as he attempted to dispel by allowing Tablighis into the largely Barelwi mosque. While the subsequent expulsion of the Tablighis was in part to remove this ambiguity, it seemed to result only in further ambiguities, with Imam Aziz now shading into Shi'ism in the eyes of the Tablighis and Deobandis and into a munafiq (hypocrite) presiding over a "Masjid Zarar" (the mosque built by hypocrites at the time of the Prophet) in the eyes of Barelwis. Given Momin Town's increasing importance within the sectarian geography of the city, national sectarian trends fed into local events as ephemeral as the rumor of a qabza. The marking of the mosque as Masjid Zarar indicated that it needed to be put under surveillance by neighboring mosques, just as Ahmadis, whose mosques were considered Masjid Zarar by the state, were being watched. While the state was anticipated in each turn in the figure of an official requesting to see if the papers were in order for the mosque, it was mobilized in the form of bored policemen, who came to lend a hand at whatever local politics were taking shape within the mosque. Their presence implied a qabza, even if one had not happened, and this only polarized the community further.

In contrast to Momin Town's closeness to the pulse of sectarian politics at the national level, the mosque in Gulshan felt like a throwback to another era, the era of the early years of constitution making when the Prophet's era seemed intermingled with Pakistan's present. The state administrative structure served as the model of government for this mosque with its upper-middle-class, largely well-to-do committee members. The members did not know about maslak differences, or if they had a vague idea of them, they did not know their finer details. When they finally learned of them, they acted as if they could deploy these religious differences to their own advantage and quickly found themselves out of their depth. The resort to legal cases, writ petitions, notices, rules, injunctions, and memorandums of understanding, suggested reliance upon legal forms and bureaucratic procedures for enforcing their picture of proper conduct and orderly change. This was a far cry from the notion that rules of etiquette and conduct were cultivated as expressed in the booklets on the history of mosques from the Urdu Bazaar, by means of which I was first inducted into the study of mosques. Or, perhaps the technical and textual engineering it now took to manage competing groups attempting to coinhabit a mosque represented another turn in that history of cultivation.

Of the three, the mosque in the Punjab Government Employees Welfare Society colony in Gauhar Town represented the most diverse milieu. While tensions were close to the surface in this colony, it was not so evidently about maslak differences as in Masjid Noor, or of class ethos as in the mosque in Gulshan. From Dr. Khan's perspective, it was about character. At times, it was a character determined by the nobility of birth or the enlightenment of education, which stood in marked contrast to the characters of those of lowly birth or those who were ignorant. At other times it was about the resolve to stay the course of a fight, descending if necessary to the level of one's enemies by employing dirty methods, or ascending by enriching one's knowledge and learning to undertake disputation. Maslak differences were simply grist for the art of war. The state was most absent in this case, having passed over many of its responsibilities to private developers who instituted little administrations of their own within the domain of the colonies.

Regardless of the outcomes of these qabzas, they provide insight into the initial striving that informed the building of mosques. Qabza made explicit the desire to stake a claim on a new nation-state, as in the case of Masjid Noor in Momin Town. It highlighted the attempt to produce an exemplary Islamic state within Pakistan and to reform religious leadership to holistically attend to the needs of a community, as in the case of the mosque in Gulshan. And it showed the encouragement of a civic spirit among a diverse group of worshipers by the attempt to have an elected mosque committee, as in the early days of the mosque in the Punjab Government Employees Welfare Society colony in Gauhar Town. These expressions of striving not only tie religious and moral development to the development of the nation-state but also to the imagination of an earlier era of Islam.

We learn of the threats to these expressions of striving by means of qabza. In the case of Masjid Noor, qabza accentuated the vulnerability of a leader's standing in the neighborhood because of the swirl of rumors about him. Qabza made evident that, long before the actual event of the seizure, the imagination of change had been compromised by a sense of middle-class entitlement and the expectation that the state would uphold the status quo in the mosque in Gulshan. The qabza of the mosque in the Punjab Government Employees Welfare Society colony loosened Dr. Khan's hold upon the world such that at a particular moment he lost faith that people were human and not animals come to attack him. But at a later point he came to be grateful for the events of qabza and even for his enemies as he learned of the richness of Islamic thought through this experience. I take this as one of those rare but decisive moments within qabza that provided an impetus for further striving.

What is noteworthy is that even if they resonated with political trends at the national level, each of these instances of qabza came from within the neighborhood, from the ties and tensions therein. In calling qabza a scene of Muslim aspiration I have attempted to draw attention to the trajectory of striving that tries to leave the ordinary behind, as a past or a sociality to move beyond, but which is shadowed by the forces informing everyday life. Insofar as qabza emerged from the neighborhood, we might also think of it as also demonstrative of the force of skepticism within social ties and intersubjective relations, of which I spoke in my introduction. To briefly illustrate what I mean by skepticism, the fact that anything could be believed about the imam in Masjid Noor suggested his community's skepticism of him. Or when Dr. Khan could not determine if those who came to denounce him were human or animals, we learn of his skeptical turn toward the world.

There were other tendencies within these neighborhoods that were in tandem with the tendency to strive. There was the resignation to a future together, as in the case of the mother and daughter in their relation to Imam Aziz; the identification with the pain of the mosque and attending to it by praying there with regularity, as in the case of the engineer in Gulshan; and the necessity that Dr. Khan felt to promise anonymity to an Ahmadi (the group that had been formally put outside the bounds of Islam) in the midst of his fights with others. In each of these gestures I find a certain resistance to the complete dissolution of social relations and modes of relatedness through the nurturing of small enclaves of tendencies counter to the mainstream ones of striving, seizing, and skepticism within everyday life. These enclaves hold out the possibility that should circumstances change they could provide the grounds for a new beginning. They held out hope for a future still open.

Chapter Two

A POSSIBLE GENEALOGY OF MUSLIM ASPIRATION

MUHAMMAD IQBAL IN HIS TIME

Iqbal as a Thought Zone

I have presented a few scenes of aspiration in contemporary Pakistan. Librarians sit around a table in the Provincial Assembly Library engaged in a heated religious argument that threatens to spill into accusations of blasphemy. Lahoris resolve to build mosques for their neighborhoods only to preside over the dissolution of their communities in their fights over the mosques. What is it that makes these sites of obvious dissonance also scenes of aspiration? It is the fact that in each of these instances each person will likely return to these situations, as they did while I was there, with as much investment in the effort of an argument or the act of constructing mosques and with the expectation that the outcomes are not entirely knowable in advance. In other words, aspiration necessitates efforts at being Muslim in the ways one knows or attaches to, which are marked by a striving to an as-yet-unattained self without presuming that this next self is the final one. This conception of aspiration, as I said earlier, is in the nature of a tendency rather than a social program or a movement. It is striving toward a determinate end while maintaining the notion of further ends and an open future.

Why would we see these scenes from this angle of aspiration when others have found them to be all-too-familiar and disturbing for speaking of a lack of consensus on Islam (Shaikh 2009)? In this chapter I argue that Muhammad Iqbal, the poet and philosopher—a central figure for Muslim thought in the region and elsewhere and ubiquitous in Pakistan—enables and hones our perception of striving in these all-too-mundane scenes of arguments and fights. While it is contestable whether Iqbal is the exclusive preserve of

Pakistan, which claims him as its spiritual founder, Pakistan—or more specifically the potential in Pakistan—is arguably better understood through Iqbal's poetry and philosophy. Iqbal offers me a theory of the creative working of time that is in close conversation with significant thinkers of time in modern Western philosophy. I place particular emphasis on Henri Bergson and Friedrich Nietzsche among Iqbal's considerable philosophical references.[1] At the same time his theory is also distinctly his own insofar as it is engaged with a long history of Islamic thought and Muslim polemics, the specificity of colonial India as the context in which he wrote, and Muslims experiencing Western modernity. Reading Iqbal reorients me to the interweaving of temporality and history, such that while we have to take seriously the historical record, we are also reminded to attune ourselves to the temporal realm of unstated intentions, unrealized potential, and faint lines of becoming, that is, the future as open, which accompanies this record.

It is not only that Iqbal helps me orient my intellectual framework toward this aspect of time as becoming. Iqbal's unique place within Pakistan ensures that the aspirations and actions of its Muslims are deeply informed by his philosophical sensibility, ideas, and gestures. The singularity of his position in the nation derives from the fact that as its spiritual founder he has an authorized presence within its books of history and heritage. At the same time he is not entirely containable within these authoritative accounts and citations of him, and his ideas circulate in ways that transgress the normative picture of him.

In this chapter, rather than reconstruct a Pakistani Iqbal and his influence from the myriad references to him within Pakistani state and society, which I do in chapters ahead, I plumb his writings for a possible genealogy of Muslim aspiration so as to recognize its presence within everyday acts of striving to be Muslim, state exertions, and the public culture of Lahore. In other words I depart from the ethnographic mode of exposition in adopting a literary, even philosophical approach to Iqbal's writings. Here I draw upon the recent edited work of the historians Sugata Bose and Kris Manjapra (2010), who show how specific South Asian intellectuals, among whom they showcase Iqbal (Jalal 2010), created zones of thought by assimilating the work of thinkers from different times and parts of the world to their own (see also Gandhi 2006). Such synthetic modes of thought helped these intellectuals develop and sustain a cosmopolitanism that exceeded the limits placed upon the imagination by colonialism or nationalism (Kaviraj 1998, Chatterjee 1993). Jane Guyer (1996) in her anthropological work in West

Africa and Souleyman Diagne (2004) in his philosophical pursuits have each suggested the importance of attending to intellectual modes of inventiveness, both in their locatedness and their translocal ambitions, in order to understand the openness and connectivity that characterizes the social (Marrati 2006, Strathern 2004). I bring together these insights in this chapter to present the zone of thought that Iqbal enabled through his politics and writings in conjunction with his intellectual predecessors and companions, in which lie the lineaments of Muslim aspiration that find their home in Pakistan.

I first present a reading of Muhammad Iqbal's relationship to Pakistan that is other than one of spiritual father. I then present the historical moment of Iqbal's emergence upon the Indian political scene, that is, the 1910s to the 1930s, which were heady decades of nationalism and anticolonialism in the late colonial era. I aim to show how Iqbal was both in keeping with his time and untimely, in the Nietzschean sense of drawing attention to the capacities of a community for good or for evil not exclusively limited to its condition or context of subjection. I next explore Iqbal's philosophy in light of the writings of Henri Bergson to suggest how Iqbal did not so much inaugurate a new project of reform for Muslims as provide a new orientation toward self-reform by means of the Bergsonian conception of time as duration. A comparison of Iqbal with Sir Sayyid Ahmed Khan and Maulana Ashraf Ali Thanawi, both famous Muslim reformers in their day, who can reasonably be said to have been at opposite ends of the spectrum of reform and whose writings continue to circulate in contemporary Pakistan, shows how Iqbal attempted a bridge between reason and revelation in the making of a new Muslim orientation to everyday life. A further comparison, of Iqbal with Muhammad Asad and Maulana Syed Abul ala Maududi, two of his contemporaries who moved to Pakistan after its formation and exerted considerable influence upon its political formation, suggests how Iqbal's picture of Muslim aspiration was one among several on offer for Pakistan, although it retained distinct qualities. Finally, I explore how the earliest constitution-making body in Pakistan used the language of experimentation to set the new nation-state on the course of an Iqbal-inspired striving to be Muslim.

Muhammad Iqbal, or Allama Iqbal as he is respectfully called, holds a special place as the visionary of Pakistan, its spiritual founder.[2] It was he who said, in a presidential address delivered at the annual session of the All-India Muslim League at Allahabad on December 29, 1930:

> I would like to see the Punjab, North-West Frontier Province, Sind and Baluchistan amalgamated into a single State. Self-government within the British Empire, or without the British Empire, the formation of a consolidated North-West Indian Muslim State, appears to be the final destiny of the Muslims, at least of North-West India. (M. Iqbal 1973: 11–12)

However, it was also he who said:

> I am opposed to Nationalism, as it is understood in Europe not because, if it is allowed to develop in India, it is likely to bring less material gain to Muslims. I am opposed to it because I see in it the germs of *atheistic materialism*, which I look upon as the greatest danger to modern humanity. Patriotism is a perfectly natural virtue, and has a place in the moral life of man. Yet, that which really matters is a man's faith, his culture, his historical traditions. These are the things which, in my eyes, are worth living for and dying for, and not the piece of earth with which the spirit of man happens to be temporarily associated. (ibid. viii, emphasis in original)

Consequently, the formation of Pakistan as a sovereign territorial entity in 1947 poses the question whether Pakistan was the fulfillment of Iqbal's vision or its antithesis (McDonough 1970, H. Malik 1971, Naim 1980, Metcalf 1982, Devji 1993). This question is unlikely to be definitively resolved, since Iqbal died in 1938, almost ten years before Pakistan came into existence. Even Muhammad Ali Jinnah, the founder of Pakistan, weighed in on this discussion by including the following introduction when he published the letters that Iqbal wrote him while Jinnah was in England:

> I think these letters are of very great historical importance, particularly those which explain his views in clear and unambiguous terms on the political future of Muslim India. His views were substantially in consonance with my own and had finally led me to the same conclusions as a result of careful examination and study of the constitutional problems facing India, and found expression in due course in the united will of

Muslim India as adumbrated in the Lahore resolution of the All-India Muslim League, popularly known as the "Pakistan Resolution," passed on 23rd March, 1940. (In H. Malik 1971: 384–85)

In other words, Jinnah's views were those of Iqbal's, which was to do what was best for Indian Muslims at that time, that is, to obtain for them a nation-state. Yet the ambiguity lingers.

As Manu Goswami (2004) has written, in the colonial period in which Muhammad Iqbal came to utter his fateful words, the expression of desire for a nation or nationality was inexorably affixed to a territory or the desire for one. Even if one militated against such an equation of nation to territoriality, as Javed Majeed (2008) has most recently shown Iqbal to do, to speak as Iqbal did on December 29, 1930, to the All-India Muslim League was to have one's words bear consequences.

Consequently, even if one could argue that Pakistan wasn't the actualization of Iqbal's ideals, it was the creation of his words. Pakistan claimed Iqbal posthumously as its poet laureate to show itself as beholden to Iqbal. And the memorializing of Iqbal continues in Pakistan, with a national holiday on his birthday, an academy dedicated to research on his work, and his presence in school curricula among the many ways in which his name is kept in circulation in both official rhetoric and everyday discourse.

Nonetheless, this degree of publicity has led his son, Javid Iqbal, to say that everyone remembered Iqbal in Pakistan but no one knew him. He reports of "a trend in Pakistan of quoting odd verses of Iqbal or talking about his ideas without having any deeper understanding of what the man actually said or meant (or in what context he said or meant)" (introduction to M. Iqbal 1961: xxvii). It appears it will not do to resolve too quickly the question of Iqbal's intention by claiming Pakistan as Iqbal's creation. The creation of a "thing" such as a nation-state, in Faisal Devji's formulation (1993), could not possibly exhaust the potential of Iqbal's thought. Rather, it is necessary to see how what Iqbal actually said or meant empirically impinged upon Pakistan's unfolding and how Pakistan's upholding of Iqbal took his thinking in new directions, perhaps unforeseen by its originator.[3] We have also to keep in mind that Iqbal has other lives and lines of thought, and that this particular actualization leaves others still to come.[4]

Can one imagine a resonance between Iqbal and Pakistan below the threshold of national events?[5] This resonance might lie in the way that Iqbal imagines a personality to develop, through the augmentation or depletion set in motion when two entities come into contact: "Man is essentially an energy, a force, or rather a combination of forces which admit of various arrangements. One definite arrangement of these forces is personality—whether it is pure chance arrangement does not concern me here. . . . That is good which has a tendency to give us the sense of personality, that is bad which has a tendency to suppress and ultimately dissolve personality" (M. Iqbal 1961: 17–19). In other words, the picture of the relationship of Iqbal to Pakistan that I present is of two entities whose proximity sets up a force field of possible influences, impingements, augmentations, and depletions between them. And relations of this nature make it likely that the resonance between the two may not always be entirely beneficial for one or the other at various points.

Reform in the Colonial Context: Historical Trajectory as Philosophical Praxis

In 1908, when Muhammad Iqbal returned to India after studying in England and receiving his doctoral degree in philosophy in Germany, the swadeshi movement had come to an end. This large-scale economic boycott of British-made consumer goods marked the transition from a previous emphasis on reform of one's religious tradition and community toward citizenship within the British Empire (Jones 1999, Goswami 2004), to that of the enhancement of one's political, economic, and spiritual abilities toward inevitable self-government (Chatterjee 1993, Sinha 2006). Among the trends of reform prevalent within the Indian Muslim community at that time were those of Sir Sayyid Ahmed Khan, who established the Muhammadan-Anglo Oriental College, later renamed the Aligarh Muslim University, intended for educating Muslim elite men to become modern colonial subjects (A. Ahmad 1967, Lelyveld 1996), and the ulama who established religious seminaries along the lines of British educational institutions toward revitalizing the traditional study of Islam with a greater focus on the Qur'an and hadis (Metcalf 1987b, Zaman 2002). Both trends aimed to purge the shadow of "custom," specifically historical accretions and the influence of Hinduism upon the tradition of Islam, from everyday Muslim religiosity. These were still informed by the earlier notion of reform, which was reconciled to the fact of the colonial state (Metcalf 1997, Devji 2007).

It was within this context that Iqbal returned to Lahore to teach. He switched his profession from teaching to that of law in 1911 and began to present his poetry in public gatherings (H. Malik 1971, Hassan 1977). It was in the midst of a new kind of Muslim political movement, one in which Muslims in India protested not their victimization as colonial subjects, nor the ambiguities of their minority status (Mufti 1995), but the situation of Muslims in other parts of the world and important Islamic sites threatened by Western encroachment, in which Iqbal's poetry found its audience. Iqbal presented his famous poem Shikwa (Complaint) in April 1909, in a poetry gathering organized by the Anjuman-e Himayat-e Islam (Society for the Support of Islam) in Lahore, following it up in 1913 by its companion Jawab-e Shikwa (Answer to the Complaint) (I examine the texts of these two poems in detail below) (M. Iqbal 1994). He followed up these public recitations of poetry with extensive collections of Urdu and Persian poetry that won him international fame and a knighthood in 1922 (Schimmel 1989).

In time, Iqbal threw his support behind the Khilafat movement, which began in 1918 to urge the British to keep intact the Ottoman Empire, the titular head of the Islamic caliphate, after the First World War. The irony of this movement was that Indian Muslims fought to keep together an empire at a time when it was undergoing internal fragmentation, from the rise of Arab and Turk nationalists who desired national self-determination (Landau 1990). However, as scholars of this movement have pointed out, the Khilafat movement did not wish to return to a previous era of Islam but sought to give shape to incipient Indian Muslim desires for a political utopia (Minault 1982). Insofar as this utopian ideal was outside of the ideal of a sovereign nation-state, it only seemed to emphasize Indian Muslim tendency toward separatism, to insist upon foreign origins when many of them were undoubtedly of Indian stock (Robinson 1974). This led B. R. Ambedkar, a famous Indian politician from the Dalit community, to finally declare support for the idea of Pakistan because a sovereign India would be more secure with its foreign and possibly disloyal elements outside of itself (1940). Yet it was not a matter of small consequence that this movement, disturbing to nationalist notions of self-rule and bounded territories, would garner the support of Mahatma Gandhi, the Indian nationalist leader, who felt that Indian Muslims gave rightful expression to their faith in protesting the treatment of their coreligionists elsewhere (Datta 1999, Devji 2005b).

In 1926, two years after the Khilafat movement finally sputtered out after the disintegration of the Ottoman Empire, Iqbal won a seat in the Punjab Legislative Council, one of the few venues for Indian self-government conceded by the British, where he served until 1930. By this time the All-India Muslim League, established in 1906 at the occasion of the All-India Muhammadan Educational Conference as a counterpart to the Indian National Congress (established 1885), had become an active presence on the national scene. Iqbal took over its leadership in 1930, during which time he gave his historic speech outlining the future of a Muslim state. Between the years of 1930 and 1932, he attended the Roundtable Discussions in Britain in his capacity as the head of the Muslim League to discuss the future of India. He was instrumental in persuading Jinnah to return from Britain from his self-imposed exile to take over the leadership of the Muslim League. Jinnah would later spearhead the movement for Pakistan. Iqbal traveled extensively, attended international conferences, met with world leaders and intellectuals, and presented six lectures in Madras, Aligarh, and Hyderabad in the late 1920s, which were later published as *The Reconstruction of Religious Thought in Islam* in Lahore in 1930 (I analyze this text in some detail below). Stricken by illness in 1933, he died an invalid in 1938. He was buried in the grounds of the grand Badshahi Masjid in Lahore, which places his mausoleum squarely within Pakistani territory.

I have given the barest sketch of Muhammad Iqbal's life in colonial India from the 1910s to the 1930s. However, even this sketch suggests a life that was involved in some way with the major religious and political movements of its day, even those whose ends were at odds with one another. The tendency in historiography has been to differentiate a later separatist Iqbal from an earlier nationalist one (H. Malik 1971, Hassan 1977). I find it more useful to see Iqbal's myriad involvements as his philosophy in practice, in which he put himself in relation to dynamic individuals and emergent movements and institutions to see how they sat with him and he with them. This was, I suggest, his mode of self-experimentation.

While Iqbal was in the advance guard of Muslim politics, scholars have long commented on the classicism and conventionality of the images that he deployed in his poetry, such as that of slavery—a trope long established in poetry for expressing the desired nature of relation to the divine—or the conservative bent of the political actions that he advocated, for instance, calling for a return to an Islamic caliphate or espousing prayer as central among the five pillars of Islam as the means to foster a sense of community (A. Ahmad 1967, Schimmel 1989). These latter tendencies do not contradict self-experimentation. They suggest that experimentation did not require the creation of the new, but rather new ways of inhabiting the fundamentals of religion toward producing the readiness for change. As Iqbal writes in his notebook: "The attitude of toleration and even conformity—without belief in dogma—is probably the most incomprehensible thing to the vulgar mind. If such is your attitude, keep quiet and never try to defend your position" (1961: 130).

A close look at some of his early poetry suggests how experimentation and convention came to be interrelated, that is, how becoming a renewed force in history required a new appreciation of one of the fundamental tenets of Islam that Muhammad was its prophet. The salience of the Prophet for Muslim aspiration has already been hinted at in the argument I witnessed at the Provincial Assembly Library and at various points during the construction of mosques. Iqbal gives both a frank appraisal of the dangers risked by the worshiper in following a prophet and possible ways to model oneself upon the Prophet of Islam to avoid such dangers.

Iqbal's Dialogue with Allah: Prophetic Guidance and Human Freedom

In 1909 Muhammad Iqbal recited Shikwa to a wide and appreciative audience. In the poem, Iqbal laments the fall of Muslims from the status of a world-historical force in upholding and spreading Islam to that of beggars, stripped of any social standing or material possessions, ghosts to the historical present:

Who were the people who asked only for You [God] and no other?
And for You did fight battles and travails suffer?
Whose world-conquering swords spread the might over one and all?
Who stirred mankind with Allah-o-Akbar's clarion call?
Whose dread bent stone idols into fearful submission?
They fell on their faces confessing, "God is One, the Only One!"
   (M. Iqbal 1994: 37)

Our complaint is not that they are rich, that their coffers overflow;
They who have no manners and of polite speech nothing know.
What injustice! Here and now are houris and palaces to infidels given;
While the poor Muslim is promised houris only after he goes to heaven.
Neither favor nor kindness is shown towards us anymore;
Where is the affection You showed us in the days of yore? (43)

Now on strangers does the world bestow its favors and esteem,
All we have been left with is a phantom world and a dream. (45)

The poem must have felt very familiar to its largely Muslim audience because it relied on imagery from the tradition of Persian and Urdu poetry, most notably those of gatherings where one met to sing praises and lament for one's beloved (that is, God) (Pritchett 1994). It also invoked and animated known events and important figures in Islamic history, such as the Prophet Muhammad and his cousin Imam Ali (Waugh 1983, Schimmel 1989). We see stock stereotypes, such as those of Muslims as sword-yielding avengers of God, iconoclasts, desirous of houris (virginal maidens) in paradise (Majeed 2007, Rustomji 2008). Interestingly, it is the stone idol, the standard representation of Hinduism in Muslim polemical literature, that Iqbal puts forward as the primary enemy of Muslims, while British colonials appear only as the strangers upon whom the world had bestowed many favors.[6] However, insofar as Iqbal had a complicated relationship to the figure of the Hindu and to Indian philosophy (Devji 2009), it would be simplistic to say that he sets up Hinduism as the natural enemy of Muslims in this poem. Rather, as I show below, the stone idol indexes the dissipative tendencies within Muslim thinking and the fossilizing of action.

Despite its familiar imagery, the poem was said to have shocked many, because in it Iqbal addresses God directly, daring to blame him for bringing Muslims to their current pitiable condition (M. Iqbal 1994). This poem is an instance of a conventional form pressed to express new feelings:

> My theme makes me bold, makes my tongue more eloquent.
> Dust be in my mouth, against Allah I make complaint. (28)

> The Koran You sent us we clasped to our breast.
> Even so You accuse us of lack of faith on our part:
> If we lacked faith, You did little to win our heart. (40)

> Your blessings are showered on homes of unbelievers, strangers all.
> Only on the poor Muslims, Your wrath like lightning falls. (41)

More challenging to piety and propriety than the verses berating God would have been Iqbal's triumphal claim regarding what Muslims accomplished at their apogee, as though undirected by God. Iqbal claims that Muslims emerged upon the scene of history at a time when people were mistaken in their thinking, for which reason the world was out of joint, a state of disorder for which Iqbal appeared to hold God responsible. Muslims inaugurated a revolution in thinking that realigned the world, rendering it natural. They did so by retelling the story of God such that His Oneness would become clear to all:

Before our time, a strange sight was the world You had made:
Some worshipped stone idols, others bowed to trees and prayed.
Accustomed to believing what they saw, the people's vision wasn't free,
How then could anyone believe in a God he couldn't see? (31)

Who routed infidel armies and destroyed them with bloody slaughter?
Who put out and made cold the "sacred" flame in Iran?
Who retold the story of the one God, Yazdan? (36)

They fell on their faces confessing, "God is One, the Only One!" (37)

Once again, Hinduism with its stone idols is the most obvious reference as the enemy of Islam, although animism and Zoroastrianism are also targeted. Iqbal hints that Indian Muslims had to battle particularly hard to install Islam in a country so given to thinking outside of the oneness of the divine. However, as I suggested earlier, Iqbal had in mind not external enemies, but internal demons that preyed upon Muslim thinking. He readily concedes to God that all revolution in thinking was beset by frailty internal to itself:

Our love may not be what it was, nor told with the same blandishments;
We may not tread the same path of submission, nor the same way give
    consent.
Our hearts are troubled, their compass needles from Mecca may have
    swerved,
Perhaps the old laws of faithfulness we may not have fully observed.
But sometimes towards us, at times to others You have affection shown,
It's not something one should say, You too have not been true to Your
    own. (49)

Shikwa gained the appreciation of its audience, it was, as noted above, also criticized, and not just for its supposed impiety. Some felt that Iqbal risked his faith in speaking to God in such a manner. Others, who felt his address to be insolent, thought he deserved punishment (1994: 59).

In 1913 Iqbal delivered a sequel to Shikwa, the Jawab-e Shikwa (Answer to the Complaint). He recited it at a political rally in Lahore to raise money for the Turkish struggle against a Bulgarian uprising, a prefiguring of the Khilafat movement. It was a public moment when a poet was called upon to recite stirring verse to move the audience in support of a transnational Muslim cause. Yet no one quite expected that God would speak through Iqbal. Iqbal had clearly assimilated the criticism leveled at his earlier poem. In this poem God rebukes Iqbal for addressing Him so impolitely, but ultimately accepts his complaints as they were spoken with such obvious pain and sincerity. This was how Iqbal explains his words finding a home in the heavens:

> Spoke the Voice: 'Your tale is indeed full of sorrow;
> Your tears tremble at the brim and are ready to flow.
> Your cry of lament the sky has rung;
> What cunning your impassioned heart has lent your tongue!
> So eloquently did you word your plaint, you made it sound like praise.
> To talk on equal terms with Us, man to celestial heights did raise.'
>   (1994: 65)

Despite accepting Iqbal's complaints, God is harsh in his rebuke. Can Iqbal not see that he is not the same as his forefathers? Does he consider himself capable of begetting the Adams of yesteryear?

> 'To every vein of falsehood, every Muslim was a knife;
> In his life's mirror, the jewel was a ceaseless strife.
> On the strength of his own arms a Muslim used to rely;
> All he feared was his God; all you fear is to die.
> If from his father's learning, a son takes no light,
> Over his sire's legacy, how can he stake his right!' (79)

> 'What kinship of the soul can there be between your ancestors and you?'
>   (80)

> 'Limitless is Our bounty, none for it will pray.
> There's no one on the seeker's path; to whom do We point the way?
> Not one proved worthy of the care with which they were raised;
> You are not the clay of which another Adam could be made.' (66)

Because Muslims were separated from their glorious past, what comes up for criticism is their regression to a pagan era and the harmful spirit of the modern age:

> 'You have no strength in your hands; in your hearts God has no place;
> On the name of My messenger, you people have brought disgrace.
> Destroyers of false gods are gone; only the idol-makers thrive;
> The sons of Abraham have departed, Azar's idolatrous breed survives.'
>   (67)

'The new age is like lightning; inflammatory is every haystack,
Neither wilderness nor garden is immune from its attack.
To this new flame old nations are like faggots on a pyre;
Followers of the last Messenger are consumed in its fire.' (85)[7]

Iqbal's triumphal claim that Muslims have inaugurated a revolution in thinking is met by God's scorn that such thinking could hardly survive without fraternity:

'You always quarrel among yourselves; they were kind and
    understanding.
You do evil deeds, find faults in others; they covered others' sins and
    were forgiving.' (81)

Thus, the promise of a new world withers for a lack of seekers:

'If there were one deserving, We'd raise him to regal splendour,
To those who seek, We would unveil a new world of wonder.' (66).

In these poems, two pictures of degeneracy face each other. None of their details would have shocked the Muslims in the audience long accustomed to chastising themselves (Hasan 1994, Jalal 2000). At the same time there were subtle but significant shifts from the complaint of the first poem to an imperative to reexamine oneself in the second poem. In the first, the lamenting Muslim asks why he is no longer a world-historical force. Has he not served God well? Did he not inaugurate a revolution in rightful thinking? What is his rightful due and how long must he wait to receive it? God quickly sizes up the Muslim's lament in the second poem. He points out that Iqbal's sole interest is in record keeping, when in reality the Muslims of yesteryear were vastly superior to the Muslims of the present era, as present-day Muslims will likely be from the youth of the future, that is, if the young even remain Muslim. Of what use is fighting over accounts of history when Muslims face the possible demise of their earthly existence, along with their revolutionary thinking and historical agency?

However, God provides a hint of a way out of this dilemma:

'Your real worth is hid, other people are yet to see what's true;
The Lord of the world's assembly has yet much need of you.' (91)

'With reason as your shield and the sword of love in your hand,
Servant of God! The leadership of the world is at your command.

The cry, "Allah-o-Akbar," destroys all except God; it is a fire.
If you are true Muslims, *your destiny is to grasp what you aspire.*
If you break not faith with Muhammad, We shall always be with you;
What is this miserable world? To write the world's history, pen and
    tablet We offer you.' (96, my emphasis)

God finally yields to Iqbal's pleadings, evincing awareness that Muslim
victories had once been great and could once again be so. But contemporary
Muslims manifest tendencies of thought that proliferate godheads. They are
judged wanting by God for their feelings of bitter resentment and postures
of frozen resignation. Such tendencies of thought, feeling, and posture
indicate that Muslims did themselves more harm than has been done to
them. And God's revaluation calls for a change in oneself so that the spring
to action could come from a newly vitalized self. To achieve this new condition, God's first imperative is to "break not faith with Muhammad." The
second is, "your destiny is to grasp what you aspire." Thus, crucial to amend-
ing defective modes of existence is the search for the proper relation between
one's fidelity to the past and one's desires for the future, between prophetic
guidance and human freedom.

Time in Iqbal's Thinking: Teleology and the Potential of an Open Future

Although God, in Iqbal's poem, obviously places great importance on the
relationship between prophetic guidance and human freedom to enable
Muslim self-transformation, this relationship is a fraught one within Iqbal's
evaluation of Muslim history and futurity.[8] In *The Reconstruction of Religious
Thought in Islam* (1996)[9] Iqbal provides an exposition of the uniqueness of the
prophet figure within Islam. Prophets are unique in that they have religious
experiences not unlike mystics, but unlike mystics they choose to return
from such privileged proximity to God in order to share their experiences
with humans: "The mystic does not wish to return from the repose of
'unitary experience'; and even when he does return, as he must, his return
does not mean much for mankind at large. The prophet's return is creative.
He returns to insert himself into the sweep of time with a view to control the
forces of history, and thereby to create a new world of ideals" (ibid., 111).
Further on, Iqbal describes the prophetic consciousness as "a mode of econ-
omizing individual thought and choice by providing readymade judgments,
choices, and ways of action" (112). However, Iqbal states, it is only after

prophets had ceased to come, that humans could finally experience genuine freedom: "This involves the keen perception that life cannot for ever be kept in leading strings; that in order to achieve full self-consciousness, man must finally be thrown back on his own resources" (113). Consequently, human freedom, earned after a long period of tutelage under prophets, must be jealously guarded. Most particularly humans had to guard against encroachments upon their freedom by forces that occasionally emerge among a people as a consequence of their historical deprivation and suffering. The one force that Iqbal singles out for trenchant critique, which he would identify with the Ahmadiyya, was what he called the "Magian crust . . . over Islam," of which he said, "one important feature of Magian culture is a perpetual attitude of expectation, a constant looking forward to the coming of Zoroaster's unborn sons, the Messiah, or the Paraclete of the fourth gospel" (126–27).

Even though a proper appreciation of the Prophet Muhammad's greatness and the necessity to mold oneself on his example remains an imperative for Muslims, Iqbal is able to more easily cast human freedom in relationship to divine providence over prophetic guidance. It is through the Muslim relationship to God that Iqbal seeks to present a new perception of reality by means of which Muslims could come to appreciate their own capacities.

A crucial way to indicate divine providence in monotheistic religions is by their teleological underpinnings.[10] Islam is strongly informed by teleology, in the sense of final causes and ends. Although the notion of a fully determined course of individual history, what goes by the name of predestination, has been differentially mobilized in Islamic history and theology, the tradition bids its worshipers to act in this world with the knowledge of the brevity of earthly existence and the certainty that they will meet their maker (F. Rahman 1979). Consequently, in addition to detailed attention to worship incumbent upon Muslims ('ibadat), there are highly developed codes to inform matters of faith and belief ('aqidat), ethical character (akhlaq), and worldly affairs (mu'amalat), among others (Thanawi 1976). These give a certain tenor and temporality to Muslim everyday life, most notably of engaging in worldly life while keeping the image of the afterlife in one's mind's eye (Hirschkind 2006).

Besides pitching numerous philosophical battles that do not concern us here, Iqbal's writings in The Reconstruction of Religious Thought in Islam are best located in the place between worldly engagement and the eye toward the otherworldly. His central concern was to provide a picture of human freedom that did not chafe under the weight of teleology but delighted in it. At the same time human freedom had to be convinced of its own capacity to effect meaningful change in this world in order to be active.[11] Iqbal worked out this problematic by thinking through Bergson's own, which was that of enabling change in the human perception of time so that humans could see how their present was charged with open-ended potential.

By the time Iqbal presented his lectures in India in the late 1920s Bergson's *Creative Evolution* had been reprinted numerous times since its first appearance in 1907. *Matter and Memory* preceded it in 1896, but it took *Creative Evolution* to make the former understandable (Bergson 1965). *The Creative Mind*, published in 1934, delved further into Bergson's concepts of "duration" and "intuition," the first being the reality of time as a dynamic continuity and the second the imaginative means by which humans could perceive duration. But it was *Creative Evolution* of 1907 that made the French vitalist philosopher famous in the world, and this text, more than any others by Bergson, showed its considerable influence upon Iqbal's writing.[12]

Bergson was an evolutionary thinker. However, in *Creative Evolution* it was clear that he did not agree with the picture of evolution as selective adaptation to a given environment or as accidental variation.[13] The first he faulted for giving too much credit to externality. It was as if a body could do no more than produce defensive reactions to its environments and all that a body could do was already in place awaiting actualization and adaptation. The second he faulted for not taking into consideration the simultaneous appearance of specific features, such as the eye in diverse forms of organic life, an original and unprecedented outcome for which no accident could account. Each of these theories lacked an account of the original impetus for evolution, that is, life. "Life . . . is essentially a current sent through matter, drawing from it what it can. There has not, properly speaking, been any project or plan" (1998: 265). This picture of life as a vital impulse through matter allowed Bergson to provide a positive account of evolution as a continual discharge of creative ideas and tendencies moving through a world of matter. Furthermore, "Life . . . progresses and *endures* in time" (ibid., 51). Thus the creativity manifest in evolution indexed the durational aspect of time as continuous and creative movement.

Within this picture of evolution, humans introduced creativity into the world through the choices they made in undertaking any action. In *Matter and Memory* (1996: 162) Bergson provided a diagram of a cone in which the summit of the cone rests on a plane. The plane is the representation of the world. The summit is the point at which the human inserts himself or herself into this world. The point of contact between the summit and the plane is the present and the outreaches of the cone are memories, some recollected, some deep in the subconscious, some having the quality of dreams. These memories crowd into the present at its point of contact with the plane, and do so at every moment of human existence. The past rushing upon the present possesses what Brian Massumi (2002) calls "potential" to indicate that its capacity was far in excess of those possibilities that had come to pass, or even those that could have come to pass.[14] In this manner we are given to see how retrieving from one's past in order to act upon the world or shape a response to it could introduce newness into the world.

Bergson (1965) wearied of trying to convince people of his understanding of time. This was, he claimed, because people are entrenched in their spatial modes of apprehending time. For instance, units of measurement lead people to concentrate on the two ends of a temporal act rather than the movement in between them, which better approximates the dynamical quality of time. And this truncation and serialization of time is the product of human intelligence. In *Creative Evolution* he writes: "Everything is obscure in the idea of creation if we think of things which are created. . . . It is natural to our intellect, whose function is essentially practical, made to present to us things and states rather than changes and acts. But things and states are only views, taken by our mind, of becoming. There are no things, there are only actions" (1998: 248). This incapacity of intelligence to grasp the durational aspect of time called for what Bergson elaborated in *The Creative Mind* (1965) as "intuition." Intuition demands that humans take a leap of imagination to immerse themselves in time as duration. Only then can humans sense this interplay of the past and the future upon their every present, an entangled temporal flow of which they are active conduits.

Intuition produces not only an experience of time as duration, but also the awareness that one is not yet a distinct self, set apart from other selves. Rather, one is in a perpetual state of becoming. As Bergson writes, "*Life does not proceed by the association and addition of elements, but by dissociation and division*" (1998: 89, emphasis in original). "We may conclude, then, that individuality is never perfect, and that it is often difficult, sometimes impossible, to tell what is an individual, and what is not, but that life nevertheless manifests a search for individuality . . ." (ibid., 15). Bergson's philosophy asserted the a priori of matter, life, and time before the individual. The individual or individuation was the propensity of matter, while multiplicity was its actuality.

Iqbal's debt to Bergson, analyzed in detail by only a few scholars (Bausani 1954, Schimmel 1989, Diagne n.d.), is evident early in *The Reconstruction of Religious Thought in Islam* when he quotes the Prophet Muhammad as saying: "Do not vilify time, for time is God" (1996: 17). Further on, Iqbal writes on the themes of life and time:

> Life, is then, a unique phenomenon and the concept of mechanism is inadequate for its analysis. Its "factual wholeness" . . . is a kind of unity which looked at from another point of view, is also a plurality. In all the purposive processes of growth and adaptation to its environment, whether this adaptation is secured by the formation of fresh or the modification of old habits, it possesses a career which is unthinkable in the case of a machine. (46)

The human being out of touch with life's vital force was simply "dead matter":

> If he does not take the initiative, if he does not evolve the inner richness of his being, if he ceases to fell the inward push of advancing life, then the spirit within him hardens into stone and he is reduced to the level of dead matter. But his life and the onward march of his spirit depend on the establishment of connections with the reality that confronts him. (19)

By seeking genuine connections to reality humans could experience time as it really was:

> Pure time, as revealed by a deeper analysis of our conscious experience, is not a string of separate, reversible instants; it is an organic whole in which the past is not left behind, but is moving along with, and operating in, the present and the future is given to it not as lying before, yet to be traversed; it is given only in the sense that it is present in its nature as an open possibility. It is time regarded as an organic whole that the Quran describes as "Taqdir" or the destiny—a word which has been so much misunderstood both in and out of the world of Islam. (49–50)

Iqbal also appears to accept Bergson's understanding of intellect as denying humans the experience of time as duration. In *The Reconstruction of Religious Thought in Islam*, Iqbal writes: "The ordinary rational consciousness, in view of our practical need of adaptation to our environment, takes that Reality piecemeal, selecting successively isolated sets of stimuli for response" (ibid.: 24). But Iqbal stops short of advocating intuition as the only means to perceive duration. Rather, he proposes intelligence as a means. His challenge to Bergson is worth recounting because it suggests how Iqbal rendered vitalist philosophy (which denied teleology) acceptable to Islam. If life is positively inclined toward human existence, Iqbal asks, as evidenced by the flourishing of humans as a species, surely it had not erred in having invented intelligence/rational consciousness/thought? In other words, intelligence was also a product of life and, as such, it ought not to be dismissed at the outset. What was needed was a careful consideration of the task that intelligence set itself: "Thought has a deeper movement also. While it appears to break up Reality into static fragments, its real function is to synthesize the elements of experience by employing categories suitable to the various levels which experience presents"(52). The work undertaken by intelligence suggested that intelligence was informed by short-term goals. And insofar as intelligence was "as much organic as life. . . . It (life) is determined by ends, and the presence of ends means that it is permeated by intelligence. Nor is the activity of intelligence possible without the presence of ends" (52). Thus, Iqbal counters Bergson's claim that life had no overarching project or plan and instead suggests that life was permeated by a forward-looking intelligence. Later, addressing Bergson more directly, Iqbal writes:

> Again, in Bergson's view, the forward rush of the vital impulse in its creative freedom is unilluminated by the light of an immediate or remote purpose. It is not aiming at a result; it is wholly arbitrary, undirected, chaotic, and enforceable in its behaviors. It is mainly here that Bergson's analysis of our conscious experience reveals its inadequacy. He regards conscious experience as the past moving along with and operating in the present. He ignores that the unity of consciousness has a forward aspect also. Life is only a series of acts of attention, and an act of attention is inexplicable without reference to a purpose, conscious or unconscious. (52)

The idea of a forward-looking aspect to the intelligence permeating life provided Iqbal with the opening to insert teleology into the Bergsonian understanding of the world as continual becoming: "Reality is not a blind vital impulse wholly unilluminated by idea. Its nature is through and through teleological" (53). This assertion further enabled him to introduce the concept of God, variously called the Ultimate Reality, Divine Self, and Absolute Ego:

A critical interpretation of time as revealed in ourselves had led us to a notion of the Ultimate Reality as pure duration in which thought, life, and purpose interpenetrate to form an organic unity. (54–55)

Nature is to the Divine Self as character is to the human self. In the picturesque phrase of the Quran it is the habit of Allah. (55)

In our observation of Nature we are virtually seeking a kind of intimacy with the Absolute Ego; and this is only another kind of worship. (56)

Iqbal was of course constrained to introduce the concept of God. After all, his project was to determine how and why Muslims had fallen out of God's good graces. Any tasks he would set Muslims to secure a future had to involve finding a way back to God. Thus it was not surprising that Iqbal would find a way to speak of God within a Bergsonian framework. Bergson briefly did the same in *Creative Evolution*, before going on to explore this possibility in *Two Sources of Religion and Morality* (1977). More interesting is the manner in which Iqbal engages Bergson to present, first, a teleological picture of Muslim striving and, second, an understanding of teleology other than that of aiming at a final end. Instead, he suggests that for Muslims an "ought to be" stands in the forefront, inflecting the present well before any final end. Iqbal writes: "The past, no doubt, abides and operates in the present; but this operation of the past in the present is not the whole consciousness. The element of purpose discloses a kind of forward look in consciousness. . . . To be determined by an end is to be determined by what ought to be" (1996: 53). In other words, it is not a final end that draws human beings inexorably toward it. It is short-term religious objectives, projected by one's own intelligence, which inform human movement in time toward God.

What had become of the teleology of final ends and causes? Of what use was even a notion of teleology if humans act according to their own motivations? As if in anticipation of such questions, Iqbal writes: "The future certainly pre-exists in the organic whole of God's creative life, but it pre-exists as an open possibility, not as a fixed order of events with definite outlines" (1996: 74). Addressing the question of God more directly, he writes:

The Ultimate Ego exists in pure duration wherein change ceases to be a succession of varying attitudes, and reveals its true character as continuous creation, "untouched by weariness" and unseizable "by slumber of sleep." . . . The "not-yet" of man does mean pursuit and may mean failure; the "not-yet" of God means unfailing realization of the infinite creative possibilities of His being which retains its whole throughout the entire process. (58)

We can better understand Iqbal's answer by utilizing Bergson's image of the cone standing upright with its summit resting on a plane. In an Iqbalian rendition of this image, the plane would be the field of God's potential. Just as the past rushes into the present at its point of insertion into the plane, so too does the field arch toward that point. The human located at that point is both active in the past and drawn to the future, which curves to meet him or her. In other words, there is mutual attraction between one's forward-looking intelligence and God's essence as a field of potential.

This formulation raised the question of God's finiteness, in that, in place of a transcendental God who was all knowing and all seeing, readers were presented with a potential-bearing God, one who was not aware in advance how this potential might be actualized (Maruf 1983). Iqbal's counter to this was to assert that there was both a durational quality to God and a transcendental aspect in which God was out of time. In this second aspect, time presented itself to God as a series of "nows." Instead of seeing these articulations as a contradiction or its quick settlement in Iqbal's thinking, I propose that we see it as an instantiation of Iqbal's nondialectical mode of thinking. As I will take up this discussion in the following section, for the remainder of this section, I ponder what ends intelligence sets itself with respect to God and what promise such a reformulation of Islam in Bergsonian terms has for Muslims fallen into degeneracy.

Bergson characterized life as steeped in multiplicity but moving forward by dissociation and individuation. This impulse to individuation is also evident in Iqbal's framework: "The ultimate aim of the ego is not to see something, but to be something. It is in the ego's effort to be something that he discovers his final opportunity to sharpen his objectivity and acquire a more fundamental 'I am' . . . The end of the ego's quest is not emancipation from the limitations of individuality, it is on the other hand a more precise definition of it" (Iqbal 1996: 173). Individuation, driven by the sense of what ought to be, aspires to actualize one of the many qualities of God (al-Ghazali 1992). As the field of potential arced to meet this line of individuation, the quality of God held in potential within this field transected with the line manifesting a distinct individual.

What manner of relatedness was this to God?

It is the lot of man to share in the deeper aspirations of the universe around him and to shape his own destiny as well as that of the universe, now by adjusting himself to its forces, now by putting the whole of his energy to mould its forces to his own ends and purposes. And in this process of progressive change God becomes a co-worker with him, providing man takes the initiative: "Verily God will not change the condition of men, till they change what is in themselves." (Iqbal 1996: 48–49)

The human toils with God to forge himself or herself as an individual. Insofar as individuation is the means of change, this copartnership implies the advancement of the self as the object of striving. Given that this self arcs toward God and partners with God in order to advance, its self-advancement implies change in the world. In other words, the creation of the self and that of the world are crucially linked. Insofar as individuation is a condition of perpetual becoming with the possibility of failure, this process implies that there are only ever limited ends and partial beings along the way and that such change is not progressive.

Iqbal's support of human freedom led him to transfigure this condition of partiality into the celebrated one of finitude: "Whatever may be the final fate of man it does not mean the less of individuality. The Quran does not contemplate complete liberation from finitude as the highest state of human bliss" (1996: 104). As such, finitude is worthy of the most vigorous protection, undoubtedly from one's external enemies but more insistently from enemies internal to one's community, those who are easily disappointed with this condition and ready to part with it at the first opportunity of annihilating themselves in the divine:[15] "True infinity does not mean infinite extension which cannot be conceived without embracing all available finite extensions. Its nature consists in intensity and not extensity; and the moment we fix our gaze on intensity, we begin to see that the finite ego must be distinct, though not isolated, from the infinite" (105).

This, in essence, was Iqbal's philosophical project, to understand how the past and the future were to be reconciled according to God's imperative in Jawab-e Shikwa. A new orientation to reality, one that experienced time as duration, would change the perspective of Muslims about their state of decline. In learning to value their intelligence, particular the value of finite ends, they would be motivated to act to better themselves. And in so doing, they would change the world.

Iqbal does hint, in this poem, that humans are to be informed by prophetic guidance. Humans protective of their finitude in the presence of the divine will recall the action of prophets who return to the people, rather than stay in privileged places of proximity to God. Is one then to model oneself on discrete actions and qualities of the Prophet, or to make the entirety of the Prophet's personality or the height achieved by the Prophet the end of one's striving? In keeping with the prophetic action of returning to the people, that is, in emphasizing the importance of the people for themselves, for Iqbal the ends of one's striving could only be one's next self. Moreover, given that change was nonprogressive, one could not assume that one's next self lay ahead of oneself. It could lie alongside of one or in one's past, requiring that one develop an attunement to one's actualized, possible, and potential selves as one strove to realize a distinct individuality. This speculation is consonant with Bergson's claim that while individuality was a propensity, multiplicity was the reality of life. As Iqbal himself said, albeit more enigmatically: "It is the inadequacy of the logical understanding which finds a multiplicity of mutually repellent individualities with no prospect of their ultimate reduction to a unity that makes us skeptical about the conclusiveness of thought. In fact, the logical understanding is incapable of this multiplicity as a coherent universe" (1996: 13).

Finally, Iqbal drew attention to the shadow of disappointment that accompanies the human condition of perpetual becoming. This disappointment makes humans vulnerable to parting too easily with the selves that they have realized. Muslims were told to be protective of themselves such that when they arrived within the presence of God, they would care enough for themselves, for the person they sought to be, not to part with their finitude too quickly.

Given this, can one still say that Iqbal's thinking was riddled by contradictions? Is it enough to rescue Iqbal from the charge of contradiction by arguing that his philosophical project was directed at subjective experience, the creation of personality, or an aesthetics of the self and, therefore, should not be held to the dry standards of reason (A. Ahmad 1967, Malik 1971, Schimmel 1989, Majeed 2009)? A brief comparison of Iqbal to Sayyid Ahmed Khan and Maulana Ashraf Ali Thanawi hints at a more ambitious project of thinking and acting nondialectically, one in which the durational aspect of God and God outside of time belong together within the same picture.

Muhammad Iqbal's focus on individuality, personality, and self, has lead to his being read as a theorist of the self, preoccupied with Muslims crafting and tethering their subjectivity to the contemporary world. However, his engagement with Bergson provides grounds for a somewhat different reading. When Iqbal spoke of a self-seeking individuation, he did not mean the creation of a modern-day identity, such as that of a rights-bearing citizen in a nation-state, or a subject distinguished by the peculiarities of his or her own way of life or point of view or a specific interiority. He meant making manifest qualities attributed to God, such as those of majesty, beauty, and grace (al-Ghazali 1992). To actualize those qualities meant to embody majesty, beauty, or grace to the best of one's ability.[16] Moreover, Iqbal conceptualized that such individuation was never complete. In other words, one never quite arrives at a bounded self, distinct from others. Instead, one formed a continuum of such qualities with others. These considerations of the aim and process of individuation lead me to speculate that Iqbal had in mind individuality marked by a certain impersonality, with the degree of impersonality achieved determining the uniqueness of the self. In other words, the more one manifests the impersonal quality of (for example) grace, the more unique one is.[17]

Experimentation and convention, fidelity to one's past and seeking one's future, prophetic guidance and human freedom, reason and revelation, teleology and open future, duration and transcendence, freedom and finitude, individuality and impersonality. These are the nonintuitive pairings that spring from my examination of Iqbal's life and works. They do not suggest contradictions seeking a dialectical resolution, in which one of the two elements of a pair is excised or the two combine to produce a third form. Nor are they in relationships in which one qualifies or limits the other, or serves as its other. Rather, the elements are drawn to each other, a mutual attraction that does not detract from the plenitude of each.[18] In this section, I attempt only a demonstration of this method of intercalating the world.[19] I will focus on reason and revelation, which have a long history of tense, even oppositional interrelatedness in Islamic theology (Reinhart 1995), but which in the context of colonial India effectively describe the point of contention between the modernist project of Sayyid Ahmed Khan and the position of traditionalists espoused, for instance, by the Deobandi scholar Maulana

Ashraf Ali Thanawi.[20] Both were lines of reform that Iqbal inherited. The question is how did he inherit them? The first position is that since religion is natural, natural reason is the sole criterion by which to judge what is authentic and worthy of upholding in the practice of the religion.[21] The second holds that since religion is the gift of God, its modes of reasoning are inscrutable to the lay Muslim; one could be guided only by a sound source, such as the Qur'an and hadis, in securing Islam from unlawful innovation and the accretions of custom in Muslim life. In The Reconstruction of Religious Thought in Islam I find Iqbal to affirm both positions, while suggesting how the two attract each other, or rather are drawn together in human nature.

In the aftermath of the Mutiny of 1857, in which a disproportionate number of Muslims were involved, Sir Sayyid became known for his stirring defense of Muslim loyalty to the British Empire (Khan Review n.d., Khan 1970). At the same time he became engaged in efforts to found an educational institution, the Muhammedan Anglo-Oriental College, which would train elite Muslim men to be modern colonial subjects (Lelyveld 1996). He also wrote copiously for a largely educated Muslim audience to provide them the intellectual resources by which to reform themselves, particularly their religious perspectives (Devji 1993). He was interested specifically in grounding Islam in science, or rather rationality, such that Muslims would be freed from the tensions perceived between the two (A. Ahmad 1967, Brown 1996). Toward this end, Sir Sayyid writes, in his "Lecture on Islam":

> The only criterion for the truth of the religions which are present before us is whether the religion is in correspondence with the natural disposition of man, or with nature. If yes, then it is true, and such correspondence is a clear sign that this religion has been sent by that person which has created man. But if this religion is against the nature of man and his natural constitution and against his forces and faculties, and if it hinders man from employing these profitably, then there can be no doubt that this religion is not sent by the person that created man, because everyone will agree that religion was made for man. You can turn this and state to the same effect that man was created for religion. (Khan 2007: 36)

While he granted that religion was made up of both revelation and reason, he felt that one's continued practice of religion had to be grounded in reason. That is, one came to attach to and uphold a religion first and foremost because it agreed with one's physical constitution, with this constitution the seat of reason. In order to be able to give the human body this status, he projected the laws of nature onto it, seeing it as informed by regularity and, therefore, given to the natural workings of reason. And this line of reasoning led him to pose the further necessity of taking nature seriously in its broadest sense, as encompassing the physical world, intellectual reason, and the capacities of the body, rather than in its curtailed sense as flawed human nature that served as an obstacle to religion, a perspective he attributed to the ulama. In other words, religion had to suit humans, rather than humans suit religion, for in suiting humans it suited nature.

One way to understand Iqbal's relationship to Sir Sayyid is in Sir Sayyid's affirmation of nature, or more crucially, the human constitution. The latter produced the discursive space for Iqbal to argue for the importance of thinking evolutionarily, rather than only historically. For Muslim thinking to be once again revolutionary, Iqbal said in *The Reconstruction of Religious Thought*, "it was in need of biological renewal (1996: 149)." What is needed was a theory of human perception that understands it within the workings of concrete nature and is not divorced from it. This theory would acknowledge the human body's natural instincts and sense perceptions, as well as its intelligence, and their place within the larger picture of natural evolution. For only then would Muslims understand how by working on oneself one could produce change in the world.[22] More fundamentally yet, Sir Sayyid's understanding of a religious life lived by the workings of reason alone gave Iqbal an affirmative picture of existence after revelation had ceased.

Sayyid Ahmed Khan repudiated the supernatural aspect of miracles, insisting that they had to conform to the laws of nature if they were to be considered a part of religion. Quoting Shah Waliullah, the eighteenth-century Indian Muslim theologian, in his "Principles of Exegesis," he writes:

> "Mujizat (miracles of the Prophet) and karamat (miracles of saints) are things causal which are dominantly characterized by fullness of causal relation." So the Shah believes that miracles are caused by natural causes and according to his view the occurrence of miracles conforms to the law of nature. We do not question this view. What we question is whether miracles be regarded as mafauq al-firta, i.e., "supernatural" in English. We negate this and consider its occurrence as impossible as the infringement of the verbal promise of God. We declare openly that there is no proof of the occurrence of anything supernatural, which, it is asserted, is the miracle. (2004: 31)

In espousing this view, Sir Sayyid would be marked, derogatively, as a *nechari* (naturalist) in the eyes of the ulama. To show how revelation was understood by the ulama, and also put into action by Muhammad Iqbal, I present the views of Maulana Ashraf Ali Thanawi. Maulana Thanawi was a reputed Islamic scholar trained in the Dar-ul Uloom Deoband. Beside his book of conduct for women, *Bihishti Zewar*, which made him a household name among South Asians (Metcalf 1997), he was most famous for his writings on *tasawwuf*, which contributed to bringing Sufi thinking and practice within the ambit of Islamic legalism.

Interestingly, in Pakistan Thanawi shares the title of Hakim ul-Ummat, "physician of the moral community," with Muhammad Iqbal.[23] And although his intellectual realm and field of influence are quite different from Iqbal's (Zaman 2008), his writings showed him to be equally, if not more so, concerned with the spiritual sickness that modernity had produced in Muslims as Iqbal. He did not simply view these as exacerbations of the doubts and anxieties that fall within the usual purview of Sufism, with its attentiveness to spiritual health, but rather much more.[24] Iqbal would have agreed with Thanawi that even the striving to overcome the sickness of modernity risked spiritual ailment. Although Iqbal's cure lay in continued self-experimentation, Thanawi's prescription lay in Muslims relying exclusively on the proper religious authorities for the rightful answers to excise doubts. Yet even so, Thanawi left open the possibility that the alleviation from sickness ultimately rested upon whether the suggested cure was to "one's taste," that is, up to the striving or sick self. As he writes in his introduction to *Answer to Modernism*: "How is it that when you are afflicted with religious doubts, you just expect that the *ulema* themselves should attend you? Why do you not turn to them yourselves? And if, during this quest, one *alim* fails to restore your health (either because his answer is not sufficient, or because it is not to your taste), why do you not seek out other *ulema*?" (1976: 7)[25]

An *Answer to Modernism* was written for the students in the Muhammedan Anglo-Oriental College, ironically, the institution founded by the man whose position he countered, Sayyid Ahmed Khan. During one of his visits to the town of Aligarh, where the college was located, Thanawi was requested by students of the college to give them a few beneficial lectures. He asked them to submit their doubts and anxieties to him so that he might answer each individually, but evidently he felt compelled to write a book addressing the main issues of doubts shared by those who came to him for guidance. In it, Thanawi attempted to undercut Sir Sayyid's highly publicized and by this time infamous position on the naturalist basis of religion in several ways. I focus on three of the strategies Thanawi employed in his defense of miracles as supernatural events.

First, arguing under the rubric of logic, that is, from within reason, he argues the possibility of something being improbable rather than impossible. This leads him to say: "The impossible is opposed to reason, while the improbable is opposed merely to habit" (1976: 20). Second, he asserts the priority of sound reports over reason:

> It is rationally possible for the Heavens to exist as the Muslims in general believe them to do. That is to say, reason does not possess any argument either to confirm or to deny this fact, but admits both the probabilities. So, in order to decide whether such a thing does exist or not, reason has to depend on an argument based on report. And such an argument based on sound report is provided by the Holy Qur'an and the Hadith, declaring that such a thing does exist. So reason must, as of necessity, affirm the existence of the Heavens. (18)

Third, he asserts that God's reality was beyond observation and empirical deduction, that is, beyond the capacities of reason. His argument provides a flavor of the religious disputations common in colonial times:

> We have already established that the material world is not eternal, but created and temporal. Now, let us suppose that the earth went on having rains in the rainy season year by year, and this became established as the habitual process. But there once came a rainy season when there was a complete drought. This had happened for the first time, and it did not as yet form a part of the habitual process. If the habit of getting rains in the rainy season was "a promise in the form of an act,"[26] how did things go against this promise?

> . . . At this stage, one may raise still another objection, and say that this did not go against the habitual ways, for the habitual way, in the real sense, is the sequence of physical causes and effects, and thence one should include all these diverse phenomena in the habitual way. To this new assertion we would reply that since physical causes themselves are in need of being manipulated by the Divine Power and of being related to the Divine Will, this principle (i.e., physical causes produce certain effects) would itself have to depend on a more basic principle (i.e. physical causes are controlled by Divine Power and Will). So, the latter alone

would genuinely be called the habitual way. And it would still hold good, even when things go against scientific laws. Seen from this point of view, what is seemingly opposed to the habitual way actually turns out to be in perfect conformity with it. (45–46)

This line of reasoning allowed Thanawi to argue for the existence of miracles, as events for which one could not provide any rational explanation but which must be accepted as the habit of Allah.

Addressing the issue of miracles, Muhammad Iqbal wrote in his notebook:

> The question is not whether miracles did nor did not happen. This is only a question of evidence which may be interpreted in various ways. The real question is whether belief in miracles is useful to a community. I say it is; since such a belief intensified the sense of the supernatural which holds together primitive societies and those societies (e.g., Islam) whose nationality is ideal and not territorial. Looked at from the standpoint of social evolution, then, belief in miracles appears to be almost a necessity. (1961: 118–19)

Iqbal may be read as making a functional argument for miracles, that is, miracles were to be believed because they were useful. However, I read him as saying that just as Muslims needed to understand the capaciousness of nature to be able to engage and value human striving, so too did they need to accord existence to the supernatural. As he quotes from the Qur'an in *The Reconstruction of Religious Thought*: "God adds to His creation what he will" (1996: 66). Without the narratives of the supernatural, one had little sense of the quality of experience one was striving for. This formulation did not place the supernatural outside of the realm of everyday life but alongside it. Again in *The Reconstruction of Religious Thought*, Iqbal writes about mystical states: "All that I mean to suggest is that the immediacy of our experience in the mystic state is not without a parallel. It has some sort of resemblance to our normal experience and probably belongs to the same category" (25). Later: "In order to achieve this intimacy thought must rise higher than itself, and find its fulfillment in an attitude of mind which religion describes as prayer, one of the last words on the lips of the Prophet of Islam" (59).[27]

I find Iqbal to affirm the contributions of Sir Sayyid and of Maulana Thanawi on the issues of reason and revelation, while taking both positions further. He accepted Sir Sayyid's claim that human nature was capable of purifying religion, and he did so by representing humans as co-workers of God in duration. He accepted Thanawi's claim that revelation preceded reason by giving God a transcendental nature, outside of time: "The eye of God sees all the visibles, and his ear hears all the audibles in one indivisible act of perception" (1996: 71). However, I would argue that the reason why such two oppositional lines of thought came to be within the realm of Iqbal's thinking and, only then, worthy of his affirmation, was that they both sensed human restlessness and affirmed it.[28] At least in the examples I have provided in this section Sir Sayyid affirms human nature, while Thanawi affirms human taste.

Thus far we have seen that although Iqbal's thinking and expressions are quite distinctive, he is hardly exclusive in the problems he set himself, that of the Muslim condition in the world; the concepts he uses, such as reason and revelation; and the affirmations he seeks to make, for instance, of human nature. These were a part of his milieu and the conversations around him. A comparison with two additional thinkers, Muhammad Asad and Maulana Abul ala Maududi, who were as involved as Iqbal in the reform of Muslims, mobilizing similar vitalist perspectives and imagery, underlines how singular, yet easily displaced the idea of an open future was within an Iqbalian picture of striving.

Islam in Its Proper Place versus the Islamic State: Asad and Maududi

Muhammad Asad, an Austrian Jew, converted to Islam in 1926 over the course of long travels and sojourns in the Middle East. He came to India in the last decade of colonialism, where he entered into deep conversation on the contemporary fate of Muslims with Indian Muslim intellectuals such as Muhammad Iqbal. He moved to Lahore after the formation of Pakistan in 1947. Although he only served the state of Pakistan late in his life as its ambassador to the United Nations, in the early years of Pakistan he was mostly known for his autobiographical and journalistic writings and his books on Islam, through which he exerted quiet but considerable influence upon debates over the future of Pakistan. Later he also came to be particularly well known for his translation of the Qur'an (Chaghatai 2006).[29]

In drawing out Asad's characterization of Muslim striving, it is worthwhile to touch on how he came to be a Muslim. He writes in *Islam at the Crossroads* (1947), a book dedicated to "Muslim youth," that he became obsessed with understanding why Muslims of the early twentieth century were in such a state of disarray despite the greatness of Islam. In the course of his search prior to his becoming a Muslim, someone remarked to him: "But you are a Muslim, only you don't know it yourself" (1947: 4). After his conversion he could provide no better explanation for it except to say, "This feeling that everything in the teachings and postulates of Islam is 'in its proper place' has created the strongest impression on us." Thus, his notion of finding a new world in the present, one in which Muslims were not in disarray, was one in which Islam would be "in its proper place" (5).

On the one hand, Asad writes, "we need not 'reform' Islam, as some Muslims think—for that is already perfect in itself" (154). On the other, he argues, "In order that they may once again become a creative force in the life of Muslims, the valuation of the Islamic propositions must be revised in the light of our *own* understanding of the original sources" (159). Between two seemingly contradictory sentences, one that posits Islam as perfect and in need of no reform, and the second that Islam should be evaluated in light of present needs, stands the figure of the Muslim who is yet to come. As Asad announces, "Our object is to make conscious, determined, deep-hearted men of action. Men and women of such a style were the Companions of the Prophet" (144). To become such a Muslim, one who might even one day "create a new *fiqh* [Islamic jurisprudence], exactly conforming to the Two Sources of Islam—the Qur'an and the life-example of the Prophet—at the same time answering to the exigencies of present life" (159), present-day Muslims "need to reform ourselves: What we must reform is our attitude towards religion, our laziness, our self-conceit, our short-sightedness, in one word, *our* defects . . . it should be a change from *within ourselves*—and it should be in the direction of Islam, and not away from it" (154–55). Moreover, this turn toward Islam had also to be a turn toward the historical moment: "If we conform ourselves to the principles of this religion we cannot wish to eliminate modern learning from our life. We must have the wish to learn and to progress and to become scientifically and economically as efficient as the Western nations are" (1974: 89). This turn was one toward human self-perfectibility providing, of course, that this perfectibility did not vie with God's perfection:

> As long as we have to do with human, biologically limited beings we cannot possibly consider the idea of "absolute" perfection, because everything absolute belongs to the realm of Divine attributes alone. Human perfection, in its true psychological and moral sense, must necessarily

have a relative and purely individual bearing. It does not imply the possession of all imaginable good qualities, nor even the progressive acquisition of new qualities from outside, but solely *the development of the already
existing, positive qualities of the individual in such a way as to rouse his innate but
otherwise dormant powers.* (20, italics in original)

A more statist version of Muslim striving is to be found in the writings of
Abul ala Maududi, the Islamic scholar, founder of the Jama'at-e Islami party
in the Indian subcontinent and the intellectual precursor to radical Islamic
thinkers such as Sayyid Qutb of Egypt (Nasr 1994, I. Ahmad 2009). Maududi
was Muhammad Asad's contemporary. At one point Asad employed Maududi on behalf of Iqbal to run a foundation devoted to fostering Muslim
thought. Both men took active part in the nationalist struggles against British colonialism although they were on opposite sides on the movement for
Pakistan. Maududi threw in his support with the Indian National Congress,
that is, for an unpartitioned India, while Asad was inclined toward the
politics of the Muslim League, that is, for Pakistan. However, after the
Partition of 1947 both immigrated to Pakistan to help create an Islamic state.
Although never an official member of government, Asad was viewed sympa-
thetically by the then administration at a time when Maududi was very clearly
in the opposition. Maududi was one of the religious leaders imprisoned over
the 1953 anti-Ahmadiyya riots in Punjab (see chapter 3) and was condemned
to be executed on grounds of treason. His sentence was later commuted and
he was released on humanitarian grounds. His ideas only really came to
influence the administration under President Zia-ul Haq in the late 1970s,
although his influence had been widespread through Jama'at-e Islami's influence upon student activism and national politics.[30]

Maududi felt that the decline of Muslims was the direct result of their
seduction by Western civilization. While championing the selective use of
the advances of the West, most notably its scientific knowledge, Maududi
advocated that Pakistanis self-consciously adopt Islam: they should increase
their attachments and observance of Islam so as to set themselves on the
right course both spiritually and temporally, to literally resume their "con-
tract" with God.

Maududi felt Muslims had degenerated morally and biologically to such
an extent as to be unable to bring about such a change by themselves.
Consequently, he laid his hopes upon the modern state to instill a turn to
God in its citizenry, for he felt that Muslims would only raise themselves out

of their current state of torpor if given clear guidelines and defined parameters. Not surprisingly, Maududi imagined an active role to be played by the state in the creation of a modern Muslim citizenry: "A state of this sort cannot evidently restrict the scope of its activities. Its approach is universal and all-embracing. Its scope of activities is coextensive with the whole of human life. It seeks to mould every aspect of life and activity in consonance with its moral norms and programme of social reforms. In such a state no one can regard any field of his affairs as personal and private." He went so far as to say, "Considered from this aspect the Islamic state bears a kind of resemblance to the Fascist and Communist states" (quoted in Adams 1983, 130). While never an advocate of totalitarianism, and in fact a proponent of constitutional politics in Pakistan (Binder 1960), he used such language to convey the sense that an Islamic state should come to bear a resemblance to the omniscience of totalitarian regimes, if necessary, to bring about a tremendous change in its subjects. But the state was not only to prescribe and punish. It had also to educate. As Ishtiaq Ahmed writes about Maududi:

> Great emphasis is laid by Maududi on education. He believes that most of the present day Muslims are ignorant of true Islam. What they follow and believe is the corrupted version of Islam resulting from the deviations of Muslims, and the influence of alien ideas over Muslim minds; the result is a 'Muslim Islam' and not true Islam. An educational programme based on Islamic values and ideology is necessary to carry out a successful Islamic revolution which transforms both body and soul, making every Muslim a vigilant defender of true Islamic ideology. (1987: 110)

Comparing the three thinkers, Iqbal, Asad, and Maududi, it is clear that each was interested in Muslims yet to come. In some ways Asad's understanding of Muslim aspiration was most similar to Iqbal's. He drew upon similar language of the need for Muslims to reconstitute themselves. He advocated a project of Muslim self-making that aligned itself both to the past of Islam and the historical present so that the new Muslim might be the best expression of Islamic renewal in the modern world. And he urged that Muslims always keep in mind their own finitude in striving toward absolute perfection.

Asad's picture of aspiration was closer to Maududi's in a more crucial respect. Both felt that Islam was perfect, but that Muslims were too degenerate to accord Islam its proper place. Both upheld images of the Muslim, if not intrinsically defective and given to weakness, quite close to such a condition. However, unlike Asad, for whom this perfect form of Islam resided internally in Muslims to be brought forth through self-transformation, Maududi believed that this picture of aspiration lay in the hands of forward-thinking religious thinkers such as himself, who were already at some remove from the madrasa-trained ulama. Rather than advocate a project of self-directed change, Maududi suggested that one erect a state to instill this change in oneself. In other words, Muslims who know themselves to be weak by constitution should set up the state that would ensure they become the persons they ought to be.

For Iqbal striving is an open field of potential in which people are bound towards individuation without ever arriving at concrete individuality. Through self-experimentation people stand not only to advance aspiration without exhausting its potential, but also to advance themselves as more and more individuated persons. So both the field of potential and people are in states of becoming. But there is another element in this picture. Those striving for self-advancement found and refound Islam without exhausting its capacity to be newly perfect. In other words, Islam was also in a state of becoming; the promise of striving was that one could not only advance oneself but also advance Islam. In comparison, lacking the idea of an open future and an affirmative picture of human nature, it is unclear how humans are to be motivated to found a perfect Islam within Asad and Maududi's pictures of striving (although Maududi espoused clearer programs than Asad).

Although all variations of Muslim striving continued into Pakistan through these individuals, the state in its early years was clearly more inclined toward Iqbalian aspiration. In the remainder of this chapter I explore how the state positioned itself to receive Iqbal's specific orientation to Muslim self-advancement, one in which the future was to be kept open through experimentation, more specifically by means of striving with myriad possibilities of becoming within it.

Iqbalian Aspiration in Pakistan

After Pakistan's formation in 1947, the nation operated under the 1935 Government of India Act, the last preindependence constitution erected by the British, while a Constituent Assembly was established to frame a new constitution. Within a year of its establishment the Assembly discussed and passed an Objectives Resolution in March 1949 that set forth the principles by which the constitution makers were to carry out their task. These principles were widely criticized for being so vague as to please all, including those seeking to make Pakistan into an Islamic state and those vehemently opposed to it, in particular those who insisted that Pakistan had been created to be a Muslim homeland (Binder 1960, McGrath 1996, Talbot 2005). However, the Objectives Resolution did make distinct statements on Pakistan's relationship to God, its position on Islam, and commitment to a Muslim way of life. These principles have been important for the history of the Constitution of Pakistan, making the constitution a significant means by which to introduce Islamic values and norms into the wider Pakistani society (Lau 2005).

If we keep in mind Iqbal's idea of striving, in particular the notion of a open future and experimentation as the means to bring this future into being, but one significantly informed by human finitude, as both a limit point and an achievement, these principles inaugurated by a speech by Liaquat Ali Khan, the first prime minister of Pakistan, are distinctly Iqbalian in spirit. I take this resonance to be only an initial indication of my sense that the Pakistani state positioned itself to absorb and express Iqbal's picture of aspiration, one that is borne out by the way in which Iqbal is deployed in later constitutional engagement with the Ahmadi question.

In the fourth line of the Objectives Resolution is an expression of hope for the coming constitution on behalf of Muslims in Pakistan: "Wherein the Muslims shall be enabled to order their lives in the individual and collective spheres in accord with the teachings and requirements of Islam as set out in the Holy Quran and the *Sunna* (The Prophet's Example)." The Resolution ends with the following hope on behalf of all Pakistanis: "So that the people of Pakistan may prosper and attain their rightful and honoured place amongst the nations of the World and make their full contribution towards international peace and progress and happiness of humanity." It is crucial to note that the principles of the Objectives Resolution espoused the spirit of *enabling*, making Pakistan available for such a life, producing the rightful environment within it, rather than one of *entailing*. This spirit was born out by the words by Liaquat Ali Khan inaugurating the document:

> It is, therefore, clear that this Resolution seeks to give the Muslims the opportunity that they have been seeking, throughout these long decades of decadence and subjection, of finding freedom to set up a polity, which may prove to be a laboratory for the purpose of demonstrating to the world that Islam is not only a progressive force in the world, but it also

provides remedies for many of the ills from which humanity has been suffering. (Choudhury 1967: 27)

While the figure of Muslim in decline is discernible in the phrase "these long decades of decadence and subjection," there was no tarrying at this point. Rather we are briskly moved into the language of Pakistan as a laboratory. It was to be a place for self-directed experimentation. And the question of ends is left intriguingly open. Only Muslims could find out for themselves what they could yet be, an opportunity for self-exploration for which they had been long seeking. That is, they alone could find out the answer to the question, "To what does a Muslim aspire?" as in God's parting words in Iqbal's *Jawab-e Shikwa*.

In just the few passages I have quoted from the early years of constitution making, we can see how two pathways open up for Muslims in Pakistan, as Muslim directed toward the Qur'an and the *sunna*, and as the people of Pakistan directed toward the world. We are provided both the teleology of Islam and the presumption of the openness of the temporal future. Liaquat Ali Khan mobilized the language of divine destiny and providence mixed with an unimaginably open future, beyond "our wildest expectations":

This Objectives Resolution is the first step in the direction of the creation of an environment which will again awaken the spirit of the nation. We, whom Destiny has chosen to play a part, howsoever humble and insignificant, is this great drama of national resurrection, are overwhelmed with the magnitude of the opportunities which are before us. Let us use these opportunities with wisdom and foresight, and I have not the least doubt that these humble efforts will bear fruit far in excess of our wildest expectations, through the help of a Providence which has brought Pakistan into existence. (Choudhury 1967: 29)

Was it then the case that the Objectives Resolution was trying to have it both ways? If it was, it was aiming for nothing more than what Iqbal was trying to achieve as well.

Chapter Three

INHERITING IQBAL

THE LAW AND THE AHMADI QUESTION

The Silent Presence of the Law

There was a moment in the scientist Dr. Khan's narrative about the disputes in his mosque in the Punjab Government Employees Welfare Society colony, Lahore, described in chapter 1, in which he tells how he informed a member of the mosque committee, with whom he was presumably fighting, that he knew the person to be an Ahmadi. Dr. Khan gave his word that he would not tell anyone. The Ahmadiyya movement emerged in the nineteenth century in colonial India under Mirza Ghulam Ahmad, who claimed to be the new prophet of Islam. Ahmad differentiated himself from the Prophet Muhammad by saying that while Muhammad was the primary lawgiver, he, Ghulam Ahmad, was renewing the law. Insofar as he claimed himself a prophet, Ahmad challenged the normative position of majority Muslims that Muhammad was the "seal of prophecy," that is, with him prophecy ended. The most immediate subtext of the exchange between Dr. Khan and his Ahmadi adversary, however, was the Penal Code of Pakistan, revised in 1984 to deny Ahmadis access to Muslim insignia and institutions, such that an Ahmadi in a mosque committee stood to be severely punished if she or he were exposed.

In another conversation, this time with a district court judge of Lahore, in which I attempted to understand why the lower courts did not seem interested in clearing the backload of cases involving mosque-related conflicts and forcible possessions, the judge said frankly, "We pursued such cases in the 1970s and 1980s when they involved Ahmadis as a way to rid mosques of Ahmadis, but now there is no such need. Now people can solve their own problems." As an indication of the extent to which the state had succeeded in severing Ahmadi relations to Islam through the constitutional amendment of 1974, lawyers in Rabwah, the Ahmadi headquarters in Pakistan, showed me extensive documentation of the widespread destruction of Ahmadi mosques following the amendment and accompanying legal acts. It was as if, their sacredness being revoked, these spaces were open to common vandalism rather than symbolic desecration.

Given my orientation to mosques as sites of striving, the fact that Ahmadi presence in mosques felt so troublesome to the state, over and above the frequent seizures of mosques, means that attention has to be paid to how Ahmadis were understood to obstruct Muslim religiosity. As the status accorded to the Prophet Muhammad by the Ahmadis was what primarily differentiated them from mainstream Muslims, we also have to understand the enduring importance and resignifying of the Prophet for Pakistani Muslims. It is noteworthy that the recentering of the prophet figure is a departure from an Iqbal-inspired aspiration, because Iqbal was more concerned to put Muslims in direct relation to the divine and went to great lengths to delimit the place of the Prophet, or any prophet, within this relationship. Iqbal's opposition to the Ahmadiyya arose less from the theological insistence that the Prophet was a seal upon prophecy and more from Ahmadi encouragement of a continued reliance upon a prophet figure for guidance. Nonetheless, both Iqbal and the state of Pakistan converged on the need to expel the Ahmadiyya from Islam, or, rather, the state took Iqbal's lead in expelling Ahmadis, given the frequent citation of Iqbal within state pronouncements on the Ahmadis.

Contrary to the writings that claim that, in making Ahmadis into minorities, the state capitulated to reactionary forces extant in Pakistani society (Lau 1996) or that it embarked on this act of labeling Ahmadis as apostates in order to secure its authority to speak on behalf of Islam (A. Ahmed 2010), I claim that the state was actually engaged in a form of striving of its own by slowly and tentatively sensing out its position vis-à-vis the Ahmadis through religious argumentation conducted by means of the law. The law was, after all, the silent presence in the ethnographic episodes with which I began this chapter (the penal code that made punishable Ahmadi presence within mosques, the courts that ferreted out Ahmadis from mosques, or the constitutional amendment that revoked the status of Ahmadi institutions as mosques). The fact that religious argumentation was undertaken by this means places law center stage in the state's efforts at striving and inflecting Muslim aspiration within everyday life.

In chapter 1 we saw how the state secured its authority in neighborhoods through the seemingly disinterested bureaucratic procedures it required of mosques. It was a requirement that the lands and committees of mosques be registered and that registration papers be available for inspection, even as mosques spanned the spectrum from legal to illegal, registration guidelines were ad hoc, and state inspection was sporadic. In this chapter I explore how the state unveiled its interested face, that of a possible aspirant to Muslim becoming. Over a well-known course of law making and legal judgments (Kennedy 1989, Lau 1996), which was spurred as much by the state's own initiative as by segments of its populace, it was the state that defined the correct mode of attaching to the Prophet. This became the means by which Ahmadis were disinherited from Islam. Given the centrality of the Prophet to Muslim modes of striving in Pakistan, as evidenced, for instance, in the argument I witnessed in the Provincial Assembly Library (see chapter 1), this legal trajectory could not but impinge upon striving in everyday life, as people sought to police their attachment to the Prophet and watch their mosques for possible Ahmadis hiding in their midst.

While I explore the consequences of this legal history for everyday life in the chapters ahead, in this chapter I stay awhile with law so as to map out the course of Ahmadi expulsion from Islam and to show how an earlier mode of relating to the Prophet was put out of reach of Muslims more generally. I show how the law delineated a changing relationship to the Prophet, beginning with the relationship espoused by constitution makers of the 1950s. This action was followed by the Munir Report of 1954, by which the state deflected the question of the proper relationship to the Prophet focusing instead on who was a Muslim. The constitutional amendment of 1974 provided a definition of the Muslim in a way that moved Ahmadis from the status of Muslim to that of minority for the purposes of the constitution or law—a measure amplified by the ordinance of 1984, by which Ahmadis' usage of signs of Muslimhood was criminalized. I explore how the law was made the site of theological disputation over the course of the 1980s as to whether Ahmadis were simply a minority or a particularly harmful minority in a series of legal cases involving the Ahmadis. I end my review of the law and its redrawing of Muslim relations to the Prophet with the Supreme Court judgment of 1993, in which the court sought an end to disputation by spelling out what manner of harm Ahmadis intended legitimate Muslims. Here we see the state as a claimant upon Muslim aspiration, not only through its efforts at attending to theological questions but also through its enunciation of a new

Muslim legal subject informed by continual experimentation. Simultaneously we see the judgment institutionalize a mode of generalized, if not pervasive skepticism toward the world.

In the final section of the chapter, I attend more closely to how the state in the 1980s and 1990s attempted to inherit Iqbal through the workings of the law and how this inheritance sat alongside Iqbal's own understanding of Ahmadism as a problem to be dealt with, as spelled out in his writings in 1935. The issue of tolerance is interestingly posed by Iqbal so as to both allow for the expulsion of Ahmadis as well as flag the concern that their disinheritance might adversely affect the tenor and scope of Muslim aspiration. This raises the question of what an Iqbalian mode of exclusion is, if it also calls for tolerance.

The picture of the law presented in this chapter is different from the studies of colonial law in the region that see it as the site of cultural codification and ossification (Cohn 1996, Kugle 2001). As we shall see from the workings of the law, the most prominent aspects of it are its capaciousness in translating and assimilating theological alterity (A. Ahmed 2010), its productivity in the Foucauldian sense of generating new legal subjects and rationale for incarceration (Golder and Fitzpatrick 2009), and its creativity in generating new possibilities for self-experimentation hitherto unthought under the rubrics of law or religious practice. I also build upon recent writings on the law inspired by Derridean philosophy that concede a horizon of aspiration to the law through the register of justice (Obarrio 2010) by showing how that horizon is often effaced by the law in its legislative and punitive workings.

Changing Relations to the Prophet

THE BASIC PRINCIPLES COMMITTEE, 1953

The constitutional history of Pakistan in which the Ahmadis became entangled was one of repeated stagings of new constitutions and their suspension and restoration by various democratic and military governments (H. Khan 2004). The first attempt at a constitution of Pakistan was undertaken by the Constituent Assembly created shortly after the formation of Pakistan (McGrath 1996). This Constituent Assembly met from 1947 till 1956. On March 12, 1949, the day that the Objectives Resolution was introduced and adopted by the Constituent Assembly, a Basic Principles Committee comprising twenty-four members was formed to prepare a draft constitution on the basis of this resolution. This committee submitted two reports to the assembly, the first in 1950, which was struck down, and the second in 1952, which was discussed in great detail in 1953 and formed the basis of the final draft of the Constitution of 1954. A comparison of the 1949 discussions on the Objectives Resolution with the 1953 discussions on the report of the Basic Principles Committee is instructive in that it shows how the Constituent Assembly considered Islam's salience for the state-yet-in-formation, in particular how the time of the Prophet Muhammad was understood to inform the present moment and the coming polity.

In 1949, the Constituent Assembly met to discuss the principles articulated in the Objectives Resolution. Many aspects of the Objectives Resolution were found troublingly ambiguous by assembly members, such as the resolution vesting sovereignty in God and giving the government the right to serve as God's trustee while allowing the government to be an elected body. This principle, some argued, left it unclear from whom the state derived its authority. Furthermore, how was such a government to guarantee the protection of minorities? Some constitutional specifications seemed to undercut the fundamental rights enunciated by the resolution. One such example brought up during the debates was that only Muslim men were to be allowed by the constitution to serve as the head of government, whereas this stipula tion went against the right of equality asserted by the Objectives Resolution.

Those who struck a more positive response to the Objectives Resolution sought to mitigate these anxieties by speaking concretely about Islam. Among them, I draw out two to illustrate a persistent mode of engagement with the time of the Prophet. Maulana Shabbir Ahmad Usmani, the only alim (religious scholar) in the Assembly, had this to say about the Islamic state:[1]

> The Islamic State is the first political institution in the world which abolished Imperialism, enunciated the principle of referendum and installed a Caliph (Head of the State) elected by the people in place of the King. . . . It is the duty of an Islamic State to fully safeguard the lives, property, honour, religious freedom and civic rights of all the loyal Non-Muslims within its jurisdiction. . . . In the glorious period of the Caliphate there was not the slightest vestige of that tyranny, oppression, treachery, despoliation, man-slaughter, destruction, mutual hate, inequality and suppression of peoples rights which is rampant in the modern world. (Government of Pakistan 1949: 46)

What is interesting about this exposition is that the speaker moves fluidly between the Islamic state at the time of the Caliphate in Arabia and the state under construction in Pakistan. The Islamic state, which was yet to be established in Pakistan, is presented as if it were already in the present, and the Caliphate, long in the past, is presented as close behind, with the actual present relegated to the menacing modern world that howled outside the citadel. The rhetorical effect is to give the impression that Pakistan was poised to take up the mantle of the Islamic state from the time of the Prophet.

The second of a series of impassioned speeches in support of the Objectives Resolution came from Sir Chaudhry Muhammad Zafarullah Khan of the West Punjab Muslim League. Ironically, he was the highly placed Ahmadi politician against whom the anti-Ahmadi riots of 1953 were directed (see below). In his speech he quoted from the Qur'an to draw out the main functions of the Prophet:

> One of the functions of this Prophet is to recite and expound divine signs which create, inspire and, sustain faith in God.

> This Prophet purifies the Muslims through his teachings, precepts and example and points out the means of their progress in all spheres.

> He expounds and teaches them the Law.

> He makes plain the philosophy upon which these teachings and laws are based. (Government of Pakistan 1949: 65)

Following on this, Zafarullah Khan attempted to calm the disquiet of minority members of the Assembly toward the Objectives Resolution by giving an example from the Prophet's life to illustrate his spirit of tolerance. He related the incident in which the Prophet granted a visiting Christian deputation the right of worship in his mosque in Medina. In this manner Zafarullah Khan placed before the Assembly "certain concrete illustrations" of the Islamic ideals contained within the Objectives Resolution in order to show that the resolution did not articulate obscure theological references to Islam in need of specialist interpreters or vulnerable to exclusionary readings.

In drawing upon Maulana Usmani and Zafarullah Khan's references to the Prophet's era, I am suggesting that Muslim ideologues circumvented their most immediate pasts and the historical past of Islam to hone in on the idealized past of the Prophet's era as the golden age of Islam (Al-Azmeh

1996). However, I am more interested in the ways in which one's relation to a tradition makes one's present moment, way of being, mode of address, or hoped-for effect in the world resonant with cherished ideals extant in the archives of the tradition. In other words, when Maulana Shabbir Usmani spoke he was indeed speaking of the Prophet's era, but he was also seeing Pakistan as poised, like the city of Medina, to receive the Prophet's guidance. Just as the Prophet gave Medina a charter, so Pakistan was to receive the Objectives Resolution. Zafarullah Khan asserted the Prophet's authority by showing him to be the link between God and the people, as sanctioned by the Qur'an. Then he drew out the Prophet's reputation for tolerance. Concurrently, Khan assumed that the Prophet's gesture of invitation conveyed his own promise of tolerance to Pakistan's minorities. In effect, the rhetorical stance within these constitutional debates worked to presence a theological/historical event through its present day animation (N. Khan 2008).

In 1953, during the Assembly discussion on the second report of the Basic Principles Committee, which laid out the constitution in draft form, it was opposition members who made explicit this resonance between the present of Pakistan and Islam's earliest era by their redoubled efforts to capture a similar resonance in their speech. We see an effort at such a resonance in a lengthy speech by Bhupendra Kumar Datta of East Bengal, one of the Hindu members of the Constituent Assembly, who vigorously advocated that there be no explicit mention of Islam in the future constitution for it automatically implied the exclusion of Pakistan's minorities. Whereas previously, in 1949, his speeches indicated he had only a very basic knowledge of Islam, by 1953 he spoke as any Muslim member might. Datta was present during the 1949 Constituent Assembly Debates and was outspoken in his criticism of the Objectives Resolution. At that time he confessed to knowing little about Islam except to say that he sensed there was great dissension among its various sects and subgroups, such that he doubted he was alone in not knowing exactly what was meant when the resolution spoke of such things as "justice" and "equality" "as enunciated in Islam." Four years later, at the time of the 1953 Constituent Assembly Debates Datta had clearly educated himself on Islam. In his protests against separate electorates for minorities, a practice with colonial roots in which minorities could only put forward and vote for representatives from their own communities for a fixed number of seats in government, he brought up one example after the other from the Prophet's era to question if such a separation of Pakistan's minorities from the mainstream of politics was indeed Islamic. In his final coup, in which we see the demonstration of a resonance between the present moment and a cherished past, Datta spoke of the charter written by the Prophet for the city of Medina and asked if such a charter was being attempted by the Constituent Assembly.

The event to which Datta alludes is when the Prophet escaped from religious persecution in the city of Mecca by going to Yathrib, a nearby city, later renamed Medina, to which he had been invited to provide leadership to a divided community. There the Prophet had to preside not only over those who had converted to Islam, but also over many who hadn't, Jewish tribes being prominent among them. In his efforts to produce leadership acceptable to all, the Prophet entered into various agreements, committing these agreements to writing. Many have seen these agreements as an instance of an early constitution in Islamic history (Watt 1981, Armstrong 1993). What this charter shows is that the Prophet was concerned not only with the good opinion of his own people, but also of non-Muslims. In effect, when Datta reminded the assembly of the Prophet's constitution he was reminding them of an event that was the source of considerable pride to Muslims. He was also reminding them of that initial and overt show of consideration to non-Muslims by the Prophet. In effect, he was taking the place of the Jews in that event in Islamic history and inviting the Constituent Assembly to extend to his community the same consideration as had been shown the Jews in Medina. According to him, such consideration could only take the form of an unambiguously worded text that promised to protect minorities in Pakistan, just as the Medinan charter had done for the Jews.[2]

So it is that in the words and gestures of a minority member of the assembly we see a mode of invoking the Prophet's era and example not unlike what we saw above with Maulana Shabbir Ahmad Usmani and Zafarullah Khan. Although many more such examples may be found in the 1949 and 1953 Constituent Assembly Debates, the few I have provided should suffice to underline my point that the time of the Prophet was crucial to the law's imagination of Islam's salience for the future state of Pakistan. The Prophet was most often invoked in his standing as a statesman, presiding over the construction of an ideal state and society. He was shown to be both shrewd and just in his dealings. He was seen to experiment with new arrangements. And, he appeared actively interested in maintaining his reputation among people, suggesting that lay people were as important to his standing as a prophet as much as divine mandate. Those aspects of the prophetic legacy that had to do with him as the receiver of divine revelation or as a miracle worker were greatly overshadowed by the emphasis on his public persona, ethical bearing, and openness to change, in other words, as an aspiring Muslim (Ewing 1983, Waugh 1983, Brown 1996).

THE MUNIR REPORT, 1954

The reconstruction of the Prophet Muhammad as a statesman was always an uneven one in Pakistan. There have always been multiple tendencies in relation to the Prophet. There were some who preferred to focus more on the Prophet's connection to the divine realm, his own divinity by contiguity, and his consequent inscrutability (Schimmel 1985). There were others who felt his spiritual presence to continue even after the fact of his physical death (Sanyal 1996). And then there were those who felt that revelation itself was a continuing boon of his Prophethood, that is to say, people continued to experience revelation, even in the form of dreams, after the passing of the Prophet (Friedmann 2003a). The prophetic legacy necessarily exhibits all these tendencies to a greater or lesser degree. The one tendency that was looked upon askance and was ultimately found to be intolerable in Pakistan was the one actualized by the Ahmadis, who had produced considerable anxiety among Muslims since their emergence in the nineteenth century. The Ahrars, a particularly radical stream within Muslim religious politics, committed themselves to fighting what they perceived to be an Ahmadi threat to the wider Muslim community (Lavan 1974). These tensions continued to surface in Pakistan after its formation.

In March 1953, widespread riots broke out in the province of Punjab that lasted until April of that year. The military intervened in certain places to establish law and order, and for the first time in Pakistan's short history martial law was declared in the city of Lahore; it lasted until May. This outbreak of violence resulted from the rejection by the governor general of Pakistan, Khwaja Nazimuddin, of an ultimatum delivered to him by a group of ulama whose primary demands were that if Pakistan was indeed to be an Islamic state then the Ahmadis should be declared a non-Muslim minority and Ahmadis in seats of government should be removed from their posts. The person they targeted was none other than Zafarullah Khan, at that time a member of the Constituent Assembly, Pakistan's foreign minister, and a self-professed Ahmadi. The government report into the disturbances described the violence that ensued: "Vast multitudes of human beings who in ordinary times were sane, sensible citizens, had assumed the form of unruly hysterical mobs whose only impulse was to disobey the law and to bring constituted authority to its knees while baser elements of society, having taken advantage of the prevailing disorder, were behaving like wild beasts killing people, robbing them of their possessions and burning valuable property either for the sake of fun or to spite a fancied enemy" (Government of Pakistan 1954: 184).

With public disorder of this scale potentially disastrous for a fledgling state, on June 1953 the governor of Punjab issued an ordinance requiring that a court be set up to inquire into the causes of violence. The Punjab Disturbances Court of Inquiry was placed under the leadership of the chief justice of the Lahore High Court, Muhammad Munir. From July 1953 to February 1954, the two-man court held 117 sittings, at which time it digested 3,600 pages of written statements, 2,700 pages of evidence, 339 documents, and numerous books, pamphlets, journals, and newspapers to write a report that was 337 pages long in its final form. This report delineated the circumstances that led to the declaration of martial law in Lahore, pinpointed those responsible for the disturbances, most notably the Ahrars, and determined whether adequate measures had been taken to prevent the riots and, subsequently, deal with the wrongdoers.

Since its publication in 1954 this report, popularly referred to as the Munir Report, has passed into folklore, for within it many find the last semblance of impartial government in Pakistan, unprejudiced by ideology, expediency, or interest. However, the salience of this report for my argument for the existence of an inclination toward Muslim aspiration in Pakistan lies in the manner in which the report addressed itself to the Constituent Assembly. It asked that constitution makers take up the question of "who is a Muslim" within the new constitution such that Muslims in Pakistan could be freed, once and for all, from the strong interventionist impulses of the Islamic state and the influence of the ulama in order to undertake striving on their own merit.[3] Most notably it converted the question of what manner of attachment one should have toward the Prophet into the question of who is a Muslim.

The Munir Report aimed to reveal the political hollowness of the religious opposition in Pakistan, claiming that its proponents did not have a viable blueprint for an Islamic state, despite their vociferous demands for such a state and insistence that they steer the nation's course. In the absence of such a blueprint from the ulama, the Court of Inquiry determined that it must explore all dimensions of what an Islamic state entailed and what that would mean not only for Ahmadis but for Pakistani Muslims more generally. The report reasoned that if a state existed at God's behest and must uphold God's commands, then it must serve the people in light of what God expected of them. In other words, the state must act upon people so as to ensure that they were living up to God's commands.

> The Semitic theory of State, whether Jewish, Christian or Islamic, has always held that the object of human life is to prepare ourselves for the next life and that, therefore, prayer and good works are the only object of life. . . . As the present life is not an end in itself but merely a means to an end, not only the individual but also the State, opposed to the secular theory which bases all political and economic institutions on a disregard of their consequences on the next life, should strive for human conduct which ensures for a person better status in the next world. (205)

As Islam actively sought better lives for Muslims in the next world, an Islamic state was enjoined to act upon Muslim bodies to ensure "prayer and good works" to secure their afterlives. "Therefore the question immediately arises [for the Islamic state]: What is Islam and who is a momin [believer] or a Muslim" (205)? This, the report proposed, was one reason to define a Muslim, that is, to identify the material body upon which an Islamic state was compelled to act to ensure its afterlife.

Within this conception of an Islamic state, the report tried to understand ulama demands that Ahmadis be declared non-Muslim and removed from prominent seats of government:

> The ground on which the removal of Chaudhri Zafarullah Khan and other Ahmadis occupying key positions in the State is demanded is that the Ahmadis are non-Muslims and that therefore like zimmis [non-Muslims] in an Islamic state they are not eligible for appointment to higher offices in the State. This aspect of the demands has directly raised a question about the position of non-Muslims in Pakistan if we are to have an Islamic Constitution. (212)

The report cites the one precedent of Muslim government in Islamic history most cited by the ulama, "the form of Government during the Islamic Republic from 632 to 661 A.D., a period of less than thirty years" (203), in other words, the Prophetic era, further illustrating how the imagination of that era informed the present. In trying to understand how that earlier era translated into an Islamic state in the contemporary world, the report states:

> During the Islamic Republic, the head of the State, the khalifa [caliph/ head], was chosen by a system of election, which was wholly different from the present system of election based on adult or any other form of popular suffrage. The oath of allegiance (bait) rendered to him possessed a sacramental virtue, and on his being chosen by the consensus of the people (ijma-ul-ummat) he became the source of all channels of legitimate Government. He and he alone then was competent to rule, though he could delegate his powers to deputies and collect around him a body of men of outstanding piety and learning, called Majlis-i-Shura or Ahal-ul-Hall-i-wal-Aqd. The principle feature of this system was that the kuffar, for reasons which are too obvious and need not be stated, could not be admitted to this majlis and the power which had vested in the khalifa could not be delegated to the kuffar. (214)

In other words, Ahmadis are configured as potential zimmis (non-Muslims) within the Islamic state yet to come and, as such, have rights of protection from the state. However, they are simultaneously configured as kuffar (disbelievers) and, as such, the Islamic state has to be protected from them.[4]

The Court of Inquiry's ambivalent position toward Ahmadis is borne out in several places within the report. Early in the report, the court declares that it will not decide whether Ahmadis were Muslims or not. "We have said before that it is not our business to give a finding whether the Ahmadis are or are not within the pale of Islam" (189). Later, however, it concedes, with obvious reference to the Ahmadi exaltation of Mirza Ghulam Ahmad, "Of course any comparison between the holy prophet and any other person, alive or dead, must cause offence to every believer" (197). Furthermore, in its discussion on the Islamic state, the report states that it is a dogma shared by all Muslims that "God has revealed Himself from time to time to His favoured people of whom our Holy Prophet was the last. . . . The true business of a person who believes in Islam is therefore to understand, believe in and act upon that revelation" (206). In other words, the report foresees that in an Islamic state committed to upholding the dogma that Prophet Muhammad was the last prophet, the Ahmadi position on the issue would be problematic. The Islamic state might have to implement policies that ran counter to modern reason, and this could have negative repercussions; thus the report cautions that conceding to ulama demands, even if grounded in a proper conception of an Islamic state, would create "a flutter in international dovecots and the attention of the international world would [be] drawn in one way or another to what was happening in Pakistan" (233).

While never clarifying its position toward Ahmadis, the report settles upon presenting them, if not as Muslims, then as those who had never harmed the cause of Islam. Defending Zafarullah Khan, the report declares: "The President of this Court [Munir], who was a Member of that (Boundary) Commission, considers it his duty to record his gratitude to Chaudhri Zafarullah Khan. . . . For the selfless services rendered by him to the Muslim community, it is shameless ingratitude for anyone to refer to Chaudhri Zafarullah Khan in the manner in which he has been referred to by certain parties before the Court of Inquiry" (197).

Earlier we saw how the report felt it necessary for an Islamic state to know who was a Muslim to better enhance his or her status after death. Furthermore it was necessary for an Islamic state to know who was a non-Muslim to better protect non-Muslims or to better protect itself from them. Turning to the ulama for a definition of a Muslim, the commission quickly learned that they could not provide such a definition:

> We asked most of the leading ulama to give their definition of a Muslim, the point being that if the ulama of the various sects believed the Ahmadis to be kafirs [kuffars], they must have been quite clear in their minds not only about the grounds of such belief but also about the definition of a Muslim because the claim that a certain person or community is not within the pale of Islam implies on the part of the claimant an exact conception of what a Muslim is. (214–15).

The report informs us that some among the ulama emphasized that a Muslim must believe in the unity of God, some put the Qur'an first, others said that a Muslim must believe that the Prophet Muhammad was the last prophet, and yet others said that a Muslim was the one who professed his faith through the utterance of the shahada (article of faith). The report comments in apparent disgust: "The result of this part of the inquiry . . . has been anything but satisfactory, and if considerable confusion exists in the minds of our ulama on such a simple matter, one can easily imagine what the differences on more complicated matters will be" (215).

The authors foresee the following bind:

Keeping in view the several definitions given by the *ulama*, need we make any comment except that no two learned divines are agreed on this fundamental. If we attempt our own definition as each learned divine has done and that definition differs from that given by all others, we unanimously go out of the fold of Islam. And if we adopt the definition given by any one of the *ulama*, we remain Muslims according to the view of that *alim* but *kafirs* according to the definition of every one else. (218)

The report concludes that it would take an act of constitution to provide a definition of a Muslim true for all and that such a definition ought to be established to protect the state from arbitrary accusations of infidelity (*takfir*) practiced by the ulama.[5]

After exploring the various ways in which the Ahmadi issue might be treated if Pakistan were to be an Islamic state, the Court of Inquiry resolved that Pakistan was not an Islamic state, nor should it seek to become one. However, it advised that even if Pakistan was not to be an Islamic state, the question of who is a Muslim should still be answered. The question must, moreover, be answered boldly, to provide a new, forward-looking orientation to all Muslims, who were otherwise in danger of becoming permanently out of step with the present world:

Pakistan is being taken by the common man, though it is not, as an Islamic state. . . . It is this brilliant achievement of the Arabian nomads, the like of which the world has never seen before, that makes the Musalman of today live in the past and yearn for the return of the glory that was Islam. . . . He therefore finds himself in a state of helplessness, waiting for some one to come and help him out of this morass of uncertainty and confusion. And he will go on waiting like this without anything happening. Nothing but a bold re-orientation of Islam to separate the vital from the lifeless can preserve it as a World Idea and convert the Musalman into a citizen of the present and the future world from the archaic incongruity that he is today. (232)

These words recall Iqbal's poetic and philosophic description of Muslims as out of step with time and in need of bringing together their past in line with their future.

The advice of the Munir Report to the Constituent Assembly came too late. Before the National Assembly could approve the draft of the 1954 Constitution prepared by the Constituent Assembly, the assembly was dissolved by the then governor general, Ghulam Muhammad. A second Constituent Assembly of Pakistan was created in 1955. It was this institution that gave the first constitution to the nation, that is, the Constitution of Pakistan, 1956. But further tribulations lay in wait for this constitution. Although the first general elections were scheduled for early 1959, President Sikandar Mirza abrogated the 1956 Constitution, dissolved the National and Provincial Assemblies and declared martial law in 1958. He appointed General Muhammad Ayub Khan, commander-in-chief of the army, as the chief martial law administrator. One of the major steps taken by Ayub Khan was the appointment of a Constitution Commission in 1960. The commission submitted its report in 1961 and on its basis a new constitution was framed in 1962, although martial law continued until 1969. The crucial difference between the Constitutions of 1956 and 1962 was that while the first provided for a parliamentary system of government, the second was weighted toward a single authority, the Office of the President (H. Khan 2004). However, even the Constitution of 1962 was to be short-lived. The question of who is a Muslim and how this definition was to hinge upon the correct attachment to the Prophet had to wait for the staging of a new constitution for Pakistan.

THE 1974 AMENDMENT OF THE CONSTITUTION OF 1973

In 1969, martial law was imposed for a second time and General Yahya Khan took over as president of Pakistan and chief martial law administrator. During his tenure, West Pakistan went to war against East Pakistan, and at the end of hostilities the Province of East Pakistan seceded to become Bangladesh. After the war of 1971, Zulfiqar Ali Bhutto succeeded as president of Pakistan, and became the first civilian martial law administrator. The first session of the National Assembly was held in 1972. This assembly formed a constitution committee to prepare the draft of yet another constitution. The draft was completed in 1972 and unanimously passed by the Assembly and authenticated by the president in 1973. This constitution, called the Constitution of the Islamic Republic of Pakistan, came into force on August 14, 1973, and remains the de facto constitution of Pakistan.

A fact often emphasized about the 1973 Constitution of Pakistan was that it had widespread approval, winning even the support of the ulama. Despite the Munir Report's dismissive attitude toward the ulama, a few of the ulama had been active participants in the Pakistan movement and in planning for the future of Pakistan in its early days (Binder 1960, Vali-Nasr 1994). While discredited and wary of the state after the events of 1953, Maulana Abul ala

Maududi still kept his faith in the constitution as the means by which to efficiently bring about a particular statist vision of Islam into Pakistan. His Jama'at-e Islami party, over other religious groups, now agitated that the new constitution take up no less than the Munir Report's advice that it address the question of "who is a Muslim" (Maududi 2000). Leaving aside the irony that a person impugned in the report was advocating the policy recommendations of the report, Maududi's challenge to the Bhutto government of Pakistan was that it should utilize this question as the means to exclude Ahmadis from the Muslim community. Maududi quoted liberally from Muhammad Iqbal's 1920 writings on the Ahmadi question as a further spur to the government to act decisively on the matter.

This pressure was brought to a head in 1974 by an incident of violence in which students aboard a train that stopped in Rabwah, the Ahmadi headquarters in Pakistan, insulted Ahmadis. On their return trip, Ahmadi youth were ready to return the abuse. This verbal altercation ended in violence that spread throughout Punjab. After the stilling of violence, another commission was set up to inquire into the circumstances leading to the violence and to provide policy recommendations to the Bhutto government. While not disclosing the report to the public, the Government of Pakistan reported that the Samdani Commission, so named after Judge Samdani, who headed the commission strongly recommended that the question of who is a Muslim should be resolved once and for all.

In 1974, the National Assembly passed, with very few abstentions, an amendment to the 1973 Constitution that read as follows:

> A person who does not believe in the absolute and unqualified Finality of Prophethood of Muhammad (Peace be upon him), the last of the Prophets or claims to be a Prophet, in any sense of the word or of any description whatsoever, after Muhammad (Peace be upon him) or recognizes such a claimant as a Prophet or a religious reformer, is not a Muslim for the purposes of the Constitution or law.

With this amendment, Ahmadis passed out of the legal category of Muslim into that of a non-Muslim minority.

The category of "minority," well within the scope of law, sat uneasily upon the theological indecision over whether Ahmadis were zimmis or kuffar, an indecision also exhibited by the Munir Report. It moved between the distinct affective nuances attached to zimmis (non-Muslims) and kuffar (disbelievers), that is to say, between nonjudgment and judgment, an ambiguity that awaited a resolution at a later period. While internationally this 1974 amendment was seen to compromise the democratic principles spelled out in the 1973 Constitution, in Pakistan it was widely seen as a triumph of democratic politics grounded in the constitution. An editorial in the Karachi newspaper *Dawn* of September 10, 1974, spoke enthusiastically about a constitution tested by fire and now available to the polity:

> An old controversy which posed a threat to public peace and tranquility and was not without elements of delicacy and complexity has at last been got out of the way. The resolution of the Qadiani question by Parliament, in conformity with the sentiments and aspirations of the people of Pakistan, is a matter of historic significance. For about 90 years the issue has been in existence like a volcano, sometimes dormant, sometimes active, but never extinct. It is of very great significance that the issue should have been settled in a Constitutional manner and through a unanimous verdict delivered by the representatives of the people. Thus when the National Assembly and the Senate passed the Constitution (Second) Amendment Bill declaring that non-believers in the absolute and unqualified Finality of the Prophethood of Muhammad (peace be upon him) would be excluded from the fold of Islam, not only was a painful chapter of religious controversy closed but a glorious example laid down for future reference and emulation. The manner in which the decision was taken augurs well for the growth of democracy in the country. Constitutionality is the breath of life in a democracy. The same decision coming as an official decree would not have meant the same thing.

The editorial suggests the widespread importance of the resolution of the Ahmadi question for Pakistanis and the turn to modern forms of law and government as the means to reach closure on lingering theological issues. Even so, the wording of the 1974 Constitutional Amendment was vague, directed at non-Muslim minorities at large, which included Buddhists, Hindus, and Christians, and not specifically at the Ahmadis for whom it was intended. It only said who was not a Muslim and that too with the following ambiguous qualification, "for the purposes of the constitution and the law." It allowed the Ahmadis to continue as Muslims in their everyday life, while taking them to be non-Muslims in the eyes of the state. Furthermore, it left unclear the acceptable mode of attachment to the Prophet.

ORDINANCE XX, 1985

General Zia-ul Haq, who came to power after overthrowing Bhutto's government, was very committed to the "finality of prophethood" movement, which had spearheaded the 1977 agitation against Bhutto. He circumvented the National Assembly of Pakistan to pass the Anti-Islamic Activities of Qadiani Group, Lahori Group and Ahmadis (Prohibition and Punishment) Ordinance of 1984, commonly referred to as Ordinance XX. This ordinance added two new clauses (298 B and C) to the Pakistan Penal Code, which asserted that certain titles, names, and practices were indeed exclusive to Muslims and made clear that their utilization by non-Muslims was punishable by the law. The second of these clauses, which specifically addresses the preaching and propagating of faith, states:

> 298-C. *Person of Qadiani group etc., calling himself a Muslim or preaching or propagating his faith.* Any person of the Qadiani group or the Lahori group (who call themselves "Ahmadis" or by any other name), who, directly or indirectly, poses himself as a Muslim, or calls, or refers to, his faith as Islam, or preaches or propagates his faith, or invites others to accept his faith, by words either spoken or written, or by visible representation or in any manner whatsoever outrages the religious feelings of Muslims, shall be punished with imprisonment of either description for a term which may extend to three years and shall be liable to fine.[6]

This amendment to the Pakistan Penal Code finally made it possible to punish Ahmadis for continuing to practice as Muslims. It effectively criminalized their everyday life. It recast the question "Who is a Muslim?" as "Who is not a Muslim?"

In this section on Pakistan's changing relations to the Prophet, as fostered by the law, I have focused on three historical moments to show how in the 1950s the Prophet was relatively freely cited in word and gesture by both Muslim and non-Muslim members of the Constituent Assembly. By the 1970s, such a relation to the Prophet, his time, and his example, had come under some strain as any claims upon the Prophet were framed by the widespread political agitation demanding the recognition of the finality of prophethood. By the 1990s, the Prophet had been successfully separated from lay Muslims, at least in the eyes of the law, as the titles, symbols, and practices associated with the Prophet and Islam came to be viewed as the exclusive legal property of authenticated Muslims. Despite their punitive edge, these legal interventions, notably the 1974 Amendment and the 1984 Ordinance, awaited court cases to make more explicit what constituted transgression by Ahmadis.

It is important to pause here to consider the parallels between the qabza, or forcible possession of mosques discussed in chapter 1, and khatm or the absoluteness of the finality ascribed to prophethood within the finality of the prophethood movement and the state's upholding of this position. These are distinct kinds of closures and they provide insight into the parlous condition of the state and civil society in Pakistan. Yet rather than only attend to their exclusionary effects, which are evident at both the level of neighborhoods and the national level with respect to the Ahmadis, I find it productive to consider them the consequences of efforts at experimentation with being Muslim. Seen from the perspective of the tendency to strive, these closures lose their finality and draw our attention to the spiral that aspiration produces, creating doctrinal and legal closures yet also spaces of doubt, uncertainty, and further experiments within daily life in Pakistan. This is nowhere more evident than in the individual pursuit of self-perfection that I focus on in chapter 4. For now we consider the state's own expression of striving motivated by its desire to enable Muslim striving by removing the threat posed to it by Ahmadis.

The Law as the Site of Theological Disputation and the State as Aspirant

Although Ahmadis were Muslims prior to the 1974 Amendment, they were never uncontroversial as Muslims. They were labeled kuffar and murtadd (apostates) by the more orthodox ulama from the moment of their public emergence (Lavan 1974). Sometimes they were viewed as Muslims who had placed themselves beyond the pale of Islam through their support of a taghut (the antonym of God, a devil, a sorcerer). Even if this were not the case, that is, even if they were minimally acceptable as Muslims, their continued support of Mirza Ghulam Ahmad made them suspect as munafiqin (hypocrites), those who cultivated the appearance of Muslims while plotting their overthrow in the early years of the Prophetic community. These categorizations of the Ahmadis as kafir, taghut, murtadd, and munafiq had an internal hierarchy, each implying a relative pariah status, moral disapprobation, and, possibly, punitive charge. At the same time, tauba (repentance) was also always a possibility, with differential availability, to allow one to overcome these characterizations and return to the fold of the community (Denny 1980).

This theological vocabulary was overlaid by the category of "non-Muslim minority" by which Ahmadis came to be known after the 1974 Amendment. This category was already in use within the constitution to designate Hindus, Buddhists, and Christians, among others, living in Pakistan. And it seemed to allow for a seamless transition of the Ahmadis from the status of Muslim to non-Muslim without the manifold characterizations and movements enfolded into the pariah status within the theological register. Despite this amendment, the Ahmadis persisted in calling themselves Muslims and undertaking Muslim modes of ritual behavior. In each of the three legal judgments I discuss in this section, from the years 1978, 1985 and 1993 respectively, there is a moment in which the judges, having exhausted all theological and legal arguments as to why Ahmadi claims upon the title of "Muslim" were wrong, ask if the Ahmadi attempting to "pass off" or even "pose" as Muslims could be considered a bad copy of the original. Could this constitute authoritative grounds for their definitive separation from Islam?

The first of the judgments appeared only a few short years after the 1974 Constitutional Amendment. In 1978, in *Abdur Rahman Mobashir v. Syed Amir Ali Shah Bokhari* (PLD 1978 Lahore 113), judges of the High Court of Lahore were asked to deliberate whether the plaintiffs had sufficient cause to file an injunction preventing Ahmadis from praying in their own mosques. On the one hand, the judges did not accept Ahmadi arguments that the amendment only made them non-Muslims in matters relating to the constitution, and that they were Muslims for all other purposes: "The learned counsel would have us believe that a person can be non-Muslim for the purpose of the Constitution and the law and a Muslim for the other purposes. Neither the law or Constitution or Islamic Shariah allows a person to remain Kafir for certain purposes and to be converted to Islam for other purposes" (*Mobashir*, 154). Neither were the judges convinced that the amendment gave authority to Muslims to police Ahmadi practices: "The authority deals only with the right to preserve continued existence of a denomination by ex-communicating the dissidents and excluding them from its place of worship. It does not confer any right on such denomination to interfere with the mode of worship of the ex-communicated dissident or with the place of worship constructed separately by him" (141).

The Specific Relief Act of 1887, one of the laws referenced by the plaintiffs, provided relief only in the event of an infringement upon one's own property, and not on that of another's, particularly that of God's. Similarly, neither did the concern for law and order in Section 91 in the Civil Procedure

Code, the second law cited by the plaintiffs, cover the hurt to religious sentiment. Moreover, the High Court judges saw no precedence for bringing Islamic law within the ambit of the constitution, restricting their judgment to the standing law.

At the same time the judges appeared to understand that the plaintiffs were in search of a law that would prevent Ahmadis from continuing on as before the amendment. They even went so far as to suggest that the plaintiffs were giving inchoate expression to something akin to copyright and trademark laws that would disable non-Muslims from encroaching upon Muslim rights over their tradition: "The suit appears to be based on some supposed right analogous to a right in the nature of trade mark or copyright or infringement of analogous rights by passing off" (139). The judges would not have any of this. "Rights in trade marks or copyrights are matters which are the concern of statutory law. There is no positive law investing the plaintiffs with any such rights to debar the defendants from freedom of conscience, worship, or from calling their place of worship by any name they like" (139). Instead, they called upon neighborliness, which, in their view, made qazi (Muslim judge) justice work at the peak of Muslim power in India and which they saw in the enjoinment to justice, equity, and good conscience in British and Anglo-Indian Law (Anderson 1959). In this approach one simply assumes that what Ahmadis do is their own business and that they mean no harm, having born no harm upon the neighborhoods of their residence and places of worship thus far. In effect, the judges advocated a staged ignorance of Ahmadi mores, which was not unlike the reasoning put into effect by the 1954 Munir Report in relation to the Ahmadis.

While cases such as these showed up periodically on the dockets, it was only in 1984 that plaintiffs who had earlier brought cases against the Ahmadis had a law in place to properly target the continued offences they ascribed to Ahmadis. As mentioned above, President Zia-ul Haq had promulgated a law, Ordinance XX, in which Ahmadis are barred from the use of any honorific titles and modes of address specific to the Prophetic community, from building mosques and calling the azan, from undertaking Muslim modes of worship, and from citing from the Qur'an and hadis. Under the new ordinance, the Penal Code was amended to provide three years of imprisonment or a fine or both to anyone caught doing any of the above.

Before they went on to fight the constitutionality of the ordinance in the Supreme Court of Pakistan, Ahmadis first disputed the Islamic basis of this ordinance in the Federal Shariat Court. Zia established this court and its provincial divisions in the 1980s to evaluate the repugnance of existing laws to Islam (A. Iqbal 1986, Weiss 1986). In 1985, in the case *Mujibur Rehman v. The Federal Government of Pakistan* (PLD 1985 FSC 8), the Shariat Court judges wrote a lengthy judgment in which they first put on trial the Ahmadi claim to be Muslim. This judgment was very much in the manner of a disputation, in that they drew on Islamic texts and legal opinions beyond the purview of the constitution before they went on to endorse the Islamic basis of the ordinance.

One of the most significant moves of the Shariat Court judges was to explore the meaning of the word *khatm* in the term *Khatm un-Nubuwwa* (finality of prophethood): "Khatam . . . means to prevent. It usually means the protection of a thing from mixing with other things. Khatam means seal too which means to prevent another thing from mixing with the sealed thing" (*Rehman*, 19). While these statements enunciate a clear concern that an object be unmixed and unadulterated, this etymological exercise implies that an object bears a seal of authentication, in the nature of a trademark, such that both the object and the seal are in need of constant protection (Coombe 1998). The court's discussion of the meaning of *khatm* in *Khatm un-Nubuwwa* thus opened up the possibility of speaking of aspects of Islam as sealed off and exclusive to Muslims.

Even though the Federal Shariat Court judges endorsed the ordinance, they struggled to give a positive spin to it so that it did not appear to place value upon aspects of Islam only after the fact of their improper use by Ahmadis. They did this by making those things now forbidden to the Ahmadis—the mosque form, the mode of prayer, the call to prayer, the honorific titles and the reverent texts—*shi'ar*, or symbols of the Muslim community (N. Khan 2008). By the end of their discussion it appears, however, that most things have come to be exclusive to Muslims only through customary practice, which does not preclude the possibility of their use by non-Muslims. Here again recourse to the idea of the copyright and trademark allowed for a certain priority of possession: "This strategy [of Ahmadis passing of as Muslims] . . . bears strong resemblance to the passing of by a trader of his inferior goods as the superior well known goods of a reputed firm" (*Rehman*, 100). As "superior well known goods" these markers were to be accorded the highest respect by all and protection by the state. The Federal Shariat Court issued a warning to the state: "If an Islamic state in spite of its being in power allows a non-Muslim to adopt the Shi'aar of Islam which affects the distinguishing characteristics of Muslim Ummah, it will be the failure of that state in discharge of its duties" (111).

In the lead-up to the final judgment I consider, cases filed against the Ahmadis and Ahmadi cases against extant laws and acts of persecution crowded the dockets of the Supreme Court of Pakistan. In 1993, the Supreme Court of its own volition took up a number of cases, criminal and civil, to provide a definitive statement on the Ahmadi question in *Zaheer-ud-din v. The State* (1993 SCMR 1718). Over the course of adjudicating on the issue of Ahmadis, the question, as we have seen, had shifted from whether Ahmadis were Muslims to whether Ahmadis were a dangerous minority or not. Over the course of delineating the dangers posed by Ahmadis in *Zaheer-ud-din*, the Supreme Court also dealt with a whole host of issues that had been before lower courts, such as whether the 1974 Amendment and the 1984 Ordinance were legal (which the Supreme Court judges declared them to be); whether these legal acts contradicted the constitutional rights of minorities (the judges ruled that rights had to take second place to the protection and proper transmission of Islam in Pakistan); and whether the Constitution of Pakistan had to be qualified by Islamic law (they answered in the affirmative). This judgment was widely read as a serious curtailment of the fundamental rights of minorities in Pakistan (Lau 1996).

I am interested in the way that the concepts of the copyright and the trademark were invoked in the judgment against Ahmadi "encroachments" upon Islam, while being devoid of any direct theological reference.[7] While the judgment revisited old territory—the disrespect shown by the Ahmadi prophet toward the Prophet Muhammad and the destructive influence of the Ahmadis upon Muslims—the judges were not concerned with disputing these challenges, as the Federal Shariat Court had done. Instead, all, except one dissenting judge, decried that Pakistan lacked the legal wherewithal to protect shi'ar-e Allah in the way that it had law to protect national insignia, original works, and markers of distinction of consumer goods, which it shared in common with the world community of nations. In other words, the theological thrust of these legal battles was entirely subsumed within the question of the protection of markers of Muslimhood.

> It is to be noted that it is not only in Pakistan but throughout the World, that laws protect the use of words and phrases which have special connotations or meaning and which if used for other may amount to deception or misleading the people.

> A law for protection of trade and merchandise marks exists, practically in every legal system of the world to protect the trade names and marks etc.

with the result that no registered trade name or mark of one firm or company can be used by any other concern and violation thereof, not only entitles the owners of the trade name or mark to receive damages from the violator but it is a criminal offence also. (*Zaheer-ud-din*, 1752)

It may appear that in calling for a legal structure analogous to copyright or trademark laws for the protection of shi'ar-e Allah, the Supreme Court was simply actualizing a potential for the use of the copyright and trademark against Ahmadis long simmering in earlier judgments. However, the Court did something significantly different. In harnessing the language of copyright and trademark to the Ahmadi question, it was making much more apparent that the intent of these transgressions, that is, the unlicensed use of titles, texts, modes, and spaces of worship, was willful deception. "Passing off" as Muslim was recast as "posing as" Muslims. The common deception of an unscrupulous trader passing off inferior goods as those of a reputed firm was now both transposed upon the Ahmadi and intensified, such that the Ahmadi's actions constitute a deliberate and shocking deception of the Muslim:

> The appellants, on the other hand, insist not only for a license to pass off their faith as Islam but they also want to attach the exclusive epithets and descriptions etc., of the very revered Muslim personages to those heretic non-Muslims, who are considered not even a patch on them. In fact the Muslims treat it as defiling and desecration of those personages. Thus the insistence on the part of the appellants and their community, to use the prohibited epithets and the "Shaa'ire Islam" leave no manner of doubt even to the common man, that the appellants want to do so intentionally and it may, in that case amount to not only defiling those pious personages but deceiving others. And, if a religious community insists upon deception as its fundamental right and wants assistance of Courts in doing the same, then God help it. (1754)

The Supreme Court fully understood that copyright and trademark law had an affective dimension that called forth a particular reception and response to its transgression. Ahmadis encroached upon Islam because they could, because neither Muslims nor the state were affectively constituted and legally armed to provide the necessary wall of protection around such objects such that non-Muslims might recoil from them. The judgment, in effect, calls for a proper orientation toward shi'ar-e Allah like that accorded copyrighted and trademarked goods, for only then would Muslims and the state have the defenses to make impossible the improper appropriation and use of Islamic insignia. More pragmatically, such a legal arrangement provides a positive angle on Muslim claims upon the accretions of their tradition as distinctive markers of their community. Their vague sense of exclusive rights was reconstituted as a proprietary right whose transgression could be easily and quickly demonstrated, judged, and penalized in the court of law.

Proprietary law was not so advanced in Pakistan at that time (nor is it now, for that matter) to have such an instinctive feel to it and recommend it as a discursive terrain adjacent to or encompassing theological questions and concerns. In calling Muslims to react viscerally, as they would to being cheated, to Ahmadi use of Muslim insignia, the Supreme Court asked Muslims to be more attentive to their nature, so as to be able to sense any danger posed to themselves. The Court's judgment further provoked Muslims to enfold the Constitution of Pakistan within themselves, to experiment on their bodily constitution such that they could develop new instincts to protect Islam from emergent dangers. Thus we see how the Supreme Court judgment poached upon the potential of copyrights and trademarks to make possible an affirmation of Muslim nature, suggesting a new horizon for striving. In so doing, I would argue, it actualized the Iqbalian vision of Muslim aspiration, which entwined reason and revelation within the biological.

This affective legal feedback loop, as I call the particular relation between Muslim nature and law, made deception out to be endemic, insisted upon its shocked reception and continual unmasking, and demanded collusion between shock and punishment. There was no scope in this relation for acknowledging that one barely knew what was in one's own mind much less that of another's. The single dissenting judge broke with this blanket reading of deception onto Ahmadi practices. Referring to one case he suggested that one might not know the circumstances that would lead someone to dissimulate:

> As regards the allegation that on being questioned and interrogated they [appellants] gave the reply that they were Muslims while in fact they were Qadiani or Ahmadis, that too will not be an offense under the law. Posing involves voluntary representation. In giving reply to a question one does not respond voluntarily but as would appear from the circumstances of these cases under threat or duress. One may hide his religion in public to

protect himself physically preferring the lesser evil of criminal prosecution or one may avoid and give an evasive reply. (Zaheer-ud-din: 1748)

The dissenting judge, citing another case in which a few Ahmadi men were being prosecuted for wearing badges showing the Muslim article of faith, noted:

The exhibition or use of "Kalma Tayyaba" correctly reproduced, properly and respectfully exhibited cannot be made a ground per se for action against those who use "Kalma Tayyabba" in such a manner. If for ascertaining its peculiar meaning and effect one has to reach the inner recesses of the mind of the man wearing or using it and to his belief for making it an offence then the exercise with regard to belief and the meaning of it for that person and the purpose of using and exhibiting the "Kalma Tayyabba" would be beyond the scope of the law. (Zaheer-ud-din: 1748–49)

The judge hinted that the context of these Ahmadi infractions may be one of threat and duress, in which case any questions of this nature posed to an Ahmadi would take on an interrogatory note beyond that of a simple request for information. Knowledge of such a context would require one to treat Ahmadi responses in a different manner than as simple statements of fact. In effect, he asked why such questions would be asked in the first place. And in questioning whether the law had the ability to enter into the inner recesses of people's minds to determine their motivation in the absence of any physical evidence or testimony to their wrongdoing, he drew attention to the overreach attempted by the law. He raised the concern as to whether the court was being deliberately complicit with forces extant in the world, institutionalizing blindness toward its own limits to know with complete certainty and its own capacities to inflict hurt.

Iqbal and the Pakistani State on the Ahmadi Question: The Issue of Tolerance

The legal trajectory that I have been sketching over the course of this chapter has most often been painted as initiating intolerance toward Muslim and non-Muslim others within Pakistan. Consequently, my argument that this trajectory also shows considerable evidence of creativity on part of the law and even striving on part of the state must take seriously this accusation of intolerance.[8] I approach this accusation by asking what tolerance is, after the event of exclusion.

Writing in 1935 to Jawaharlal Nehru, the future prime minister of India, who publicly raised questions about Muslim mistreatment of Ahmadis, Iqbal was responding to half a century of public debates on the Ahmadiyya movement in colonial India. He took part in the debates almost reluctantly, to staunch the flow of criticisms leveled at Indian Muslims, both nationally and internationally, for their opposition to the Ahmadis. In trying to show how the needs of modern Islam, of the necessity to set Muslims on the course to self-striving, demanded the expulsion of Ahmadis from the fold of Islam, he argued that this expulsion was not a lapse into a medieval inquisitional mode by Muslims. It was instead an entirely contemporary need. To understand the necessity for such a forceful action by the Muslims, he urged a twofold inquiry. He advocated a psychological study of the self-proclaimed prophet Mirza Ghulam Ahmad, because only close attention to his psyche would reveal the true force behind his convictions. He also called for a diagnosis of the Muslim condition in colonial India to understand why a people could be drawn to someone he considered a dangerous doppelgänger of the Prophet Muhammad.

While Iqbal left the psychological study of Ghulam Ahmad for others to undertake, he did try to show how the Ahmadiyya movement was in fact organic to the Muslims of India although in such a manner as to be "life-destroying" rather than "life-giving." He associated the beginnings of Indian Muslims' lapse into decadence with the defeat of the Muslim leader Tipu Sultan at the hands of the British in 1799; Tipu Sultan's collapse marked the moment of the political and psychological subjugation of Muslims. In Iqbal's view, the Ahmadiyya movement can be traced to the need felt by such a subjugated people to explain to themselves their state of decline in India and to live in flight from it. Writing about Mirza Ghulam Ahmad, Iqbal says:

> I dare say the founder of the Ahmadiyya movement did hear a voice; but whether this voice came from the God of Life and Power or arose out of the spiritual impoverishment of the people must depend upon the nature of the movement which it has created and the kind of thought and emotion which it has given to those who have listened to it. (1974: 17)

Further on, in his diagnosis of the "kind of thought and emotion," that the Ahmadiyya movement inspired he writes:

> It is a strange mixture of Semetic and Aryan mysticism with whom spiritual revival consists not in the purification of the individual's inner life

according to the principle of old Islamic sufism, but in satisfying the expectant attitude of the masses by providing a "Promised" Messiah. (20)

Iqbal pinpoints the constant waiting for a messiah as the Ahmadiyya's pernicious effect on Muslims. People preferred to wait for guidance than move forward with the necessarily solitary task of becoming Muslims liberated from the dictates of another. This negative enlightenment had the trappings of striving, but lacked the openness of the future so significant to it: "This reaction carries within itself a very subtle contradiction. It retains the discipline of Islam, but destroys the will which that discipline was intended to fortify" (20).

Iqbal argues that the historical moment demanded Muslim solidarity in India. Drawing a comparison between Muslims in colonial India to the Jews of Amsterdam who were compelled to excommunicate a "God-intoxicated Spinoza" to keep intact their beleaguered community, Iqbal advocates that Muslims expel the Ahmadiyya from their midst. It was to be a defensive action, to prevent the disintegration of the Muslim community: "It is in the interest of this eternal solidarity that Islam cannot tolerate any rebellious group within its fold" (30–31). Iqbal felt that Muslim reaction against Ahmadis was instinctive, an activation of their biological instinct that Mirza Ghulam Ahmad was hostile to the faith of Muhammad. They needed to bring these instincts to the light of experience and rational thought so that they could speak for modern Islam and not simply react as Indian Muslims. Only in this way would Muslims stay the course of healthful evolution.

I see the law in Pakistan taking up Iqbal's provocation in three different ways. First, and most obvious, the amendment and ordinances effectively expelled the Ahmadis from the Muslim community, as Iqbal had desired. Second, there was a distinct effort within the legal judgments to put Mirza Ghulam Ahmad to psychological scrutiny. Finally, the 1993 Supreme Court judgment put in place the modality by which Muslims could affirm their instincts by bringing them within the scope of the law by means of copyright and antifraud law. So it would seem that Pakistan did manage to attend to Iqbal's vision of what had to be done to undertake striving. And their actions precipitated both legal and practical expressions of intolerance as evidenced by the routine incarceration of Ahmadis and destruction of their places of worship in Pakistan.

There were, however, subtle differences between Iqbal's position and that upheld by the 1993 Supreme Court judgment. In Iqbal's writings on the

Ahmadis, he makes two moves in relation to the concept of tolerance. In the first, he scoffs at the Western notion of tolerance: "There is the toleration of the man who tolerates other modes of thought and behavior because he has himself grown absolutely indifferent to all modes of thought and behavior" (1974: 4). As Muslims could not abide by such tolerance in the face of the ill treatment of Islam, Iqbal would not affirm such tolerance. Of the concept of tolerance that he did affirm Iqbal writes: "True toleration is begotten of intellectual breadth and spiritual expansion. It is the toleration of the spiritually powerful man who, while jealous of the frontiers of his own faith, can tolerate and even appreciate all forms of faith other than his own. . . . Only a true lover of God can appreciate the value of devotion even though it is directed to gods in which he himself does not believe" (1974: 4–5). In his poem *Jawab-e Shikwa* this attitude was epitomized in the generosity of Muslims of a previous era:

> You always quarrel among yourselves; they are kind and understanding.
> You do evil deeds, find faults in others; they covered others' sin and
>   were forgiving. (1994: 81)

In making this double move to tolerance, first putting it aside and then reclaiming it for Muslims, Iqbal may be taken as saying that after the decisive action of expelling the Ahmadis, Muslims had once again to repair to the issue of tolerance, to ask what called for tolerance and how they should render it? In other words, the further questions for Muslim aspirants were, first, had the act been done in the right spirit, that is, to protect Islam and not out of resentment or specious theological reasoning? Second, had the act left Muslims spiritually powerful? These questions could only be answered by examining the instincts underlying the act. In other words, rather than take striving to be progressive, Iqbal suggested how returning again and again to one's past actions, submitting them to scrutiny, could perpetuate striving. But it also meant taking up the question of how Ahmadis were to be reaccommodated in everyday life after their disinheritance from Islam and if their accommodation accorded with Iqbal's expectations of tolerance.

Chapter Four

THE SINGULARITY OF ASPIRATION

A FATHER, A CHILD, AND A JINN

The Posture of the Nonconformist

Following our consideration of Muhammad Iqbal's writings and his assimilation into Pakistan through the efforts of the state, we return to the city of Lahore, in which my interlocutors took to theological argumentation or fights over their mosques. In this chapter I focus on a pious individual navigating such disputatious events and sites that were both enlivened by an Iqbalian mode of striving and limited by the state's pronouncements on the correct way to attach to the Prophet. Farooq sahib began as my Urdu teacher but quickly took over as my research guide as I surveyed neighborhoods for mosques to research. He initially came as my guardian to mosque visits and interviews but in time became skilled in conducting interviews with me. These sometimes resembled a thrust and parry quite different from the sedate, semistructured interview form I had learned during my training in anthropology. After Farooq sahib had passed me on to his eldest son, Adeeb, to help with my various research needs, Adeeb also very often took the initiative in directing my research. For instance, he requested that I send him to conferences and public disputations so that he might record the events and went indefatigably in search of the source of posters on religious polemics we saw plastered on the walls of mosques. I often felt I was his patron supporting his efforts at becoming a knowledgeable religious disputant. It was he who detoured to take me to Masjid Noor in Momin Town, later embroiling me in the rumor mill through his strenuous efforts to ascertain who had seized the mosque. Thus, over the course of my field research I learned about Farooq sahib and his family, as I did about the librarians in the

Provincial Assembly Library, mosque-related conflicts within various neighborhoods, Muhammad Iqbal, and state efforts to apostatize Ahmadis.

Farooq sahib was fond of quoting Iqbal to me, never more than a few lines here and there and often the same ones, perhaps substantiating the complaint of Iqbal's son, Javid Iqbal, that people remembered Iqbal in Pakistan but did not know him. One fragment of poetry that Farooq sahib often recited from Iqbal's *Bang-e Dara* stood out as particularly appropriate for my research into mosques, not only in substance, insofar as it addressed mosque construction, but also in the spirit I had come to associate with Muslim aspiration:

> They built the mosque overnight, these men fired by religious zeal
> But the mind, confirmed in sin, would not yield to prayer and worship.
>   (2006: 357)

The weary self that could not be roused to piety by religious zeal strikes a posture as much of resignation to sin by a nonpracticing Muslim as of a certain pride of withholding oneself from conformism. If one goes to prayer in a mosque it is by one's own choice. Thus this resignation is also an exaltation of self-willed spiritual effort. Iqbal's words, issuing from the lips of Farooq sahib who was very pious and unlikely to miss a prayer implies a kind of respect for those who take a nonconformist stand, driving home the fact that one's spiritual bearing is ultimately only one's responsibility. Farooq sahib's quotation of these lines suggested an assimilation of Iqbal beyond the context of the poem, to the point at which they become a definition of Farooq sahib himself.

At the same time Farooq sahib was quite committed to the Deobandi pathway within Sunni Islam. He had been integral in helping me understand the theological nuances of the differences among the major maslak-based identitites within Sunni Islam in Pakistan, including the Barelwi and the Ahl-e Hadis. He would not let me slip into a comfortable pose of dismissing these differences as the political expressions of the petit bourgeoisie, as identity politics. It was through his very confident articulations and heated conversations with others that I came to understand how ontological these differences were and learned to be attentive to how they expressed different lived relations to the time and personality of the Prophet.

Nonetheless, Farooq sahib could not help but be influenced by state pronouncements on the Ahmadis in his approach to the Prophet. This was not because of their particularly punitive edge, for Farooq sahib was among those who supported state action against the Ahmadis. We have to recall that many Pakistani Muslims, although not all, were in favor of a constitutional resolution to the Ahmadi question, as captured in the editorializing of the national daily *Dawn*. Rather, even though the state had claimed to have determined the correct mode of attaching to the Prophet Muhammad, ambiguity still ruled on this matter. In the face of such ambiguity, Farooq sahib harnessed a jinn (genie) to guide him in his efforts to model himself upon the Prophet. This was unusual, to say the least, and Farooq sahib worried that his efforts at bettering himself as a Muslim in this manner might have put him at odds with the state.

One can see how seeking guidance from a jinn for pious pursuits would be at variance with an Iqbal-inspired aspiration, given Iqbal's disapproval of guides in general. It was also frowned upon within the Deobandi maslak that insisted upon a direct relation to the divine. And although the state's punishment of the Ahmadis likely did not extend to such unusual means to access the Prophet's example, atypical practices always ran the risk of being misunderstood within a context both sensitive to blasphemy and speedy with blasphemy charges. Consequently there was something quite singular about Farooq sahib's efforts at improving himself as a Muslim. It was as if he had not simply affirmed the posture of the nonconformist within the verse from Iqbal's *Bang-e Dara*, he had put it into effect.

I place Farooq sahib's encounter and relationship with the jinn at the center of this chapter to draw out a picture of striving that, although grounded in the texts in citation and circulation at the time and informed by the usual catalog of religious differences, also modeled becoming so as to show us Iqbal's philosophy in practice. At the same time the entry of the jinn(s) into the family shows how family life enfolded religious differences and conflict. From the study of mosques and their qabza I had come to understand how dissonance within neighborhoods might constitute a scene of aspiration and provide the impetus to further striving. From Farooq sahib's family I learned the extent to which the domestic modulated the shape and intensity of these conflicts and, thus, the course of striving. At the same time, Farooq sahib's own anxieties about the jinns reflected the state's fears expressed through its constitutional reforms and legal judgments that the milieu was pervaded by non-Muslim others posing as Muslims. In fact, the jinns made vivid the skeptical experience of everyday life as a place of illusion and trance.

In this chapter, I first explore the sudden eruption of the jinn(s) into my research project and provide a short anthropological account of jinn society.

I then follow them into Farooq sahib's home and family, to study in turn how his daughter Maryam served as their medium, how the jinns were harnessed to Farooq sahib's efforts at pious striving, how familial relations and tensions enfolded religious differences and strife and modulated striving, moving finally to an analysis of how Farooq sahib's strivings actualized Iqbalian aspiration while demonstrating statist anxieties about striving in everyday life. I end with a consideration of how the family's treatment of the jinns compared with the treatment of Ahmadis within Pakistan to attend again to the question of the correct, even tolerant mode of accommodating Ahmadis after their apostacization, a concern flagged by Iqbal.

The Unexpected Entry of the Jinns

I had been in and out of Lahore over the course of two years doing research on neighborhood mosques. It was summer, and my days of racing around the city, rushing in and out of mosques, libraries, government offices, bookstores, and courts were coming to an end, stilled by the intensity of the heat and the sandstorms that sprang up unexpectedly and that made it hard for Farooq sahib to navigate his scooter and for me to hold on to my seat on the pillion. Instead we would duck into a bank to pay a bill or linger at a bookstore to catch the cool waves of the air conditioner. Most afternoons, however, I spent in Shabbir, one of the many dense unauthorized urban settlements around the Mall in Lahore, at Farooq sahib's house, which was forever being vertically expanded. I would trail his wife and daughters in their continual movements up and down their house and on their rare trips outside. On occasion I would take them to the local ice cream parlor so we could refresh ourselves with a *faluda* drink. I would also go to speak to the men of the house in the small, sparse room (decorated solely with a poster of the Prophet's mosque in Medina) allotted for their work on the two computers owned by the family. In addition to teaching me Urdu, guiding me in my studies of Islam, and teaching Islamiat (Islam as a school subject) at a local school, Farooq sahib to make ends meet ran a small business of what was commonly called "compositing." Compositing consists of typing handwritten Urdu texts, generally religious in Farooq sahib's case, into the computer before these texts went out for printing to the numerous small publishers crowding the Urdu Bazaar in Anarkali.

Our days were punctuated by the call to prayer, the men leaving for the mosque for each prayer and the women snatching time out of their schedules to go off to a quiet corner of the house to pray. I was, in a manner of speaking, in a powerhouse of religious rectitude, with everyone in the household a declared Deobandi, and the sons of the household active members of the Tablighi Jama'at (Metcalf 1993a, Masud 2000). They traveled regularly through mosques in and around the city preaching to Muslims to return to the right path, to expunge their religious practices of bid'a, the accretions of customs in the form of innovations, or shirk, associating an object or person with God. Oftentimes when I sat in a horse and buggy or a rickshaw with Adeeb, en route to an interview, he would strike up a conversation with the driver that would end by Adeeb urging him to go to his local mosque. "You will find solace there from your daily life," Adeeb would say quietly.

Imagine my surprise when Farooq sahib and Rahima, his wife, walked in one afternoon into the room in which I lay dozing, speaking between themselves about the ants they had seen on the steps of the house. I wasn't paying attention. "Ants?" I asked, half asleep. Farooq sahib, putting on that voice of his that always indicated to me that I ought to be taking notes, declared,

> Naveeda, did we ever tell you that we had jinns living with us? We got them from an acquaintance who had inherited a group of jinns from his father, a famous 'amil [healer-magician]. But he has no use for these jinns so he gives them to whomever he thinks will benefit from them, providing the recipients are good Muslims. Each of the men in this family was given a jinn. Hostile jinns once attacked our house posing as ants. We knew they could not be just ants because they would bleed when we killed them, whereas ants do not bleed. Thankfully, our jinns helped us to get rid of them.

By this time I was sitting up. At my look of shock at what I was hearing, he assured me that the jinns had since returned to their original guardian.[1] Farooq sahib had made no subsequent efforts to bring them back since he felt that they were leading his family astray, that is, his family had ceased to make entreaties directly to Allah because of their growing reliance upon the jinns. "Our 'aqida [faith] had become weak and our 'ibadat [worship] was suffering." However, he continued exasperatedly,

> For a while we were the most besieged house in this neighborhood, with the women dropping by all the time to ask us to locate lost keys, secure marriages, get their husbands jobs, like we were 'amils or something. If

the women could, they would have the jinns undertake 'ibadat on their behalf.

Mildly intrigued by my interest, Farooq sahib's family related stories upon stories to me about the jinns who had shared their home with them. "Oh, we hadn't told you about them," they said. Over the next two days their interest began to wane. "Naveeda, better get back to your research," Farooq sahib declared.

What Form of Life Is a Jinn?

The introduction of the jinns into Farooq sahib's family did not raise disquiet at the outset for the family. A ready explanation for this was that jinns date to the time of the Prophet and were a form of life recognized within the Islamic tradition. Yet what form of life were they? And what nature of influences did they introduce into human lives?

The most important verification of jinns is to be found in the Qur'an in Sura 72, titled Al-Jinn, which opens thus:

Say: It has been
Revealed to us that
A company of Jinns
Listened (to the Qur'an).
They said, "We have
Really heard a wonderful Recital."

And, further on,

There were some foolish ones
Among us, who used
To utter extravagant lies
Against Allah;
But we think
That no man or jinn
Should say aught that is
Untrue against Allah.
    (The Holy Qur'an: 1830–31)

The most cited hadis in support of jinns was the one in which the Prophet asks his assembled companions who among them will come with him to a gathering of jinns. When none volunteers, he presses one among them into service. The two walk till they have left human settlement far behind and find themselves in a desolate area. There, in an open field stand tall figures who strike fear in the heart of the companion. The Prophet recites the Qur'an to the silent receptive crowd, after which he turns back toward the settlement. When he is a short distance from the figures, he picks up a piece of wood and some dung from the ground and flings them at the junns. He tells his companion that he has asked God that the jinns be able to get sustenance from wood and dung during their travels. In other words, he has interceded on their behalf to God (El-Zein 1996: 332).

These two texts provide the strongest textual verification of the existence of jinns within Islam. It has been said that belief in the existence of jinns is one with that of the existence of angels, which is within the primary articles of faith in Islam and, consequently, it is incorrect to disbelieve in them (El-Zein 1996).[2] I provide here a few commonly known characteristics of jinns from the enormous library of religious commentary, prophetic tales, magicians' manuals, folklore, and ethnography that has emerged around them in order to facilitate our acquaintance with the jinns who came to live in Farooq sahib's house.

Many Muslims believe jinns to be a species of spiritual beings created by God out of smokeless fire, long before he created humans out of mud, to whom he gave the earth to inhabit. By constitution jinns are drawn to both good and evil. That is, they are unlike angels, who were given the heavens to inhabit, and who were created out of pure light, and are hence incapable of evil (Hughes 1885, Encyclopedia of Islam 2003: s.v. djinn). In many ways jinns are the equivalent of humans in that they are endowed with passions, rational faculties, and responsibility for their own actions (El-Zein 1996). Biologically, they eat, grow, procreate and die much like humans. Socially, they organize themselves also much like humans (Westermarck 1926). However, unlike humans, jinns are capable of shape shifting, fast movement, great acts of strength, long lives, and are also known to eavesdrop on the angels in the lower reaches of heaven, thereupon acquiring limited knowledge of the future (Hughes 1885, Westermarck 1926, El-Zein 1996, Encyclopedia of Islam 2003). These two types of being, humans and jinns, inhabit the earth together, although jinn haunts are primarily desolate places, such as forests, ruins, and graveyards. The relations of humans and jinns range from mutual indifference to wars between collectivities in the distant past, relations of love and guardianship between individual humans and jinns, and the disruption of one another's lives, most visibly manifest in spirit possessions (Seigel 1969, Crapanzano 1980, Boddy 1989, Bowen 1993, El-Zein 1996, Rothenberg 1998, Pandolfo 2000). And it is to harness their powers that humans have long struggled to bring jinns within their possession. However, as we shall see, these relations between humans and jinns were constantly evolving.[3]

The word of Islam was brought to jinns as to men through the Prophet Muhammad. After the introduction of Islam, jinns became divided between those who became Muslims and those who did not. But a more distinctive shift in the concept of the jinn from pre-Islam to Islam was that jinns began to be much more unequivocally associated with evil, whereas previously both good and bad had been ascribed to their constitution. There is an early theological debate, as yet unresolved, as to whether the devil, more specifically Iblis, originates from jinns (Hughes 1885, El-Zein 1996, *Encyclopedia of Islam* 2003). Some claim that Iblis was allowed among the ranks of angels because of his immense devotion to God and was later banished from the heavens after his refusal to kneel before Adam. This possible association of jinns with Iblis hints at the anxiety that currently attends to the existence and disruptive tendencies of jinns. Another classical theological debate that continues into the present deliberates whether jinns are indeed a different category of being from humans, or whether they are forces of nature or projections of human interiority, in the Muslim sense, notably of the little mischievous *nafs* (spirits) that make up a self (Bowen 1993, El-Zein 1996; see Metcalf 1997 on nafs).

I generally found an acceptance in South Asia of the anthropomorphic existence of jinns, intermixed with a wariness that this acknowledgment of alternative worlds should not be seen as yet another marker of Muslim irrationality. Be that as it may, I do not here attend to this sense of insecurity, which arises from an almost quotidian acceptance of jinns, nor do I do justice to the rich anthropological and psychological literature that sees in the belief of jinns complex arrangements of cultural memory, political strategy, mental illness, and individual subjectivity (see Siegel 1969, Crapanzano 1980, Boddy 1989, Bowen 1993, El-Zein 1996, Rothenberg 1998, Pandolfo 2000). I take for granted the existence of jinns in an effort to learn more about the family that adopted them and their efforts at striving.

Besides his wife and himself, Farooq sahib's immediate family comprised his two sons and three daughters (born in that order) at the time the jinns came to be with them, some seven years prior to my initial acquaintance with them. At that time, Maryam, the second of Farooq sahib's daughters, was an eight-year-old girl and had been their conduit to the jinns. By the time that I met Maryam, she was fifteen, and had ceased her education at a private school for girls after passing her metric examinations. Her elder sister, who was sixteen, was to be married shortly, so Maryam had assumed many of the household duties she once shared with her older sister. Even at this more advanced age, Maryam was viewed as the most spiritual of the girls, akin to Adeeb, her eldest brother, who had gained a reputation for great piety from an early age.[4]

Although I did not observe Maryam's transition from childhood to adulthood, I imagined how it must have been for her by observing the family's treatment of their youngest daughter, Farah, who was eight at the time I met her. At that age Farah did not as yet observe purdah (the veil), frisked around in frocks and high heels and even occasionally dabbed on some lipstick. Previously readily held and kissed, indulged, and asked to perform na't (a form of poetry in praise of the Prophet) in public, by the end of my stay, when she was almost ten, she was already being pulled, protesting, out of her sleep to say her prayers with the family, since she would soon be "accountable."

To clarify this in brief, according to Islamic principles, children, although born free of sin and with the ability to communicate with divine beings (Das 1989), are considered beings without 'aql (reason), that is, they are always under threat of being easily led astray (Lapidus 1976, Aijaz 1989, Devji 1991). Consequently, in addition to the azan being said in their ears to mark them as Muslim, Islamic and Qur'anic instruction has to begin as early as four to ensure that children are provided guidance from early in their lives. However, Muslim parents are urged by the ulama to hold their children responsible for any missed religious duties, notably the reading of the Qur'an, prayers, and fasting, when they reach the age of ten, as by that time they are considered to have reached the age of sexual maturation. According to a hadis quoted in a manual titled *Muslim Children—How to Bring Up?* "The Prophet (S.A.W.) has said that we should call upon our children to offer prayers when they are seven years old and when they are ten years they should be punished for missing prayer and should have separate beds" (Aijaz 1989: 32). By this time parental entreaties could be replaced by punishment if children had not formed the habit of prayer and fasting (ibid.: 30).

It was Maryam who communicated between the jinns and her family. As an eight-year-old, she had a window into the spirit world. While at times she would look into the palms of her hands to see what the jinns would have her see, at others, the stories seemed to suggest that she was attuned to the ways in which this world, and the jinn world, a mirror of this one, were intertwined. She saw jinns interspersed among her family members. She relayed the requests of the human world to the jinns, bringing forth advice, instructions, and sometimes expressions of desire from the jinns. For instance, one day she told her father that one of the jinns wanted to taste human food and with her father's permission she instructed the jinn that he could enter her father's body. That day, as Farooq sahib later related, he had an appetite that frightened him with its insatiability. He felt that if the food had not finished he would have stayed rooted to his seat on the floor and continued eating through the night.[5]

Let me pursue briefly the specific relationship of ventriloquism between the jinn and Maryam. In the case of Maryam there seemed to be no question that her reported speech represented the voice of the jinn. It was as if Maryam was effaced the instance that she reported on the jinn. Yet, such transmissions were not free of ambiguity, for there were recorded cases in which other spirits slipped through a ready medium. Also, what would enjoin her family to attend so closely to her words if not the fact that they knew her so well as to trust her transmission? In other words, there was an accepted contiguity of jinn and human selves and the possibility of a plurality of voices in Maryam's mediation.

A fruitful comparison can be made between the Ahmadi-Muslim dyad explored in chapter 3 and that of the jinn-Maryam. While it was acceptable that the jinns could be conterminous with Maryam, in 1993 the Pakistani Supreme Court struggled to make it such that the figure of the Ahmadi could not be conterminous with the Muslim. In explaining its ruling, the court cited the Ahmadis' claim that they were the only true Muslims. The court argued that to accept the Ahmadi claim to be Muslim was to accept one's own annihilation as Muslim. While the basis of this argument of the court was questionable, after as the Munir Report showed each Muslim group to claim themselves the truest of all, my juxtaposition of the Ahmadi-Muslim dyad with the jinn-Maryam one raises the question of the limits of the contiguity of different forms of life, that is, when was copresence tolerable and how was it made intolerable?

Farooq Sahib's Pious Pursuits

When the jinns first came to Farooq sahib's house, the family's curiosity would compel them to spend long hours conversing with the jinns about their lives in their world. It was in the course of these initial introductions that it emerged that one among the jinns was a sahaba jinn. The title sahaba refers to a close companion of the Prophet or one who was alive at the time of the Prophet, thus having the opportunity to see him and relay his teachings. Moreover, certain hadis attest to Muhammad's conversion of tribes of both people and jinns to Islam. Given the long life attributed to jinns, it was conceivable to have a sahaba jinn alive today.[6] It was with the sahaba jinn that the family was most taken. In fact Maryam would spend most of her time describing Sulayman, as this jinn was called.[7] He was tall, I was told. He had a long beard that he kept well groomed. He was always dressed in spotlessly clean clothes. He kept his face arranged in a serious expression, careful not to indulge in loud outbursts of laughter. Although he looked stern, he smiled easily. He would sit down to drink his water or to partake in food. And he was very gentle with Maryam. She said she never felt frightened in his presence. She rewarded him by claiming him as her friend.

The family was captivated by these details of Sulayman's comportment, much more so than of the extensive physical landscape and social structure of the world of jinns also available to them. In fact, father and sons would attend to Maryam's descriptions taking them as examples of the correct way to emulate the Prophet. I understood Farooq sahib's preoccupation with the Prophet's example. In chapter 3, I showed how the Pakistani state attempted to uphold striving, as inspired by Muhammad Iqbal, by ensuring that Muslims relate correctly to the Prophet. The state punished the Ahmadis, whose relationship to the Prophet was faulted first and most urgently for claiming Mirza Ghulam Ahmad as a prophet, and second for compromising individual striving by passively seeking guidance through revelations. This event showed that although upholding the Prophet's example was an important modality of Muslim striving, there was by no means a foregone conclusion how one should pursue this upholding.

Farooq sahib was by no means a religious scholar, but he took scholarship seriously. He was a sayyid (noble-born, those who claim descent from the Prophet), a calligrapher by training, a teacher of Urdu and Islamiat by vocation, and a compositer of computer-generated religious texts by profession. For him calligraphy in the Islamic tradition was the textual expression of that which is enjoined upon every Muslim, *imitatio Muhammadi*. Just as the calligrapher, now compositer, sought to make the most perfect copy of a text without introducing any novelty into it, so too Farooq sahib and his sons struggled to make themselves the perfect emulation of the Prophet, to uphold his sunna (example) without introducing any innovation into it, providing us yet another instance of how a library of texts enfolded everyday action and behavior (Messick 1993).

By the time I met Farooq sahib he had already tried out a mode of emulating the Prophet, different from the Deobandi maslak and within Sunni Islam in Pakistan, through passionate love for and ecstatic identification with the Prophet. This was the Barelwi maslak (Sanyal 1996, Buehler 1998), into which he was born, which was generally recognized to be infused with Sufism. In this path the Prophet was immanent in the world, present everywhere, of course with the permission of God so as not to grant God's powers to another. Farooq sahib's own family, that is, his parents and sisters and brothers, who had stayed behind in Delhi at the time of the Partition of 1947, had remained Barelwi. Farooq sahib moved to Lahore in part so that his wife could be closer to her own family and in part so that he could ply his profession as calligrapher, later compositer, in a place where Urdu would be the lingua franca of the nation. However, through his ceaseless copying of religious texts, old and new, authentic and inauthentic, in Pakistan, Farooq sahib had come to realize that Barelwism was not the correct path by which to experience the Prophet.

Farooq sahib was then persuaded by the Deobandi maslak, in which the Prophet called forth a love—not *fana-e rasul* (self-annihilation in the Prophet) as in Barelwism, in which one was oblivious to one's being in the world in one's passionate embrace of the Prophet (Ernst 1995), but rather a love that compelled one to literally embody the Prophet in this world. It was the imagination of simultaneously seeing the Prophet in one's mind's eye and imitating him. In it the Prophet was not immanent in the world, although he was alive in his grave in Medina from where he was witness to the world, once again by God's permission. Thus, although one could legitimately dream of the Prophet, if the Prophet so wished to bless one with his presence, one could never call him forth, as Barelwis believed could be done through prayers in a mosque. Both these paths accepted jinns as having a dynamic if disruptive presence within the human world, alongside those of angels and saints (waliullah, literally friends of Allah) whose shrines were scattered across the country. Deobandis, however, felt that Muslims risked angering God with their excessive reliance upon jinns, angels, and saints, for it was God who alone ought to be relied upon (Metcalf 1997).

The Deobandi imagination with regard the imitation of the Prophet differed also from that of a third maslak within Sunni Islam in Pakistan, the Ahl-e Hadis; Farooq sahib had been a traveler also on the Ahl-e Hadis path for a very brief period before he embraced Deobandism. The Ahl-e Hadis believed that the Prophet was a man, albeit a great man, who demanded not love but respect (Metcalf 1982, Brown 1996). So when one imagined the Prophet (as my friend Akbar, the librarian and a self-identified Ahl-e Hadis, once described to me), one imagined oneself riding behind the Prophet as though on horseback, being lead by him. The hadis intermixed by sirat (biography of the Prophet) were the only legitimate means to access the Prophetic will. That is, there could be no other experience of the Prophet other than through the record of his words and deeds simply because, in Akbar's words, he was quite dead and turned to dust. So, for the stricter members of the Ahl-e Hadis, dreaming of the Prophet was sheer fancy. Every time I mentioned the topic of jinns to my Ahl-e Hadis acquaintances they would repress superior smiles, although I knew that a few of them were not averse to activating these forces when they had the need.[8]

It was in and through these varied affective relations (ecstatic love, reverential love, respect) to the Prophet that the variations among the Sunni paths became clearer to me. But the enmity that had developed between the two major Muslim sects, Sunnis and Shi'as, in the 1980s and 1990s was also part of the relations among the travelers of these three paths, although this enmity did not take the form of a unified Sunni versus Shi'a conflict. So, for instance, at one point Adeeb contemptuously referred to the Barelwi practice of celebrating the Prophet's birthday (Milad-un Nabi) with processions of models of the Prophet's mosque in Medina as repressed Shi'ism ("They just want to be like the Shi'as") because it resembled the procession of Shi'a taziyas (models of the tomb of Hussain in Karbala) during Muharram. In another instance, an Ahl-e Hadis acquaintance commented that the Barelwi and Deobandi belief that the Prophet was alive in his grave was akin to Shi'a notions of the Hidden Imam, giving his Barelwi and Deobandi colleagues in the library in which they all worked a real fright. This one comment generated one of the bitterest debates in which I participated in my time in Pakistan, which I have analyzed in my introduction. Thus, even within the daily struggle to affirm the presence of the Prophet with a certainty that only faithful emulation could provide, there were considerable concerns on how to ground this emulation in unwavering religious authority.[9]

Each of the Sunni masalik had evolved complex procedures to buttress its individual modes of imitatio Muhammadi. For the Deobandi this involved face-to-face relations with the ulama-e salih, the rightful scholars of Islam, for only through their teachings and behavior could one have concrete examples of how to emulate the Prophet. Given the Deobandi emphasis on face-to-face learning from the ulama, what startled me was that Farooq sahib would take his cues on the Prophet's example from a faceless and voiceless jinn with his child serving as its medium. One way to approach this would be to say that Farooq sahib was doing what many others do in activating several even competing bodies of knowledge and sets of relations in the hope that one of them will pay off (Ewing 1997). However, I had come to know Farooq sahib quite well by this point and I knew of his insistence upon a modicum of consistency in his life. I knew, for instance, that he struggled with the fact that he did not wear a beard, although he was strongly urged by his sons to do so as it was a practice of the Prophet. And given his disapproval of overreliance upon jinns to get things done, it seemed strange to me that he would allow jinns into his home in the first place. Let me simply flag this discrepancy in Farooq sahib's actions, postponing my interpretations of it for later. For now let me point out that Farooq sahib's careful delineation of the promises and pitfalls of each path and sect within Islam suggested stable and enduring differences. However, as we know from mosques and their qabza, the sources of tensions and conflicts could not be religious differences alone and that these differences often received great impetus from other facets of people's identities and social arrangements.

Tensions within the Family

Farooq sahib's immediate family consisted of him, his wife, and five children. Although this was not a joint family arrangement, that is to say, only one family ever resided in the house in Shabbir, the exact number of inhabitants remained in flux.[10] Relatives came and went as the family retained close ties with its extended family as far afield as Multan, Karachi, and even Delhi in India. Furthermore, there was an expectation of future growth, as the adult sons would soon have their families within this household.

Over the period of time I was in Lahore, the unproductiveness of the sons was a continual source of tension within the family. While Farooq sahib toiled at numerous jobs, Adeeb spent much of his time undertaking pious, but unremunerated work, taking private lessons with a well-known alim; doing gasht (the beat) of the neighborhood, that is, inviting male members of households to come pray in the mosque; preparing dars (lessons) with his Tablighi sathis (companions) in their markaz (center) in Lahore; going on chilla (forty-day trips) to convert errant Muslims in other parts of the country and abroad; and even on occasion, sitting 'etikaf, that is, retreating to the mosque for prayer and contemplation, for the Islamic month of Ramzan (Ramadan) (Metcalf 1993a, Masud 2000). While the family was very proud of his spiritual strength, they also felt his meager contributions to the family coffers very keenly. Of late Adeeb had gained a lot of weight, which, combined with his beard, head cap, and loose flowing tunic made him look older than his twenty years. People, even his parents, had started to teasingly refer to him as a mulla, once a title of respect but now a derogatory term for a religious personage who was seen to mostly sit around the mosque (Ewing 2003).

His younger brother, Ali, was not doing much better. At the beginning of our acquaintance he was ambivalent about being openly pious, preferring to spend his free time hanging out with his friends, watching pirated Hindi films, and generally exploring avenues to leave Pakistan. When, by the end of my trip, he turned more strongly toward his faith he tended to be drawn to the more strident aspects of the Deobandi path that sought to police members of the other Sunni paths for their misuse of fiqh-e Hanafiyya (a school of Islamic jurisprudence).[11] Fashioning themselves on the Sipah-e Sahaba (warriors of the Sahaba), the incipient group called themselves Sipah-e Hanafiyya (warriors of Hanafiyya). One time, disgusted by Adeeb and Ali's meager financial support of the family, Farooq sahib spat out at them, "Why don't you call up jinn bhoots [ghosts] to make some money?" In other words, if they considered themselves too superior to take up regular jobs then why didn't they simply resort to being 'amils to make some money? By this time the jinns had come and gone from the family and, from what I could make out, the family had seen it beneath themselves to profit monetarily from them. Although Adeeb had shown some talent in the profession, chalked up to his great piety, to turn to 'amiliyat now would be a considerable step down for these sayyid (noble-born) boys.

By the end of my stay the young sister of Farooq sahib's wife, Rahima, died quite unexpectedly in nearby Multan. Rahima's family grieved her loss. She had left behind two young children, a boy and a girl, who came to live with Farooq sahib and Rahima shortly after their mother's death. Farooq sahib, in keeping with his generosity, agreed to keep them and even adopt them if necessary. From what I gathered in conversation with them, the children pined for their father. At the same time there was some concern: how would Farooq sahib manage financially if they did come to live with him permanently? No one dared approach the children's father about this matter. Instead they sat around speculating whether he planned to remarry and forever abandon his children.

To remind the reader, by this time the jinns had returned to their original guardian (the 'amil who had entrusted Farooq sahib's family with them) and Maryam had ceased to be of the correct age to serve as a medium.[12] However, in discussion the family struck upon the idea of speaking to the jinn Sulayman about what lay ahead for the young children. The family decided to take Farah, Farooq sahib's youngest daughter to speak to Sulayman, to transmigrate to Multan with him if necessary, to see what was in the absent father's mind. However, Farah did not fare as well as Maryam. She was alternatively frightened of the jinns and upset at them for not taking her to Medina, as they had earlier promised. Amid much regret that Maryam was no longer capable of serving as a medium, the family sent the two children with Sulayman. When they returned to their bodies, they described how they had seen their father in their house packing his bag. This was followed by an exuberant hope that he was packing to come pick them up, as indeed he did shortly afterward, but then just as quickly sent them back. Through the time that I was there, the children remained in limbo among several households.

Keeping this unresolved tension of the children's fate in mind and the challenge their possible integration offered to the straitened state of finances within the family, I turn briefly to a third story, that of withholding of forgiveness. Rahima's mother, Farooq sahib's mother-in-law, became the de facto guardian of the children. A beautiful old woman quite untouched by the ravages of time, she had returned to mothering, she said, when she ought to be knitting sweaters. Her own arrangement was a continuing source of tension within Farooq sahib's household. She lived in Lahore with her eldest son while her husband, whom she referred to only as "he," lived with Farooq sahib and Rahima, in whose house he generally kept to a dark corner. He would emerge only to go to the mosque to pray. The husband and wife were estranged and had been so for almost a decade. Farooq sahib's mother-in-law refused to speak to "him" for whatever untold miseries he had heaped on her.[13] As he got older and, apparently more concerned with his mortality, he felt the need to reconcile with his wife before he died. Of late he had developed a cough that racked his body and he sensed that he might die soon. He had sought out his wife on several of her visits to Farooq sahib's house, but, as she told us, although she wanted to do the right thing by him his presence made her sick. Spurred on by Rahima, Farooq sahib attempted to reconcile the two. When all the stories of the jinns were being told to me, Rahima's mother came to me and said almost ruefully, "Naveeda, I too was offered a jinn once. Now what is a jinn but a man. And I don't want to have a relationship with a man ever again."

These stories, of parental disappointment with sons, of children's possible abandonment by their father, and of a wife's estrangement from her dying husband, hint at the tensions that tear at families, even one as close-knitted as Farooq sahib's, of the ambiguities that undergird lived relations. A final story suggests how these familial tensions and the tensions between Shi'as and Sunnis, or among Sunnis, graft onto one another, or how religious differences are exacerbated by familial tensions. This additional story dates to the time when Maryam still served as the family's medium, long before I came into the picture. Farooq sahib had traveled to India to spend time with the Barelwi side of his family there. Maryam remained restless the entire time he was away, scared that he might never come back. She asked her mother to take her to their 'amil friend almost every day so that she might speak with Sulayman. Every day she would whisper something to him. Meanwhile, Farooq sahib tried to get his Indian visa extended to allow him to spend more time with his family in Delhi. However, it seemed to him, particularly in retrospect, that his every attempt failed. Dejected he returned home on the very day that his original visa expired. Maryam rushed to greet him at the door of the house but then she fell back screaming. Apparently a thirty-feet-tall *churail* (witch)[14] had followed Farooq sahib back from India. Farooq sahib immediately dropped his bags at the doorstep and without pause rushed to the mosque to say his prayers. When he returned home, Maryam assured him that the witch had left him. If at that time Maryam had still been frightened, he said, he would have had to tear up the city looking for someone to rid him of the witch, but thankfully his prayers had helped him. When I asked Maryam why she did not want her father to stay on in India, she replied that his family there was not going to let him go and that they had literally bewitched him because they were jealous he was returning to his other family. When I asked Farooq sahib what he thought of this suggestion, he shrugged and thought it genuinely possible that his Barelwi family would pull such a prank because they did not take his being a Deobandi seriously enough. I pushed him on this statement. After all, it was a grave accusation to make against one's own brothers and sisters. "Jealousy is a strong force. Sometimes those who are jealous do not even know how they bind others up," he replied. I wondered if he wasn't also thinking of Maryam when he made his observation. Similarly, the attack on the family by jinns posing as ants, with which Farooq sahib and Rahima had begun telling these stories to me, was taken as another indication of the force of jealousy, this time emanating from their Barelwi neighbors who wished to test the truth of the Deobandi family's claim of having jinns in their possession.

The Unfolding of Farooq Sahib's Striving or Becoming Jinn

To return to my deferred line of inquiry, what do we make of Farooq sahib's impulsive gesture of bringing the jinns into his home in the first place? In the anthropological literature, occult manuals, and encyclopedia entries I have read on jinns, sustained contact with jinns augurs madness. The average 'amil undergoes considerable pain and deprivation to be able to lay claim upon a particular force, and undertakes continual exercises of the body and mind to control it (Shurreef 1823).[13] However, Farooq sahib did not train himself to be an 'amil, in fact, he still retained his sense of distance and disdain of the profession. He allowed the entry of jinns into his home without the armature of the average 'amil. He appeared to have knowingly risked the potential disruption of his family, their succumbing to madness, which was not unimaginable in the realms of jinns, or, at the very least, the possibility of his family being permanently affected by this encounter. Consider the danger to Maryam in being made to face the jinns on a regular basis.

One way to read his actions is to acknowledge the casualness with which he took on the jinns. It was nothing special, speaking to the ordinariness of jinns within the landscape of Lahore. The mainstream Urdu press carried stories of jinn sightings and abductions interspersed with regular stories of family feuds, political rivalries, and sectarian violence. Often, to caricature the gullibility of the ordinary Pakistani and to make fun of the Urdu press, the English press, the exclusive preserve of a cosmopolitan Pakistani elite, would plant stories in their pages about their correspondents attending jinn weddings.

A second, more productive way to read Farooq sahib's decision is to see it as the extraordinary efforts of a Muslim to keep on the straight path. It involved Farooq sahib's abdicating his position of authority within his family to attend to his daughter's words of guidance. His turn toward Maryam may be taken to be a turn away from the present, an admission that his everyday life did not have the spiritual riches and authoritative accounts he desired to make himself a better Muslim. I have suggested above how ambiguity plagued daily struggles to ground the pious emulation of the Prophet in proper religious authority within each of the Sunni paths. Moreover, the state's policing of one's attachment to the Prophet intruded upon these struggles, making all the more tenuous any textual or extratextual claims to authenticity. One might develop a sensibility finely attuned to theological differences so as to ascertain whether such claims to authenticity were from within one's particular path, over those of others. But there were such claims, even under the rubric of one's maslak, that were equally productive of *shakk-o shubha* (doubts) as of certainty. Farooq sahib was fully aware of this problem. Together he and I had mulled over many "authorized" posters affixed to Deobandi mosques, which left him worried about their possible reception. In turning toward Maryam, Farooq sahib appeared to give expression to his sense of the illusory quality of everyday life, where things were not as they appeared to be, and people were not who they appeared to be.[16]

In such a situation, guidance might well come from an unexpected source from an unexpected place, and one had to know to accept it. For a short period of time jinns provided the solace that one was on the correct path and this was well worth the disruptions they introduced into Farooq sahib's life. Sulayman's welcome into the family suggested how pursuits of the self might productively incorporate the unexpected, to the extent of abdicating full control of oneself. The encounter with Sulayman further showed how tense religious differences did not betoken the fragmentation of a family, though they nonetheless infiltrated the weave of familial relations. At the same time the familial relations that formed and frayed around Sulayman suggested that putting oneself together with others did not necessarily protect one from becoming estranged from them. Thus Sulayman's appearance illuminated an entire field of striving with doubts and uncertainties woven into it.

But what do we learn about the nature of Farooq sahib's individual striving over the course of his family's encounter with the jinns? Farooq sahib appeared to stand beside himself, to be quite otherwise than the reformed Muslim he claimed to be, when he first brought the jinns into his family's life after espousing derision for those who did so. Then he moved again from his position as a pedagogical figure to become a pupil to his daughter, newly moved herself by the force of the jinn. He returned to a position of authority when he decided not to attempt to bring back the jinns after they returned to their guardian. But it was no longer the position he occupied before the jinns came. He had seen his milieu through a different set of eyes. He had moved through positions unfamiliar to him. The genetic elements in his milieu and within him had reorganized around him. He sensed the block of becoming-jinn that has asserted itself into this milieu within him ex-pressed in his confession: "Our 'aqida [faith] had become weak and our 'ibadat [obligatory worship] was suffering." There was also something of the quality of becoming mad at that time in his and his family's life. This was communicated to me through my conversations with Farooq sahib's col-leagues. They told me that they steered clear of him, scared that their pre-vious light teasing of him on account of his religiosity might bring forth a vengeful response from him.

To better explain what I mean by the change induced in him and his milieu as a result of this encounter, I return to Iqbal's picture of striving, presented in chapter 2. Within a Bergsonian model of time, one's actualized past, thronged by possible pasts and others held in potential, crowd in on one in the course of daily life. Iqbal's contribution to this model was to suggest that it wasn't only one's past that inflected one's present, but that one's imagination of the future also stood to inflect this present. Although this future was perhaps more informed by an undifferentiated potential than the past, it was not without concrete possibilities insofar as Muslims sought to actualize one of the many known qualities attributed to God. Further-more, one was never fully individuated, manifesting aspects of a quality while shading into other qualities or versions of the same quality held by others. If we were to place Farooq sahib's movements within this frame-work, we can see him inhabiting a present informed by a capacious past and future. In other words, his past selves ran into his present self as he was drawn toward his future self. He existed with these versions of himself, which accompanied him insofar as they were durationally part of him. In bringing a jinn into his life, he brought it into a series with him. It became a version of him joining other versions of himself with whom he was bound.

Consequently, even though he later set the jinn apart from himself, the memory of absorption and the quality of shading into this other form of life became a part of his makeup as of his milieu.

In Farooq sahib's moves next to himself I choose not to see contradictory positions to be resolved in a final form but rather different versions of himself internal to his being. He showed himself to be continually striving, while not discarding these versions of himself. These became side movements of which he was also capable. Moreover, his arcing toward a future self, relative to his prior self, perhaps even looping back to one of his prior selves, gives me to believe that his future world did not lie beyond the present one, but was held in potential within it. To my mind this modality of striving provides a vivid instantiation of Iqbal's account of Muslim aspiration, in which striving to one's next self and one's finitude were equally exalted. Yet the question remains, what practical relations could one maintain to a different form of life after it was set apart from oneself?

The Quality of Friendship

Thus far I have considered familial relations at some length. Let me now consider friendship as one more element of this milieu. Unquestionably, friendship has a place of privilege within the Islamic tradition. One cannot control the family into which one is born, nor the family one begets. Earlier, I cited an injunction that deemed it best to disown one's children if they continued to resist parental authority to mold them into pious Muslims (Aijaz 1989). However, good friends aided one in the pursuit of piety. In his commentary on the collection of hadis *Mishkat ul-Masabih*, Maulana Fazlul Karim writes: "A trusted friend is a safe treasure in the world and his companionship is to be greatly valued. This is possible only in good fellowship for good and pious works" (1989: 549). Certainly, friendship nourished Farooq sahib's son Adeeb, providing a resolution to a standing tension within the family over the sons' unproductiveness. It opened up a future for Adeeb to continue to be pious in the way he desired. After I left, he met and befriended a young industrialist in his travels with his Tablighi companions, who gave him a job as the imam of a mosque on his industrial estate in the fringes of Lahore. Adeeb became a mulla. He also finally accepted his talents as an 'amil and began to dispense cures and spells to the workers in the estate. He married the younger sister of the industrialist. He secured a marriage for Maryam with another of his Tablighi sathis. Maryam had a child, and she and the child often returned home to stay with her parents for extended periods of time while her husband traveled to spread the word of Islam.

What nature of friendship did Maryam share with Sulayman the jinn? Maryam did not seem to remember much, busy playing the role of the only grown daughter in her parents' home at the time I left, now busy playing the role of a wife and mother. Yet here too something was changing. When I next went back to Pakistan, she readily claimed a friendship with Sulayman, thankful that he never frightened her in their many interactions. She missed him after he left. Farooq sahib and Rahima recalled her crying herself to sleep for weeks after. She claimed to have had dreams, such dreams. She just recalled the sense of those dreams with a shiver, while making us tea.[17] This memory was also to be in her past. During another return visit to Pakistan, Maryam blushed when I asked about Sulayman because what could a married mother of two have to do with a jinn?

Did Sulayman simply aid her in the family's pursuit of piety? In place of her words, I imagine a certain friendship, derived in part from my own readings of *Arabian Nights* tales and from the insight that perhaps she herself was not unfamiliar with these stories. As in the famous tale of Aladdin and the magic lamp, familiar to the contemporary imagination through Disney World's animated movie, a child found a genie and could be literally pulled out of a humdrum existence to soar the skies. She shared in his joy of discovering human food. She got to whisper her secrets into his ears and make him complicit in her projects. She got to go to places with him, although Sulayman said that he would not go to the United States. She got to help out her family and her neighbors. And, she got to temporally take leave of her body that was changing beyond her control. Soon she would not be able to access this spirit world anymore and I imagine her father was not averse to the jinn's leaving before this inevitability, so that she would not be faced with a sense of loss.

Was Sulayman then about the inability to acknowledge friendship over time? This question gains poignancy when one recollects that once it became conceivable to think that Ahmadis were not Muslims in Pakistan, friendship seemed to be the only positive way to relate to them. This was the formulation of the Munir Report of 1954, in which the judges stated that one should not estrange the Ahmadis for they had been loyal friends of Pakistan. However, as this story reminds us, there are always irreparable betrayals and disappointment within friendships. Sulayman left this family in disappointment over their behavior, and Maryam repaid his betrayal by forgetting him. Nonetheless Sulayman endured for Farooq sahib, by being assimilated within the series of selves that constituted Farooq sahib. Yet, what understanding and acknowledgment did the enduring elements of Sulayman within Farooq sahib call for?

Chapter Five

SKEPTICISM IN PUBLIC CULTURE

FROM THE *JAHIL MAULWI* TO MULLAISM

She Sits with Mullas

By the end of my time in Lahore, Pakistan had returned to its usual state some two years after General Pervez Musharraf first declared martial law in the country. I now had before me a military-run state that lacked credibility and failed to provide for everyday security, at times exacerbating already tense relations; an uprise of sectarian violence that made it unsafe to attend Friday prayers; and a people apparently mute in the face of the tensions and troubles that thronged them. Muhammad Iqbal's writings, abundantly available, even as graffiti on walls, spoke of a different moment in Muslim history, of a time of colonial domination, but were suffused with an awareness of suffering at the level of gesture and affect. For instance, the difference between his poems Shikwa and Jawab-e Shikwa was decisive in orienting one to the colonial landscape from a perspective other than of Muslim decline and degeneracy. If the first poem spoke of Muslim bewilderment and anger at their state of decline, the second continued the rage, this time directed at Muslims for bringing this decline upon them. But the difference lay in the urging in the second poem to not bemoan one's existence but to affirm it and to return again and again to what was incumbent upon one as a Muslim with the expectation that in doing so one was participating in change. The significance of these movements cannot be understated, as Giorgio Agamben reminds us in his reflection on gestures, because they are the mute inhabiting of potentiality (2000: 84).

To be attuned to the aspiration to strive to be Muslim in this landscape takes an awareness of gestures and the realm of the potential being attempted to be inhabited by these gestures and their enfolding within texts and narratives. In my own work, it also took an awareness of affect. I have, thus far, presented four scenes of aspiration: librarians engaged in argumentation over the nature of the Prophet's body after his death, neighborhoods embroiled in fights over mosques in attempting to prescribe the rightful atmosphere for prayer, the state drawn into theological disputation and legal experimentation over how one should attach oneself to the Prophet, and a pious man trying to seek guidance on how to be Muslim from an invisible being. In each situation, I took the gesture—that of argumentation, seizure, legal experimentation, or search for guidance—as illuminative of striving. But it was affect that communicated to me that striving hung in the balance in the first place. The intensity of seriousness, sincerity, excitement, disappointment, and sense of loss accompanying these scenes alerted me to attend more closely to their narratives and the gestures therein.

There were also other commitments in the air, most persistently commitments to friendship, neighborliness, and familial ties. In all four scenes of aspiration skepticism was also expressed. In the case of the Assembly Library, the librarian Naz felt in the narrowed eyes and clinched faces of those with whom he argued the force of skepticism about his rationality and grounds for his beliefs. In the case of mosque seizure (qabza), Imam Aziz fell prey to a skeptical situation, to which his own actions contributed, in which anything could be said and believed about him. In another instance of mosque seizure, the government scientist Dr. Khan took a skeptical turn toward the world when he felt that everyone around him had transformed into animals. And Farooq sahib, my Urdu teacher and research guide, acted on the presumption that everyday life was one of illusion and appearances, illustrating skepticism of daily existence. None of these instances brought skepticism into being, but each did actualize the potential for skepticism that existed in the social fabric. Furthermore, they illuminate the point emphasized by Stanley Cavell (1982) that the actual expression of skepticism is a datable event tied to the specific arrangement of people and circumstances. In other words, these were not chance occurrences or pervasive conditions.

But what was I to make of all the mirth that accompanied my research? "You work on mosques?" sputtered some. "She sits with mullas," declared others in introducing me. Soon I was the subject of more jokes about what happened in mosques and what the mulla in the mosque was up to than I had bargained for. Horror stories and psychological profiles of mullas quickly followed. Once alerted, I began to quite enjoy the weekly skewering of mullas in the cartoon strips of the Friday Times, a Lahore-based magazine. This humor entwined with outrage was in some ways class-coded, being the preserve of upper-class Pakistanis. But I also heard jokes from many from the middle and working classes, and once, I even heard a few "mulla jokes" (as I called them) from an imam. There is, after all, a large arsenal of off-color jokes about specialist figures of all religious traditions in the popular culture of the subcontinent (as elsewhere).[1] Perhaps these stories introduced a necessary levity to the continuing efforts to be Muslim in this milieu. They also served as political commentary, if not outright criticism, that religious forces had usurped Pakistan, making familiar figures and institutions of Islam unfamiliar, even threatening. This was certainly one way to understand the oft-stated comment I analyzed earlier in the book that Pakistan was a mosque that had undergone qabza.

What I found perplexing in almost all instances of this ubiquitous stereotype of the mulla that I encountered was that the mulla was to blame for everything that was perceived to be wrong or going wrong in Pakistan. When I heard the very same imam who cracked jokes about mullas also blame mullas for the decline of Pakistan, I felt compelled to ask him who or what was this mulla at whose feet all blame could be placed. Distinguishing among the ulama (religious scholars), the imam of Neela Gumbard Mosque, a historic mosque in Anarkali Bazaar, who would become a close informant said, "There are those who are in the right and those who misinform. Even though people think that they mean the second when they call someone a mulla, they don't mean either, I don't think. They mean someone who looks overly religious according to them, because the person wears his cap in a particular way, keeps his beard a particular length, wears his pants this high, you know what I mean. This person doesn't actually have to be an educated religious scholar. If he looks a certain way, then people fear he is going to act a certain way." "What way is that?" I interjected. "It's hard to say in shorthand. You can only know by watching him. He is most likely going to be a bad-tempered religious person [bad-mizaji dini banda]." Thus it would appear that striving Muslims had their other not only in the shadowy Shi'a, or the deceiving Ahmadi, but also in the bad-tempered mulla.

In this chapter I first explore the semantics of the term mulla to sketch the transformations that have occurred to give the word its present-day negative connotation. I mark a shift from the view of Iqbal, who understood mullaism to mean the ossification of the institution of the ulama, to that of the Pakistani state, which identified mullaism as the ossification of commentary upon Islamic texts. The state, more specifically President Zia-ul Haq, later extended this tendency to ossification to include the wider populace. I provide ethnographic examples of mullaism to show how this condition operated within everyday assertions that one's religiosity was superior to others, alongside the struggles of the Urdu author Mumtaz Mufti with his internal mulla. I track the mulla across the registers of jokes, horror stories, and cartoons to show how the figure transmuted across these domains to become a full-fledged malevolent persona considered to reside in every Pakistani Muslim. If the state's interjections into the Ahmadi question accentuated the sense of everyday life as one of deceptive appearances, the treatment of the mulla in the public culture of Lahore rendered mullaism as a condition that could befall anyone, transforming that person into a bigot. I end the chapter with my conversations with young maulwis (scholars of religion) who feel the death dealing effects of the stereotype of the mulla.

The central claim of this chapter is that the public attitude toward the mulla transformed into a mullaism that threatened one from within and without as a result of the emergence of a pervasive skepticism directed toward oneself as to others. This skepticism was markedly different from the specific kinds of skepticism that emerged within the weave of social relations that I spoke of above, although it was not different from the skepticism authorized by the state with respect to Ahmadis. And this all-pervasive skepticism had to have consequences for Muslim aspiration, putting all striving under the shadow of skepticism. I explore this pall on striving and the efforts made to address it in greater detail in chapter 6.

I focus on the figure of the mulla as its ubiquity allowed me to traverse the fragmented public culture of the city, with its enclaves of opinions and textual productions, to see how this fractured landscape came together at points in collective fear and revulsion toward this figure. While my archival work and textual analysis yielded up instances of the citation of mullaism, I plumbed my fieldwork for moments of enactment of the posture of the mulla. I added the study of President Zia-ul Haq's speeches to my existing research work when I realized how many of the jokes I was hearing originated in his time and how often he was said to have chastised the public for their joking demeanor toward icons of religiosity. I trolled the city for jokes, stories, and cartoons, also speaking to cartoonists and storytellers. I also returned to the ulama of my acquaintance to ask them their thoughts on the proliferation of this mocking image of them. While a few among them, particularly the younger ones, spoke of the ambivalence shown them by

Pakistani society as a lack of acceptance of their own claims upon striving, the more learned ones directed me to texts, either their own handwritten responses to specific inquiries or books in circulation. In these texts the effort was to return the gaze of the public to its involvement in theological speculation and argument and to exhort Muslims to consider the severe consequences of "chatter." In other words, the ulama turned the gaze upon Muslim aspiration. Two ulama, the owners of a famous Islamic bookstore in Anarkali, who delighted in directing my readings, pointed me to Mumtaz Mufti's writings as an instance of a contemporary Urdu author with good insights into the experience of being Muslim in Pakistan.

Ulama/Maulwi/Mulla: A Semantic Constellation

The term *ulama* is used for the community of religious scholars who serve as the guardians, transmitters, and interpreters of the Shari'a (Islamic law), with specific claims of knowledge upon *tafsir* (commentary upon the Qur'an), *fiqh* (jurisprudence), hadis (sayings of the Prophet), and *kalam* (speculative theology). Ulama usually include such figures as the *mufti* (interpreter of the Shari'a), *muhaddis* (expert on the hadis), and *mutakallim* (expert on kalam), and are usually located in religious seminaries or cognate institutions. In Pakistan the term *ulama* also came to include the personnel in a mosque, including the imam (the prayer leader), the *khatib* (who gives the Friday sermon), the *qari* (reciter of the Qur'an), and the muezzin (the person who gives the call to prayer). Although not formally organized, there is a clear hierarchy among them while they share a group identity. For instance, an imam of a mosque, a friend of my teacher Farooq sahib, once made an offhand but proud reference to being part of the *ulama baradari*. The term *baradari* is a kinship term in Pakistan that refers to a patrilineage of those who likely share common descent but who now share only in the collective reputation of their descent group (Alavi 1972). While the ulama do not belong to any specific baradari, the use of the term indicates the strong nature of identification the imam felt with other ulama.

Maulwi, a term used interchangeably with *mulla*, technically means learned master. It was once broadly used as a title of respect but has increasingly come to refer to those who are educated in the religious sciences, such as the members of the ulama. In its attenuated form, it refers more specifically to ulama of low- to middle-class origins who have not completed the course of study to make them experts of the highest ranks, or to ulama who simply provide for the ritual needs of a community. Further mutation of the term maulwi or mulla pushes it almost entirely in the direction of a derogatory reference to one who is overzealous in upholding the letter of the Shari'a. Along these same lines, it is also used to mean a bigot, a censor, or even a person who exacerbates differences among Muslims through his insistence on the right way to attend to religious obligations.[2] I most often encountered the terms maulwi and mulla in their derogatory sense, with the additional connotations of a qabza agent (one who undertakes seizures of properties), a sodomizer (one who rapes men), a naive fool out of step with his time, among other such depictions, a range which I explore below.

This figure of the ignorant master is no newcomer to the realm of character stereotypes (Mills, Claus, and Diamond 2003). Eighteenth- and nineteenth-century Urdu poetry often speaks of the shaikh (venerable old man) who sits piously in the mosque all day but is to be seen at wine gatherings in the evening, invariably in a state of drunken disrepair. Children from Iran and Afghanistan have long been entertained by the fictional accounts of Mulla Nasruddin, the religious master who gets by in life through hypocrisy and cunning, outsmarting those of noble birth and high cultivation. But the shift internal to the terms maulwi and mulla from one of respect to one of derision may be most effectively mapped onto changing notions of what counted as authoritative knowledge within British colonial politics in South Asia. As the notion of "useful education" took hold within the colonial administration and the wider Indian milieu, the knowledge to which the ulama were privy came to be seen not only as outdated but deliberately obscurantist and the ulama came to be jahil (ignorant) maulwis (Viswanathan 1989, Ewing 2003). From being treated as towering figures of religious authority with vast familial and scholarly connections, they came to be described in the following way by Denzil Ibbetson, the colonial officer who compiled the Punjab Census Report of 1881: "The ulama (caste no. 70)—This is a perfectly miscellaneous assortment of people, many of whom cannot claim to have any priestly character. Any divine learned in the faith of Islam claims the title of Alim. . . . But on the frontier any person who can read and write and possesses sufficient religious knowledge to enable to conduct the devotions in a mosque claims the title" (1974: 166, quoted in Ewing 2003).

From the Mulla to Mullaism in Pakistan

The negative stereotypes of the ulama and the devaluation of their forms of knowledge continued into the postcolonial period. Yet it wasn't the ulama who were directly targeted as the potential drag upon Pakistan within state discourses. Rather, the state targeted a condition called mullaism. Muhammad Iqbal had identified mullaism as one of the three forces, the other two being mysticism and Muslim kings, against which the "world of Islam" was in revolt. He writes:

> Mullaism.—The Ulema have always been a source of great strength to Islam. But during the course of centuries, especially since the destruction of Baghdad, they became extremely conservative and would not allow any freedom of ijtihad, i.e., the forming of independent judgment in matters of law. The Wahabi movement which was a source of inspiration to the 19th century Muslim reformers was really a revolt against this rigidity of the Ulema. Thus the first objective of the 19th century Muslim reformers was a fresh orientation of the faith and a freedom to reinterpret the law in the light of advancing experience. (1974: 21)

Following Iqbal, this perception of mullaism made numerous appearances within the debates of the first Constituent Assembly. As this is the assembly that I identified as the source of the idea that Pakistan was to be a laboratory for Muslim self-experimentation, it bears drawing out what the state meant by mullaism and what relation it bore to Muslim experimentation. In the Constituent Assembly debates, mullaism was often described as the fossilized state of knowledge on Islam. Dr. Omar Hayat Malik, an assemblyman, provides an instance of the official use of the term:

> Religion all over the world has become a phenomenon, in the sense that religion comes with a Prophet and the Book. Then the prophet passes away and the Book is commented upon. When the commentaries are commented upon, there are new commentaries and so on, until in the end people forget the original source and get wedded and attached so much to the commentaries that they forget the real source. That is why the religion gets fossilized. . . . The same process has occurred in Islam for hundreds of years. Now ijtihad has been banned and a class of people have arisen who think that ijtihad is sinful. We must adopt the interpretations which we made several hundred years ago. I do not say that they

were not the final arbiters of what is meant or not meant by Quran and Sunna. This is what is really called Mullaism. I do not know what it means when we hear it from the mouths of the detractors of the Islamic State, but I think this is Mullaism and this kind of Mullaism we must try to eradicate. (Government of Pakistan 1953: 269)

The speech was a direct rejoinder to those in the assembly who worried that bringing Islam into the wording of the constitution would inevitably produce a theocracy. Malik portrayed mullaism as historical accretions in the form of religious commentaries upon foundational texts, which were now outdated and could be eradicated. Implicit in this speech was the idea that modern Muslims needed to access the Qur'an and the hadis directly without the mediations of these commentaries and, by association, the commentators. A fresh interpretation of Islam without the obstruction of mullaism in the form of mediating texts would prevent any possibility of a theocracy. If we recall, Zafarullah Khan made a similar argument in these debates when he cited an example of tolerance exhibited by the Prophet Muhammad.

The movement from mullaism as ossified knowledge to mullaism as a condition of zealotry to which even lay Muslims were vulnerable was already under way when the Constituent Assembly debates were in progress. The authors of the 1954 Munir Report inquiring into the causes of the anti-Ahmadi disturbances in Punjab in 1953 issued the following warning to the state of how a people in the grips of mullaism were likely to behave: "If there is one thing which has been conclusively demonstrated in this inquiry, it is that provided you can persuade the masses to believe that something they are asked to do is religiously right or enjoined by religion, you can set them to any course of action, regardless of all considerations of discipline, loyalty, decency, morality or civic sense" (Government of Pakistan 1954: 205). In 1995, Aitzaz Hasan, a senior lawyer and one-time member of the National Assembly of Pakistan, provided a lurid description of those in the grips of such a condition in the context of a public discussion on the future of religion and secularism in Pakistan:

What are we? A man goes on the loudspeaker and starts calling people that Dr. Sajjad has burnt the Quran. And they start passing it on to others. A stampede, a madness follows. Nobody inquires and nobody cares; and before someone stops them, the man is pulled out and stoned to death. He is tied behind a motor bike, taken through half a city. Half a city means people like you and me living there, it is not just a mulla, it is all of us. There is a little mulla in each of us. (Jan 1998: 97)

In these descriptions mullaism isn't only the historical accretions on foundational texts that separated Muslims from their tradition and that could be eradicated by a fresh interpretation of Islam. It is also a tendency in each Muslim, educated or otherwise. Once activated it could spread like contagion with violent effects.

Coordinates of the Little Mulla in Each of Us: A Hint of Skepticism

In 1995 Aitzaz Hasan warned of the little mulla in each Pakistani. But self-awareness of this internal stranger was engendered by none other than Zia-ul Haq, the military leader of Pakistan from 1977 to 1988. Zia-ul Haq fashioned himself as an Islamic leader and gave considerable place of importance to the ulama in the administration of the country. It was in his time the perception emerged that the ulama bore the brunt of responsibility for Pakistan's deteriorating political condition. Here the specific reference was to Zia's decision to involve Pakistan in a war in Afghanistan between the invading Soviet government and the Afghan mujahedin (warriors in the cause of Islam), and his domestic efforts at Islamicization, which gave rise to sectarian violence between Shi'as and Sunnis in the 1980s (M. Ahmed 1998; Nasr 2000a, 2000b, 2002). I quote from one of Zia's speeches to the nation that attempted to address growing hostility toward the ulama through the figure of the maulwi in television. Of particular interest to me is his mixed address to "the people," which conjured up a split self at whom his communication was directed:

> People think that they have cracked a big joke by branding Radio Pakistan or Pakistan Television as a religious school which will be greeted by peals of laughter by others. But alas, these people are a joke themselves. The people of Pakistan can discriminate between good and bad; they don't laugh at them but they only feel sorry for them. They say what kind of people are they who have a grouse against the ban imposed in Pakistan on the performance of vulgar dances, on night clubs and dancing houses? Lashes are administered for drinking. Films are properly pruned and edited before they are shown on television. The call for prayer reverberates from radio all the time. *The Maulwi has got stuck on the T.V. screen; and let me tell you he will remain stuck there.* (Government of Pakistan 1982: 25)

These words provide us the first hint of the complex coordinates of the figure of the maulwi. In speaking of those who joke about the maulwi, Zia refers to them as "people." Yet later he says that the "people of Pakistan" felt sorry for the "people" and that they wondered what kind of "people" complained about the maulwi's cultural vigilance. There are two sets of confusions here. First, it is unclear who the "people" are in each instance. Are the people in the first reference not people of Pakistan? Or, is Zia hailing one and the same people, albeit as a split self, a private self that laughed and a public that disapprovingly shook its head at the private self? This split address, I argue, was aimed at quietening protest since it captures a common suspicion that Pakistanis often express about themselves, that they are hypocritical.

Second, what could Zia have meant when he said, "the Maulwi has got stuck on the T.V. screen"? In one sense he might have been quoting words attributable to those people who make jokes. However, I argue that in speaking so knowingly Zia might be productively read as saying that the joke was on the people. The maulwi on the TV screen is only a reflection of them, that is, of their inner mulla. It is not only that Pakistanis are likely hypocritical, but they do not know themselves. More specifically they do not know that they harbor a mulla within themselves or that they might even desire such a mulla.

We see how Zia hails Pakistanis as Muslims in this speech and implicates them in his worldview. Turned in upon themselves for daring to laugh or joke, they are lured into uncertainty: is the maulwi actually stuck in the television or is it in reality themselves or their object of desire? In effect, Zia attempts to reinstate the figure of the ulama in state and society, casting the condition of mullaism in favorable light as one to be cultivated by individual Muslims. However, the ulama's ubiquitous appearance in the television screen indexes a general uncertainty in relation to the world, whether things are really as they appear to be, whether people even knew themseves.

This constitutes our first hint of skepticism as a pervasive condition, a skepticism within the context of public culture that spoke to a world in which one might not know oneself and would find intolerable this unknowable aspect of oneself. Yet it wasn't as if each instantiation of mullaism was skepticism at work. It was, rather, one's inability to relate to the possibility of foreignness or strangeness within oneself that carried the threat of skepticism.

Everyday Embodiment of Mullaism

In this section I explore instances in which people assumed the posture of a mulla in the variable sense I have been exploring, of one who claimed privileged access to the tradition, professed ultimate knowledge on religious issues, or censored others. In *The Idea of an Anthropology of Islam* (1986) Talal Asad states that a discursive tradition, such as Islam, is grounded in argument that anticipates resistance in the form of doubt, indifference, or lack of understanding. It employs the force of reason to bring forth the willing performance of a practice. At the same time, orthodoxy is central to this tradition. Where Muslims judge or evaluate correct practices, and condemn or exclude incorrect ones, relations of power emerge and the domain of orthodoxy is produced. I restrict myself to three moments from my research on mosques in which people derisively evoked the stereotype of the mulla or assumed the posture of a mulla, that is, made a bid for orthodoxy to make a point decisively. Their action suggested how the aspiration to be a better Muslim flirted with the production or imposition of orthodoxy.

In my efforts to offset my exclusive focus on mosques, which were primarily male spaces, I sought out the few spaces in the neighborhoods I was studying in which women led others in instruction and prayer. These were not mosques, nor did their patrons seek the status of mosques. These spaces were more informal, seeking to provide a space for girls and women to further their education, either secular or religious, although they tended to privilege religious education. The women who ran them were most often self-educated or came from families in which education and the giving of instruction were held in high esteem. While in some instances these informal sites were loosely affiliated with a specific mosque, a particular alim, or even a maslak, more often than not their patrons saw these sites as distinct from and even in some cases superior to mosques or madrasas. This was because they felt they were voluntarily teaching about religion, their students came without compulsion, and their study circles could address themselves more pointedly to everyday life, thus better stitching religious obligation to individual needs and daily rhythms. Yet even such spaces experienced qabza, as for instance when my landlady in Lahore reported to me that women in her Qur'an study circle were demanding to learn from a specific 'alim because they felt that the older women leading the circle was misinforming them, perhaps even deliberately leading them astray. Thus these spaces were implicated in the aspiration to striving with its attendant anxieties.

I was taken to one such place close to Momin Town, the site of Masjid Noor, by Urush, the daughter of the Ahl-e Hadis family who had been excluded from the neighborhood through the efforts of Imam Aziz. She felt that I ought to know a more enlightened face of the neighborhood than what I was being shown through my dealings with Masjid Noor. And that was how I met Baji Zahura, who ran a tuition center for those girls whose parents did not want them to attend school but wished for them to sit the national examinations. Early in our acquaintance she told me that she had read the entire Qur'an in Urdu translation. As we talked, she suddenly spat out, "My husband, he considers himself a Deobandi and is a card-carrying member of the Sipah-e Sahaba [the political party responsible for targeting prominent members of the Pakistani Shi'a population]. But he has never read the Qur'an in translation. He doesn't know its meaning. He is a *katar mulla* [hardcore mulla]." The other woman around her reprimanded her, saying that one should not speak ill of one's husband, but she was unrelenting.

Baji Sonya gave religious lessons in Baji Zahura's tuition center. She was an extremely accomplished speaker and a sensitive interpreter of religious texts and drew many women and girls from the neighborhood to her study circle. Once when I was visiting with her, her husband joined us. In the midst of our meandering conversation, he impatiently interrupted to inquire: "I want to know, how exactly are you carrying out this research of yours into mosques in Lahore? Have you tried to find out how many mosques there are? Have you figured out which belong to specific *firqas* [sects] or *maslak*? Do you know we are Ahl-e Hadis?"

I was startled because in the weeks I had been coming to visit Baji Sonya she never once mentioned which maslak she belonged to. I looked at her to find her nodding in affirmation. "Do you know only Ahl-e Hadis allow men from their community to give sermons and lead prayers?" her husband continued. "And what is more, the Ahl-e Hadis are the only ones that encourage women to come to the mosque to pray." After her husband excused himself, I asked Baji Sonya whether she was Ahl-e Hadis. She said, "Women do not have the capacity for such certainty. They are plagued by doubts."

The third instance of the figure of the mulla that emerged in my fieldwork came when Farooq sahib had the idea of interviewing some imams of mosques in his neighborhood, men with whom he was well acquainted. "This will help you cover more area in your research," he declared. In each of his interviews Farooq sahib played the role of a maulwi baiting the other to reveal his positions on controversial issues of doctrine and practice in order to challenge their textual basis. After goading each imam to confess that his positions on various topics were closely tied to his maslak affiliation—that is, although the latter claimed to speak about Islam to all Muslims, he only spoke of Islam through a particular lens and to only specific Muslims— Farooq would back down. He would bring the interview to a close by generously praising his opponent, but clearly triumphant in his sense of victory that he had destabilized their attempts to speak for all.

I present these examples from my ethnography because they suggest how it is that striving to be a better Muslim came to bear a relationship to orthodoxy. In the case of Baji Zahura, although she called her husband a bigoted mulla, it was she who asserted orthodoxy in stating the correct way to be a Muslim. She took on the persona of the enlightened Muslim, one who knew to read and understand the Qur'an rather than simply read it uncomprehendingly in the original. But more important, she enacted the state's position in its early years when it sought to separate out the aspiration to be a Muslim from mullaism, the transmission of ossified knowledge. In the case of Baji Sonia, it was her husband who assumed the role of the mulla, not only directing maslak-related questions at me but also informing me of the superiority of his own maslak. Baji Sonia's statement in this occasion, that women are assailed with doubts, undoubtedly reproduced the gendered conception of piety, that men's faith was stronger and purer than women's. But she was a formidable religious scholar, one who had arrived at her position of a neighborhood teacher after a long career in the Jama'at-e Islami, Maulana Abul ala Maududi's political party. In contrast to Baji Zahura, whose striving had orthodox undertones, Baji Sonia's actions of nodding, reaffirming her husband while inserting a caveat for women, suggested how a striver could weave her words through those of orthodoxy, staying close to assertions of certainty but never reaching certainty herself. This was interestingly akin to the position advocated by the dissenting judge in the 1993 Supreme Court judgment relating to Ahmadis, in which the judge reminded the bench that they should keep in mind the limit placed by human finitude on absolute and certain knowledge.

In contrast to both, Farooq freely took on a disputation style. In so doing he enacted the mulla just as Baji Sonia's husband did. However, Baji Sonia's husband spoke with a certain authority, no doubt derived from the fact that he acted as a prayer leader on occasion and that, even as he spoke to me, he was preparing to give a sermon in his local mosque. He represented no one but himself. Farooq, on the other hand, shrank from such direct self-representation, given the Deobandi disapproval of unauthorized religious speech. In the company of friends and neighbors who could perhaps not be fully alienated, he ventriloquized the mulla for his own pleasure.

In each of these instances there was a figuration of the mulla within speech and deeds. At the same time this figuration was not the unexpected, unknowable, loathed foreign element within oneself of which Zia-ul Haq warned. Rather, there was an embrace of the posture, even a cleaving to orthodoxy, in an affirmation of the individual right to strive.

Mumtaz Mufti's Internal Demons

In contrast to the affirmative enactments of the mulla explored above, Mumtaz Mufti, a beloved Urdu literary figure in Pakistan, provides a more troubled response to one's inner mulla. I explore an early work, *Labbaik* (1975), which takes its title from the religious pronouncement uttered in the occasion of arriving at Mecca for the pilgrimage, meaning "I am present." As the title suggests, the book is an account of his hajj experiences in Mecca although as we shall see later it is not a typical account or a literal travelogue but one intermixed with Mufti's awareness of an enchanted world.[3] In *Labbaik* one finds stereotypical depictions of the ulama and comical demonstrations of mullaism among lay Muslims. Mufti further shows how these figurations shift and transmute by incorporating the changing physical environments and landscape of affects of Mecca. This shape-shifting mulla abroad nicely resonates with the various permutations of the figure of the mulla and dreaded others in the public culture of Lahore. But of particular interest here is the manner in which the foreign within oneself makes its unexpected appearance within Mufti's account of his time in Mecca and how he reconciles himself to its presence within himself.

At the start of his book, Mufti explains how in the mid-1960s he was struck by the unexpected desire to go on hajj. This desire was a surprise to him because he was an indifferent Muslim, not given to any strong religious inclinations. After a long wait and a string of failures in winning one of the coveted slots allotted by the Saudi Arabian quota system for Pakistanis to go on hajj, he imposed on his close friend, Qudratullah Shahab, who was a high-ranking civil servant, to secure a slot for him.[4] The matter-of-fact manner in which Mufti gives us this information suggested that life in Pakistan was shot through with moral compromise such that even his sincerest desires and efforts at making his own way to Mecca could not get him there, unless he resorted to personal contacts to make his dream a reality. What was ultimately more important to him was that he went on hajj, rather than the mechanics of how he went. We are introduced quite early in the book to this morally ambiguous position. It suggests that Mufti would not step down from the task of looking brutally honestly at himself and his companions in the midst of the global flow of humanity moving purposely to a designated meeting time and place with God.

In his trips to various government offices in Pakistan to prepare for his journey to Mecca, Mufti came face to face with the group of ulama who were making the trip with him. Like him, they, too, had managed to be invited as guests of the Pakistan government. In his mocking descriptions of them he captures the sense of the world as one of theatrical unreality with the ulama generating this sense. Mufti writes:

> They are not like us. They are not like the common people, from among you and us. Their clothes are different. Their manner of living is different from us. The rhythm of their voice is different. Their voice comes from the lower levels of their throat—it does not simply come, it is made to come out so. And this requires much exercise and exertion so that their voice appears distinguished. . . . Their make-up makes them look like a different creation of God, perhaps a better creation, between a human and an angel. Or perhaps they are costumed actors in a play. Certainly the heaviness of their make-up surpasses that of film stars. (1996: 44, my translation)

In his flight out from Lahore to Jeddah, Saudi Arabia, to begin his hajj Mufti senses the phantom presence of the ulama among the passengers in the passengers' reverent silence. These people are en route to meet God. Instead of exuding excitement and happiness, "respect, decorum and gratitude had cut the wings of happiness" (13). It is as if the pilgrims have been warned not to misbehave, or else the ulama would tell on them to God.

In Mufti's descriptions of the ulama thus far into Labbaik he sets them apart from people, seeing them as imposing their authority upon Muslims. Gradually, however, as he experiences the Saudi Arabian landscape, he comes to concede that animus lies in the world, not as easily identified and set apart as the ulama. He sees a pagan idol beckoning him from atop the Ka'aba, the sacred cube-shaped building at the center of the Masjid ul-Haram in Mecca. He flees from the shrieks for attention emitted by objects displayed for sale in the markets surrounding the sanctuary of the Ka'aba.

Even in his silent hotel room he is not free from the seductions of the houri who mysteriously follows him in his mind's eye.

It was in the city of Mina that he is finally able to identify this animus with the workings of Iblis (Satan). A man he runs into at a café assures him that the strange agitation that he is experiencing and the discord he sees among his fellow travelers is the habitual condition of Mina. Nobody can reside here permanently because it was here that Iblis tried to weaken Prophet Ibrahim's will to sacrifice his son at God's command. And here Iblis still resides, although rendered into stone. Nonetheless, his influence is everywhere, making Mina an uninhabitable city, a dreaded stop. Through his description of Mina, Mufti provides us our first orientation to a self that is penetrable by forces extant in the world: "This is a city of whispers [waswasen], a city of mad possession [shar], a city of deviation [ilhad], a city of anxiety [tazabzub], a city of dispersion [intishar]" (137). We are given to understand that Satan's influences were dispersed further afield, most certainly in Pakistan.[5]

Back in Mecca from Arafat, Mufti goes to register himself with the guide provided to him. In the façade of the institution where such guides are to be found, he sees numerous open windows, into which, it seems to him, people are tirelessly expressing their encounters with these same forces: "windows of regrets [hasraten], windows of complaints [shikayaten], windows of pain [dukh)] and happiness [sukh], a small recess for memories [yaden], windows of fear [khauf] and anxiety [khadshat], windows of paranoia [vahm] and suspicion [guman], windows of ambition [tama']." (114).

The sight of all these people busying themselves in this way leads Mufti to ponder the nature of presence in Mecca. The most important act by which pilgrims initiates their hajj is by pronouncing "Labbaik" (I am here [to follow your orders]), thus announcing their presence to God. However, windows serve a different purpose. They provide an escape from one's present into the past or the future, and in opening them, one absents oneself from the present. To speak into windows in Mecca is to risk one's absence, even temporarily, before God.

As he stands pondering the role of the window at the guide's office, Mufti runs into Waqar, an acquaintance from Lahore who has come to make a complaint. The travel agency in charge of his stay in Mecca was destroying his hajj by "inflicting a lump of filth by their side, thus, making the purity of this environment fetid for them." His story involved a Pakistani woman traveling without a male companion with whom his wife and he were staying in a compound for pilgrims. One day a strange man came to see her and she let him in then shut the door to her room. The door remained shut for a long time. The next day the strange man moved in with the woman. Both Waqar and his wife were deeply shocked by these developments and consumed by the desire to forbid the sin being undertaken in this most holy land. Not daring to confront the woman directly, they kept watch day and night on the comings and goings of the woman and her paramour. Waqar had come to complain about this woman to his guide so that this sin might cease and the sanctity of Waqar's hajj be upheld.

It is this story that alerts Mufti to the little mulla within each, one who could deny oneself the pleasure of presence before God. Upon hearing this story, Mufti wonders about the mysterious nature of the window that Waqar had opened for himself, although he dares not tell his enraged friend that he should shut the window right away. Only once does Mufti murmur, "Waqar sahib! Let them get on with their lives in that closed room. You should take pleasure in the *Haram Sharif* [Noble Sanctuary]. Why are you forsaking the Ka'aba for that closed room?" (117) Waqar is dismayed by Mufti's lack of concern, given the difficult time his wife and he are going through and leaves in a huff, prompting Mufti to ask, perhaps of God:

> Filth and sin are indeed obstacles. However, what is this injustice that innate politeness, piety, and cleanliness become obstacles as well? Why is it that the perception of sin becomes a wall? Why is it that those who have not committed any sins halt in their steps in the presence of those who have sinned? Perhaps the sin of the residents in the closed room is not important. In fact perhaps it is put there to debase the journey of innocent neighbors. What is this mystery? Why does it exist? Why have circumstances cast your pious and innocent worshipers into such perplexity? (117)

In other words Waqar strikes the classic pose of "encouraging good, forbidding evil" that is the duty of all Muslims, but which leaves him paralyzed, unable to go forward in his hajj.

In the final episode that I provide from *Labbaik*, Mufti discovers that he is no different from those around him, that he too bears an inner mulla. Mufti describes how he goes to a famous mosque near the Holy Mosque to pray. While silently pronouncing his intention to pray, he starts to hear a loud buzzing around him. As the buzzing grows more distinct, he hears voices saying: "This man, here . . . !" "What nerve!" "Get him out of here." "Throw him out." Then the voices address him directly, asking him how he dare enter smelling as he does and urging him to leave the mosque. He too begins to smell the stench of putrefaction coming from his body. It is as if his body has dissolved into a heap of rot. To be saved from these insistent voices, he tries to prostrate in prayer, but his forehead will not touch the ground, no matter how hard he presses his body forward. Instead he feels himself being lifted and hurled through the air. Startled, he leaps up and leaves the mosque in a hurry, taking refuge in the Holy Mosque.

Later, Mufti recounts his painful experience to Qudratullah Shahab. When he stretches his hand forward to provide proof of the smell pouring out of him, his friend can't smell anything. However, Sahab congratulates him, saying that the opportunity to smell himself was a tremendous favor bestowed on him by God. When Mufti wonders whether this was truly a favor or cruelty on God's part, his friend explains: "This is a tremendous favor, not cruelty. To emit a smell, to actually perceive one's own smell is a great thing. Our biggest misfortune is that we do not smell ourselves. We can only smell others" (104).

Mufti remains unconvinced as he feels betrayed that his own body had turned against him smelling of rot in such a way so as to reproach him, perhaps for the state of his spirituality. For Sahab, the ability to smell oneself is a boon to enable one to experience oneself as other. For Mufti, it is a trace of the unfamiliar within himself, his affliction by the dreaded condition of mullaism and its judgment of him.

If, as I have said above, we think of skepticism as the fear that mullas are everywhere in evidence, even within oneself, then it is this final hajj encounter that best presents the conundrum of skepticism within everyday life. Skepticism can be a paralyzing condition, undermining striving by the intensity of judgment it directs at oneself and others. At the same time it is an opportunity to experience one's unfamiliarity to oneself, to develop this opportunity into a new relationship to oneself. In accepting that one has internalized such a form of life, one is in effect accepting that one can, indeed must, live with skepticism. Yet not all expressions of skepticism provide for the opportunity for such affirmation of striving. In the following section I follow the figure of the mulla as it transmutes across the registers of oral and graphic narratives to show how public culture could well amplify skepticism as a pervasive condition.

Earlier, we saw President Zia-ul Haq reproach the Pakistani "people" for making jokes about the maulwi who is stuck in the television screen. I knew jokes about the mulla were a part of public culture of Lahore and relished by many, even by the ulama, because many of my acquaintances regaled me with jokes about the mulla.[6] The jokes and what I am calling horror stories, for their particular mix of fear and revulsion, crowded in almost as soon as I started to inquire about mosques. At the same time, as I mentioned earlier, I regularly ran across political cartoons, rich in representations of the ulama. While it is beyond the scope of this book to attempt a lengthy genre-specific analysis of each, I use the following distinctions among these genres to aid my analysis. In keeping with the Freudian theory on jokes, I take jokes to have an eruptive quality, that is, they erupt into everyday life as if from elsewhere.[7] The sensation of horror in the stories I read as the return of the repressed, with the repressed most productively understood as coming face to face with one's ordinariness.[8] Unlike jokes and horror stories, which are verbal in nature, political cartoons are visual representations. They create maximum effect through a minimum of details, encouraging the viewer to see and imagine more than what is presented.[9] In what follows I investigate horror stories for how they bring threats to everyday life into focus, and cartoons for what they have us imagine as outside its frame or within its empty spaces and jokes for the manner in which they introduce a further action into the picture of the world created by horror stories and cartoon images, that of exiling the foreignness within.

HORROR STORIES

One story that kept resurfacing involved a mulla who had illegally seized multiple properties in Lahore on which he had built mosques for each of his sons. My interlocutors called these "bread-and-butter mosques." One could countenance the truth of such a story, for it was not inconceivable that there was a land-grabbing group of mullas given how rife mosque-related qabzas were. However, the frequency with which I heard this story, and in relation to mosques that I knew to be legitimate to the extent of the law, made me listen to these stories more carefully. On one hand, the storytellers were invariably outraged at the legal impunity with which the ulama appeared to operate under Zia's regime, their commercialization of Islam, and the hint of hereditariness their actions introduced into the institution of the ulama. On the other, they perceived the burgeoning of ulama presence in the public sphere as threatening to their everyday life.

One particular mosque, grand and iridescent in an upscale shopping center in Lahore, was regularly pointed out to me as the base of a venal mulla who extended his sphere of influence in the city through the control of commercial property outside the gates of the mosque. Although the property seemed to hold no more than ten tin sheds where roses were sold, I was told that one could paralyze a city such as Lahore during the wedding season by cutting off the supply of flowers. Such an event had reportedly never taken place, but the visible link between a site that caused disquiet and weddings, an essential feature of Pakistani society, suggested a constant seepage of some unknown toxic substance into everyday life.

There were other stories that suggested the substance being seeped was not entirely unknown, that it was a certain moral perversion. Consider the story told to me about a rapacious mulla, which was supposedly reported in newspapers. In the story there was a village girl who was slightly unbalanced. Her parents wanted her to get better before they got her married. They had heard of the curative skills of a mulla in Lahore and traveled far to bring her to him. He took a liking to the girl's looks. Instead of saying a prayer over the girl and dismissing her, he recommended that the family leave their daughter with him so that he could fully cure her. They returned each day to check on their daughter's progress, but kept hearing more and more baleful accounts about her deteriorating mental condition. Finally, when they became suspicious they had the local police raid the mosque. They found their daughter tied up, with her clothes in shreds. She had gone stark raving mad.

Both these stories, of the mosque in an upscale shopping center and the sexually predatory mulla, spoke not only of the perception that there were places in Pakistan where vice was allowed to grow unchecked, but also of the menace the ulama introduced into everyday life. These stories had the effect of keeping public attention upon possible sites and agents of corruption, but also of putting everyday life into question, as to whether it was what it appeared to be.

POLITICAL CARTOONS

The cartoons I discuss here are drawn from the weekly paper The Friday Times, published in Lahore. For the past fifteen years the staff cartoonist, Sabir Nazar, has produced a cartoon image in full color for the cover of each

Figure 1. *The Friday Times*, vol. 14, no. 49, January 31–February 6, 2003, p. 1.
Courtesy of Sabir Nazar.

issue and a comic strip in black and white under the title "True Lies" inside
the paper. While one could do an extensive analysis of Nazar's rich and
imaginative archive of cartoons, I limit myself to two whose basic elements
are often repeated. As opposed to the stories, which focus attention upon
everyday life, the cartoon images draw attention to what is left outside of the
frame and allow our imagination to fill in. The cartoons reproduced here
imply that Pakistanis are caught in someone else's game.

Figure 1 shows President Pervez Musharaf, the military general who
seized power of Pakistan in 1999, as he appeared on the front page of *The
Friday Times*, sitting in front of a game of chess. To judge by the dismayed
look on his face, he is clearly losing. And the person to whom he is losing is
portrayed as a blond Caucasian man wearing a shirt emblazoned with the
name of Nancy Powell, the U.S. ambassador to Pakistan at the time. Behind
Musharaff squat two mullas, each with a hand reaching out from under
Musharaff's arms, as if they were Musharaff's surrogate hands, moving the
chess pieces for the dictator.

At one level the message is balefully obvious. Mullas stand behind the
dictator forcing him to play a losing game. At another level, I suggest that it
projects an unreality, in that the mullas resemble the racist stereotype of
Africans that used to be common in the United States, in which faces bear a
distinct similarity to those of apes. When I asked Sabir Nazar why he had

Figure 2. "True Lies," *The Friday Times*, vol. 14, no. 21, July 19–25, 2002, p. 8.
Courtesy of Sabir Nazar.

chosen to give the mullas such faces, he said that although he scrutinized
contemporary ulama closely to discern the stylistic means they chose to
differentiate themselves, it was not unusual for him to model his mulla
representations on apes because he had such a low opinion of the ulama.
While the racist depiction of Africans was undoubtedly fashioned on sim-
ians, and while Nazar probably chose this imagery without being conscious
of its specific racist reference, the mullas as squatting Africans facing an
apparently American white man have the effect of suggesting a racist American game being played out on Pakistan's turf. Although the cartoon image is
shot through with an excess of visual detail, the detail only hints at an
unassimilable foreignness of this scene, which appears to be taking place
elsewhere than in Pakistan.

A second cartoon by Sabir Nazar for *The Friday Times* (see figure 2), a
three-part black-and-white strip for the "True Lies" feature inside the paper,
posits a possible line of connection between the mullas in the first cartoon
and the everyday Pakistani. In the first frame, a man with long hair is seen
walking with a girl past a disco. Given that Pakistan is a largely conservative
society, discouraging of both long-haired men and the free mixing of men
and women, this image immediately gives us to understand that the man is a
westernized Pakistani. In the second frame we see him alone, sauntering
across our line of vision and smoking casually. This last detail further suggests that the man is indolent and wasteful. The final frame shows him still
walking, but this time he is beaming and his hand is outstretched to give
money to a mulla collecting funds for jihad.

One reading of it this cartoon is that even the most modern among

Pakistanis are complicit in religious politics. As one of the fears about the routine requests for funds to support various Islamic causes is that the donated money is channeled to violent efforts, we may understand the man to be openly providing his support of such politics. In this reading, the modern Pakistani would be homologous to Pervez Musharaf in the first cartoon.

In the context of the growing unfamiliarity of Pakistan, to which horror imbued stories draw attention, particularly the sense that there are secret enclaves of corruption and vice making inroads into everyday life, it is most likely that this second cartoon posits a relation between the young man and the mulla. The outstretched hand linking the two figures could mean that the mulla is pulling at the hand, as a puppeteer would that of his puppet. The cartoon also mocks Pakistanis by implying that there is a mulla inside them who knows to respond to the claims of other mullas. While the stories I have presented suggest an everyday life as yet distinct from the mulla, the cartoons give expression to a full-blown fear of mullaism saturating everyday life and contaminating people.

JOKES OF EXCESS

Jokes give far fuller descriptions of the physiognomy of the loathed mulla than do the other genres. Consider the following joke, in which a group of ulama are assembled to discuss the merits and demerits of having a nuclear bomb, dubbed "the Islamic bomb," in Pakistan. In the center of the conference table is a large plate of halwa to be served as refreshment at the conclusion of the meeting. While all those gathered squirm in their seats, clearly desirous to eat rather than engage in the discussions, no one can pluck up the courage to demonstrate his greed so openly. Except for one! He gets up and strides over to the plate. He sticks his finger into the mound of halwa quickly separating it into two halves. Addressing the room he says, "Let us take one half to be India and the other Pakistan. If India were to drop its bomb on us, it would certainly make a big hole in our country." On saying this, he scoops up a handful of halwa and pops it into his mouth. He continues, "But if we were to drop our bomb on India we would make a much bigger hole in that country, inshallah." And with that he gathers up the entire pile of halwa designated as India and pops it into his mouth. However, in his swiftness he accidentally puts the part he has designated as Pakistan into his mouth.

These jokes are more or less aimed at the body of the mulla, which is seen to bear the marks of its lack of productivity (for what did a mulla do all day, I was told, but sit in the mosque?) and moral degeneration. And to the historical charges of ignorance heaped upon the mulla were added those of sinfulness, sexual voraciousness, cunning, gluttony, political ambition, worthlessness, corruption, and self-destruction.

This degree of detail did not suggest to me an everyday familiarity with the ulama. Rather, the jokes suggested continuous efforts to set the mulla outside of oneself so as not to have to ask what it means to have a mulla within oneself. This effort at putting mullas on a different ontological plane from lay Muslims is most apparent in the following joke. A few mischievous college boys approach the imam of their neighborhood mosque, confessing that they had sex with a chicken. They want his advice on what they should do to repent. The imam asks them to return the following day to give him time to consult the relevant books of hadis. When they return, they find him all scratched up and bandaged. Looking accusingly at them, he charges, "You lied. It is not possible to have sex with a chicken." While the joke makes the imam out to be clueless, it also definitely shows that the mulla is of a different order of life than these boys, deficient in reason, with no possibility of sympathy between them. While negative stories and cartoons express various degrees of skeptical orientations to the world, jokes give fullest expression to skepticism. With their descriptive density, they cast out this element of the unfamiliar within oneself, making it so grotesquely other that it became inconceivable to imagine any points of relatedness to this figure.

The Ulama in the Shadow of the Mulla

In *On the Postcolony* (2001) Achille Mbembe states that the elements of the obscene and the grotesque that inform public culture in the postcolony do not easily lend themselves to a politics of transgression as has often been claimed. Rather, popular tropes such as scatological jokes, the reworking of official rhetoric for ludic effect, and the exaggerated performance of power exist in a relationship of "conviviality" with the realm of official power (110). But vulgarity has the long-term effect of the "zombification" of official figures (104). In other words, vulgar depictions of official figures eventually rob them of their humanity, such that they cannot be apprehended except through the caricatures of them.

With Mbembe's astute analysis in mind, I turn in this final section to the religious subjects of caricature to see if they exhibit a similar "zombification." I elicited responses from young maulwis, whom I most often met in religious seminaries, bookstores, or publishing houses, where I went to search out writings on mosques. A few spoke defensively of their efforts at educating the public about Islam. In conversation with a young mufti in training in Jamia Madania, the young scholar said:

> We know that we cannot get votes. Why should we get votes because it is the politicians who can guarantee schools and roads to people? People are smart. They will vote for those who can get them things. But people still love us. I don't mean to say that they love us personally, but that they love what we represent to them. We represent Islam. Or else how do you explain the money that pours in from them, even in these hard times, to pay for our madrasas?

In the cramped office of *Haqq Chariyya*, a Deobandi magazine with a long history of "exposing the false claims on Islam" made by other Muslim groups, the editor, a young man with some madrasa training, asked: "Why does the government want us to teach science, math, engineering, etc. in the madrasas? That's what the schools and universities are for. Our work is to teach *din* (religion) to people."

These defensive assertions on behalf of the ulama and madrasas differ in tone from other statements that express greater eagerness for acceptance and circulation within wider Pakistani society. My close acquaintance, the imam of the Neela Gumbard Mosque, who was given to telling me jokes about mullas and who described the stereotypical mulla as a bad-tempered bigot, often said to me: "I am not your usual maulwi. I am the only one from my family who went into this line of work. Outside these walls, I sit among regular men, I smoke, and I talk of Urdu poetry and Pakistani politics." These words resonate with those of the son of the head seminarian of Jamia Naimia, a well-known Barelwi seminary, who insisted I take a tour of the seminary, including its computer laboratory, before using its library. He said worriedly: "I am concerned that our graduates be able to mix among people. I don't mean that they should be scientists or doctors but that they should know how the world works." While these words offer two different reactions to the mockery of the ulama in Pakistani society, one defensive and the other eager for incorporation within the mainstream, there is a curious affinity among these young maulwis from different pathways and disparate locations. It lies in their desire for belonging to Pakistan, as expressed in their disappointment that their striving as Muslims and representatives of Islam was unacknowledged. One could not help but feel that all four sensed a certain chill of the figure of the mulla standing over them, making them memorials of an Islam of the past, rather than its flesh-and-blood present-day representatives. But turning to the elders among them to elicit their response to the stereotype takes us to their criticism of the lay mode of debate and argumentation and identifies it as the real culprit in leaching out not only the blood of humans but also the solidity of the world.

Chapter Six

SKEPTICISM AND SPIRITUAL DIAGNOSTICS

IQBAL, THE ULAMA, AND THE LITERATI

Literature as Spiritual Diagnostics

Setting out to understand how Pakistan is experienced as a mosque, I have looked at the formulation "Pakistan is a mosque under qabza" from various angles. It is useful to bring together the strands of my analysis to understand how the original impetus to aspiration that informs Pakistan's beginnings has fared in history and into the present. In one reading of this formulation I have shown how forcible possession paradoxically reveals Pakistan's centrality for the striving to be Muslim. In other words, in being so central the nation was subject to multiple claims upon striving and vulnerable to violent impositions of particular pictures of striving. While such impositions would seem to obviate any pluralism, the process of possession is important in making explicit the various strands of striving that inform efforts at being Muslim. At the same time the effort to impose an exclusive picture of striving also sometimes unexpectedly produces a renewal of efforts at striving. Thus, "Pakistan is a mosque under qabza" speaks of the continuing work of striving, fighting for what one considers to matter, renewing one's picture of striving, and risking violent exclusion. In other words, the aspiration to strive remaining intact, qabza was symptomatic of the threats and possibilities that ordinarily beset striving.

Along a second line of analysis, I find the formulation "Pakistan is a mosque under qabza" to speak to the sense that Pakistan is enduring illegitimate usurpation by various figures, notably the state, the Ahmadi, and the mulla. The emphasis here is on striving as indefinitely suspended, in which to strive to be Muslim is to be always disappointed with oneself and to be faced with the incredulity, doubts, disappointment, even the mistrust of others. In this case, I find qabza to be symptomatic of a wider malaise in which skepticism reigns as the pervasive condition.

My research in Lahore sustains both lines of analysis, of Pakistan as the site of ongoing aspiration as well as widespread malaise. But more often than not, I found that a skeptical reading of Pakistan was privileged over the acknowledgment of striving within it. For instance, even discounting the many dismissive, even skeptical comments directed at the Ahmadis or the Shi'a, the two groups who have historically been at the center of religious tensions in Pakistan, Imam Aziz of Masjid Noor was considered to be dissimulating in the manner of a Shi'a person no matter what he did to make clear his commitment to his neighborhood, and his mosque was called Masjid Zarar, the denigrating name given to Ahmadi places of worship. In another telling example, Adeeb, my research assistant, attempted to give himself a religious education in short bursts of oral instruction and religious disputation in the midst of all the demands on his time and labor, but his efforts were often greeted with mockery, in which people said he was becoming a mulla. His expansive girth and style of dress made him an easy target and made his strenuous efforts at self-education seem absurd.

These examples provide us two strains of skepticism. In the first case, the fear that there is a potential Shi'a in each person or that Ahmadis seek to deceive Muslims, might be understood as a fallout of state efforts to seek certainty on who is or is not a Muslim and assure the safety of Muslims from those not Muslim. In the second, the fear of becoming a mulla was born of the feeling that striving was compromised by the condition of jahalat (ignorance)—of which the government scientist, Dr. Khan of Gauhar Town, spoke most often—and individual hypocrisy and bigotry, of which Mumtaz Mufti, the Urdu writer, was the most fierce diagnostician; this fear leads one to be as suspicious of one's own efforts at striving as those of others. The fact that I found such distinct strains of skepticism supports my claim that the state does not exclusively dictate the terms of everyday religiosity. Rather, both the state and everyday life collaborate in sustaining striving, producing blocks to it, and generating skepticism. At the same time the skepticism that each produces resonates with the other, amplifying the sense that striving is indefinitely suspended.

If striving is a widely embodied but unremarked tendency and is now considered to be difficult, if not impossible, then who or what provides a diagnosis of this blockage of striving from within Pakistan? Attention to texts, affects, and gestures allowed me access to the dimension of striving in everyday practices of religiosity. Attention to diagnostic statements, such as "He has done qabza on us," uttered by the mother and daughter about Imam Aziz of Masjid Noor, or "Our 'aqida [faith] had become weak and our 'ibadat [worship] was suffering," often cited by my teacher, Farooq, to explain why he released the jinn Sulayman from the obligation of service to his family, serve as examples of everyday evaluations of the state of striving. What makes these statements diagnostic is that they imply a self standing beside itself, taking stock of its metaphysical state by means of its physiological and psychological condition. This taking stock is critical of the forces at large that produce this condition and also ameliorative of the excesses produced by this condition. I call this self-analysis combined with therapy "spiritual diagnostics," and find it to be resonant with Iqbal's words, quoted in chapter 2, on how to gauge the rightness of something for oneself:

> Man is essentially an energy, a force, or rather a combination of forces which admit of various arrangements. One definite arrangement of these forces is personality—whether it is pure chance arrangement does not concern me here. . . . That is good which has a tendency to give us the sense of personality, that is bad which has a tendency to suppress and ultimately dissolve personality. (1961: 17–19)

Spiritual diagnostics or the assessment of the state of one's personality result in the sense that one has been dispossessed of a self or that a version of oneself has become absent, as evidenced by the above-mentioned statements "He has done qabza on us" and "Our 'aqida had become weak and our 'ibadat was suffering." The early work of anthropologists of religion exploring the expressions of disease and anomie accompanying rapid cultural change (Lessa and Vogt 1979), or even the more recent anthropological work on trauma and psychosomatic diseases (Antze and Lambek 1996, Kleinman 1997), is important in drawing our attention to the moral register of such statements, insofar as they point to the larger context of the politics of forcible seizure and the perception of the difficulty of being Muslim under contemporary conditions.

In my searching and analyzing statements for this exposition of spiritual diagnostics, I also draw on Gilles Delueze's account of "symptomatology" (1983, 1991, 1997). Delueze considers it a fundamentally creative act to put together disparate symptoms to name a condition. The practice of symptomatology is thus like literature, which not only brings a condition into being but also makes visible the forces that beset it and suggests modes of cure, or what Deleuze calls lines of flight, internal to it. Deleuze further proposes that symptomatology is a political act insofar as it makes viable a realm of potential previously unnoticed, or even nonexistent, and does so in the name of a people yet to come. In other words, it produces a centralizing line through dispersed phenomena serving as the means for individuals or a people to follow this line wherever it may lead.

Spiritual diagnostics, as I understand it, does not necessarily take on the burden of creativity and politics. This is not to say that it isn't creative or can't serve as political action but it is often tied to specific events and experiences of striving and serves to provide warnings or remedies for the excesses produced by striving. I have cited further examples of diagnostic statements ascribed to specific people and places, from Sayyid Ahmed Khan, Iqbal's intellectual predecessor in colonial India, who suggested that Muslims pursue only those practices of religion that sat well with their reason or their bodily constitution, and from Maulana Ashraf Ali Thanawi, another of Iqbal's forerunners, who urged that one treat doubts by seeking out those religious scholars or spiritual specialists who were to one's taste. Here too we see the focus on the physiological as the register of spiritual health. What I take from Deleuze, however, is that literature has great capacity to yield a diagnostics that can apprehend blockages to striving and provide therapies, much in the manner in which Iqbal's literary and philosophical writings provide us an orientation to striving. Moreover, such diagnostics may provide the imagination of political action, perhaps as an unrealistic expectation but that nonetheless births a new possibility.

In this final chapter I apply spiritual diagnostics to a few literary and religious texts attuned to the excesses of striving within Muslim lives. If my effort in chapter 2 was to characterize the Iqbalian notion of aspiration, this chapter develops its accompanying tendency of skepticism. Therefore I return to Iqbal to show how he not only inaugurated Muslim aspiration but also anticipated the spiritual exhaustion that could befall it. While Iqbal's engagement with Bergson gave us the lineaments of aspiration, his engagement with Nietzsche gives us a sensitive reading of the condition of malaise that accompanies striving, which I identify as skepticism. I also turn to the writings of the ulama who feel the chill of the stereotype of the mulla, to see how they respond to this particular strain of skepticism in everyday practices of religiosity. The three ulama presented here, Maulana Muhammad Yusuf Ludhianvi, Mufti Muhammad Abdul Wahid, and Maulana Ashraf Ali Thanawi, each of whom has a public presence in Pakistan and specifically in Lahori lives, provide astute portrayals of the skeptical condition, its precise threat to the social, and pragmatic techniques for living life in attunement to one's capacity for skepticism. Their writings suggest how the institution of the ulama may retain its vitality for contemporary Muslim striving, even as individuals are mocked and feel keenly their exclusion from striving. Finally, I turn to the writings of Mumtaz Mufti, the Urdu author examined in chapter 5. Mufti's writings are exercises in living in a Pakistan that disappoints and which is disappointed in one, that is, a Pakistan in the grips of skepticism. His experiments at reinhabiting Pakistan are instructive, not only about ways of living with skepticism but also on how striving may be sustained under such circumstances. In conclusion I claim that the diagnostics of the ulama and the literati enact Iqbal's call to Muslims to inhabit and reinhabit everyday lives and religious practices to produce the possibility of an open future.

Iqbal's Nietzschean Commitments

We saw how Muhammad Iqbal delineated Muslim aspiration without asserting a final end to striving. Within the context of his engagement with Henri Bergson, even the perfect man (kamil insan) becomes less of an ideal and more the ceaseless and noble activity of tracing and retracing the self toward self-perfectibility. At the same time Iqbal acquired, by means of his intellectual engagement with Friedrich Nietzsche, his sense that humans might fail in the face of such continuous striving. Nietzsche well understood that the spiritual exhaustion experienced in the face of continuous striving followed from the failure to concede time as becoming. Most important for Iqbal, Nietzsche provided the diagnostic criteria by which to tell apart the debasement of striving and ordinary mental ailments. In this section I propose to attend closely to Nietzsche, as I did to Bergson and others prior, to locate the precise points of interrelatedness between Iqbal and Nietzsche, and thus delineate Iqbal's mode of spiritual diagnostics in the face of an exhausted striving.

The Will to Power (1968) is the compendium of Nietzsche's early aphorisms, posthumously compiled, which contain the seeds of his subsequent books (Kaufman 1974). In it Nietzsche writes of life as an endless process of becoming. He almost anticipates Bergson when he writes "that becoming has no goal and that underneath all becoming there is no grand unity in which the individual could immerse himself completely as in an element of supreme value" (1968: 13). If Bergson charged intelligence with spatializing time, robbing it of its durational quality and introducing teleology to it, Nietzsche too writes:

> In our thought, the essential features is fitting new material into old schemas, making equal what is new (273).

> The fundamental fact of "inner experience" is that the cause is imagined after the effect has taken place (265).

In his writings Henri Bergson often sounds quite sanguine about the human capacity to grasp the durational aspect of time, that is, time as a continuous flow rather than say the clock's representation of time as truncated and progressive. The examples he gives of duration, such as the famous one of waiting for the train as an example of being caught in the time of another, are often plucked from everyday experiences. Such examples underscore how durational experiences of time are within close reach of human imagination and intuition. It takes Nietzsche's dark insights into human nature to appreciate that a perception of durational time that is different from the usual experience of it may not be so easy for humans to sense, much less, participate in: "Duration 'in vain,' without end or aim, is the most paralyzing idea. . . . Let us think this thought in its most terrible form: existence as it is, without meaning or aim, yet recurring inevitably without any finale of nothingness: *the eternal recurrence*" (1968: 270; emphasis in original).

Nietszche writes that philosophy, morality, and religion, the objects of his greatest ire, have crafted a world beyond this one, so that the human need not take the full measure of this world. Over time this other world has come to pass judgment on this one, spurring self-abnegation by means of nihilism, bad conscience, resentment, and decadence, among other modes of self-destruction that Nietzsche outlines. Nietzsche, the physician, alights upon these escapist tendencies and modes of self-abnegation that sustain the world beyond this one:

> One longs for a condition in which one no longer suffers: life is actually experienced as the grounds of ills; one esteems unconscious states, without feeling, (sleep, fainting) as incomparably more valuable than conscious ones. (1968: 27)

Such a desire for escaping the world to alleviate suffering calls for self-examination:

Tremendous self-examination: becoming conscious of oneself, not as individuals but as mankind. Let us reflect, let us think back, let us follow the highways and byways. (316)

It is important to note that Nietzsche does not wish away every form of self-abnegation. He concedes that there is a time and place for some decadence:

Decadence itself is nothing to be fought; it is absolutely necessary and belongs to every age and every people. What should be fought vigorously is the contagion to the health parts of the organism. (26)

And a too-hasty view of the world may yield an impression of widespread decay when there is really self-experimentation at work (a worthwhile perspective on Pakistan):

If this is not an age of decay and declining vitality, it is at least one of headlong and arbitrary experimentation:—and it is probable that a superabundance of bungled experiments should create an overall impression as of decay. (40)

Therefore, the work of the diagnostician is as much about allowing some things to be as excising others.

The most powerful means of excising self-abnegation is self-affirmation. I take the method of self-affirmation to be at work in the two concepts most famously associated with Nietzsche, that of eternal recurrence and the Übermensch, concepts to which Iqbal was also attracted.[1] Nietzsche speaks very briefly and elliptically about eternal recurrence in The Will to Power (1968: 35) and Thus Spoke Zarathustra (1961). However, rather than see Nietzsche as speaking of the cyclical quality of time, as is sometimes done, it is more interesting to see his picture of time as an anticipation of the Boltzmanian probabilistic universe, in which any arrangement of matter within a given space experiencing forces of diffusion will return to this particular arrangement given sufficient time (Prigogene and Stengers 1984). This is not to say that time moves backward, for time is progressive, but that any random ordering is as likely to reappear as not. Within Bergson's picture of time, it is possible to imagine an order to return, if not within the dimension of actual time then within time held in potential. That is, any past arrangement exists in potential and may be actualized at any moment. Thus eternal recurrence seen from this perspective supports the picture of life given by Bergson as continuous unfolding.

Unlike Bergson, however, Nietzsche does not require that humans develop a better comprehension of the workings of time. He recognizes that such a task may be too terrible to undertake, reinforcing the pointlessness of life for a mind used to being directed toward clear ends. His desire is that humans simply affirm this aspect of time for itself.

> Can we remove the idea of a goal from the process and then affirm the process in spite of this? (1968: 36)

This is easier said than done. To affirm existence requires freedom:

> To endure the idea of the recurrence one needs: freedom from morality; new means against the fact of pain (pain conceived as a tool, as the father of pleasure; there is no cumulative consciousness of displeasure); the enjoyment of all kinds of uncertainty, experimentalism, as a counterweight to this extreme fatalism; abolition of the concept of necessity; abolition of the "will"; abolition of "knowledge-in-itself." (546)

And the affirmation integral to eternal recurrence takes the form of saying that I willed the past, I take responsibility for this present, and I lay claims upon the future come what may:

> To transform the belief, "it is thus and thus" into the will "it shall become thus and thus. (324)

It is noteworthy that Nietzsche understands the past to lie alongside the present, as did Bergson, and that his concept of eternal recurrence supports the idea of continual retracings of what had come before to make possible new horizons for the self, as in Iqbal's conception of striving.

In addition to the eternal recurrence, Nietzsche's second concept important for Iqbal, as for many others, is that of the Übermensch or overman, who exceeds the ordinary man: "The higher man is distinguished from the lower by his fearlessness and his readiness to challenge misfortune. . . . Abundant strength wants to create, suffer, go under" (1968: 12). Nietzsche has most often been understood as advocating an aristocratic elite at the expense of the masses. I believe that this concept acquires a different inflection if placed in relation to Bergson and Iqbal. The idea of the overman does not speak to the mere biological or economic survival of the fittest. Rather, it speaks to the hoped-for, but ultimately unspecified moment of arrival of human perfection that defies simple biology or economy. And this idea of a higher point of human perfection fits well Bergsonian conceptions of evolution in which life arcs toward perfection in excess of what is needed to simply endure.[2] This perfection is not assured, for life generates many responses that are as likely to be unsuccessful as successful, but it is characterized by continual striving.

Here we see how the Nietzschean idea of the overman is consonant with the Bergsonian picture of life as becoming, but takes it further in making manifest the perfectionist tendencies of life in the figure of the overman. Therefore, Nietzsche contends, such superior beings may be anticipated without lapsing into entelechy, as Bergson feared would happen if the analyst personified life. Moreover, it is such persons who would be able to look upon time as duration and not be cowed by it. As Nietzsche says in *Thus Spoke Zarathustra*:

And he who wants to create beyond himself has the purest will. (1961: 123)

I am of today and before . . . but there is something in me that is of tomorrow, the day after tomorrow and time to come. (128)

In reading Nietzsche one assumes that the overman is beyond man. Yet Nietzsche also writes in *The Will to Power*: "My hypotheses: The subject as multiplicity" (1968: 270), which is an assertion that suggests that the body is an entire society. If the subject is multiple and the body is a society, can one imagine that the path that arcs toward an overman is an aspiration to one's next finite self, as in Iqbal's notion of striving?

While it takes a close examination of religion, philosophy, and morality to get past self-abnegations in order to initiate striving, such striving is not free of debasement from within. This is the third Nietzschean committment espoused by Iqbal. In other words, while striving has to battle against the degradation imposed upon it by history and culture, it can also produce its own debased forms of aspiration. For instance, it can generate doppelgängers, those who impersonate the better selves to which one aspires without the struggle it takes to achieve such selves. And the striver has to be able to tell the lure of doppelgängers from exemplars or one's unattained selves.

One such doppelgänger in Nietzsche's world is the ape of Zarathustra, who follows Zarathusta wherever he goes but to whom Zarathustra has this to say:

Even if Zarathustra's words were a thousand times right, still you would always do wrong with my word. (1961: 178)

I despise your despising; and if you warned me, why did you not warn yourself? (197)

Zarathustra did not even consider the ape a worthy enemy:

You shall have only enemies who are to be hated, but not enemies to be despised; you must be proud of your enemy. (209)

At the same time the ape is kin to Zarathustra insofar as it is clearly the product of Zarathustra's words, even if a debased version of it. And Zarathustra feels compelled to address it whenever he encounters it.

I have already been anticipating Iqbal's points of convergence with Nietzsche. Of particular interest is the manner in which Nietzschean perspectives enable Iqbal to articulate his preferred mode of relating to the Prophet. The Nietzschean notion of eternal recurrence accords with Iqbal's quest to understand how one might relate to the Prophet's time, project it forward, yet not introduce the death grip of finality upon the future. In other words, the concept of eternal recurrence gives one to see that even if prophesied and presaged, the future is yet undiscovered and open to unexpected happenings. What is important in one's relation to time is one's stance toward this future. However it comes to pass, one must have the courage to say, "I willed it so."

Earlier we saw how the overman need not be a distant projection to which to aspire. Rather, it may be one's next self, a finitude to be anticipated, lived, and embraced. Again in Iqbal's terms, this Nietzschean conception of the overman would lead one to see how the perfect person is any number of one's possible selves, with the Prophet as the embodiment of this perfect person in all these possibilities. One does not have to erect mediators between the Prophet and oneself, nor does one have to have a prophet to manifest the Prophet. Rather one should take him to be standing next to oneself. In other words, the Prophet is available to every Muslim in many possibilities, as one's next self, the one after this one, and so on.

In agreement with Nietzsche, Iqbal understood the need for a certain amount of decadence. As he told Reynold Nicholson, the translator of his 1915 Persian poem The Secrets of the Self: "Buddhism, Persian Sufism, and allied forms of ethics will not serve our purpose. But they are not wholly useless, because after periods of great activity we need opiates, narcotics for some time" (1978: 20). He was also cognizant of the chronic weaknesses that plagued the striver and the necessity for a complete and regular diagnostics of spiritual exhaustion. His criticism of the Magian tendency, and later the Ahmadiyya, was premised upon a recognition that powerful forces of negativity, that is, the desire for self-annihilation or the search for ultimate guidance served as a drag upon striving. These forces were doppelgängers like the ape of Zarathrusta. Their debased figurations took on features of striving, but they rang hollow for not having the proper hook to the world, for continuing self-abnegation even as they proclaimed their break from the old ways of being. The correct relation of striving to these debased figures is to find a way to warn them, even to despise them, but not to deny one's kinship with them. This is how Iqbal describes the mode of tolerance that Muslims had to strive for after expelling the Ahmadis:

> True toleration is begotten of intellectual breath and spiritual expansion. It is the toleration of the spiritually powerful man who, while jealous of the frontiers of his own faith, can tolerate and even appreciate all forms of faith other than his own. His own faith is synthetic and for this reason he can easily find grounds of sympathy and appreciation in other faiths. . . . Only a true lover of God can appreciate the value of devotion even though it is directed to gods in which he himself does not believe. (1975: 5)

The only way to effect such tolerance is to claim one's doubt as one's debased form, which has come into being as a product of one's striving and whose presence can only be gleaned through an examination of the striving that birthed it and cast it out. The denial of relationship to one's doubts and their figuration, say in the form of the deceptive Ahmadi or *katar mulla* (prejudiced religious figure), will produce only strangers out of kin. In a situation of estrangement from one's debased forms, this kinship can be sensed only through the feeling of foreignness that roams abroad and inhabits one's inner recesses.

Both Bergson and Nietzsche served as worthy disputants for Iqbal. At certain moments of his writings, Iqbal was generous toward them, but at others he was quite hostile, particularly to Nietzsche. This hostility was not due to a misunderstanding of Nietzsche. I would argue that he understood Nietzsche all too well and even decried Nietzsche's misunderstood status within Western philosophy. In *Javid Nama* (1966) we find Iqbal mourning Nietzsche as an unappreciated sage, who was himself lost:

> No Gabriel, No Paradise, no houri, no God
> Only a handful of dust consumed by a yearning soul. (111)

An ecstatic born in the West . . .
A traveler gone astray in his own path. (112)

Revelation embraced him but he knew it not. (113)

Iqbal's occasional hostility toward Bergson and Nietzsche may have had to
do with his own ambivalence in feeling affinity with thinkers whose thought,
taken to its logical conclusion, spoke of the irrelevance of God. The later
Bergson of *The Two Sources of Religion and Morality* (1932) would not have been
averse to Iqbal's deep attachment to Islam. However, Nietzsche would likely
never have been as amenable to the idea that religion, any religion, was
possible and necessary for life. Yet he was not resistant to being taken for a
worthy enemy, for such an enemy could serve to bring forth new potentialities. In Iqbal's words in *The Secrets of the Self*:

> Whosoever knows the state of the self
> Considers a powerful enemy to be a blessing from God
> To the seed of men the enemy is a rain-cloud
> He awakens its potentialities. (1978: 83)

To summarize, one way to understand the links between Iqbal and Nietzsche is to think it was a Nietzschean Iqbal who provided the ammunition for
the constitutional expulsion of the Ahmadiyya in 1974, just as it was a Nietzschean Iqbal who provided a diagnosis of the condition subsequently produced of that constitutional act. Yet, insofar as Iqbal's call to maintain
vigilance toward one's debased forms paralleled the Supreme Court of Pakistan's call to Muslims to be vigilant against dissembling non-Muslims, it
makes one realize how closely striving is tracked by that against which it has
to be vigilant. The difference between the two calls, however minute, is
crucial.

The Spiritual Exercises of the Ulama

In chapter 5 we saw that Iqbal, although appreciative of the efforts of the
ulama in sustaining Islam and the Muslim community through previous
periods of dissension and fragmentation, viewed them as an ossified institution. Perhaps this, more than any other statement on the ulama, helped
ground the common perception of them as survivals. Moreover, few ulama
were in support of the formation of Pakistan and those who migrated to
Pakistan after its formation were immediately under suspicion of being un-

patriotic, a suspicion extended to even those subsequently born and raised in Pakistan. The ulama were involved in the anti-Ahmadiyya riots of 1953 and in subsequent agitations to have the group expelled from the fold of Islam. Their organizations pursued the criminalizing of Ahmadi everyday life. They were integrated into various institutions of government under the efforts of President Zia-ul Haq, producing the public perception that the face of the mulla was stuck on the television screen. As we saw in chapter 1, they were also involved in mosque-related struggles in many ways, from spearheading violent seizures of mosques to maintaining a quiet but strong hold on mosques. While Muhammad Qasim Zaman (2002) rightly warns against treating the ulama, even of one place, as a unified and homogenous group, in the instances I provide above they were addressed and treated as a troublesome collective by the wider public. Consequently, their positioning in Pakistani society makes tenuous any claims that they themselves might make upon striving. The few times I heard the ulama quote Iqbal it was to make doleful pronouncements about the proliferation of soulless striving, such as:

The custom of *azan* remains, but not the spirit of Bilal.

Philosophy remains, but not the religious instruction of Ghazali.

Their retort to the stereotyping of them was to refuse it, to displace it, as did my friend the imam of Neela Gumbard, upon a person who only looked the part of an alim but did not have the credentials or the commitment to be one. Many among them blamed those who acted the part of the alim, even embodying the stereotype of the mulla, for proliferating sin and producing dissension among Muslims. Given the general ambivalence, if not loathing of them as an institution, the denial of striving to them and their own critical assessment of disputatious modes of striving, what, if any relations could they bear to Muslim aspiration?

Anthropologists who study religious figures who produce repugnance in others (Faubion 2001, Harding 2001, Povinelli 2001) tend to emphasize their incommensurability within extant societies and political arrangements. The ulama well fit the conceptualization of repugnant others in the sense that Susan Harding (1991) provides, that is, both out of step and out of time with respect to the general populace and for whom we can claim a certain incommensurability with respect to everyday life and public culture in Lahore. Mumtaz Mufti provides a vivid sense of this aspect of the ulama in his description of them as actors in heavy makeup, as we saw in chapter 5.

However, I claim that the ulama can be placed in productive conversation with Muslim aspiration. More specifically, I claim that it is necessary to attend to their writings, as these acknowledge the intensity of the desire to be Muslim within lay efforts at striving while subjecting existing modes of striving to critical analysis of the kind that I associate with spiritual diagnostics. In other words, they attend to the excesses of striving through theological argumentation, by means of the physiological and psychological effects such argumentation produces. They thereby provide both avid descriptions of skepticism and bold strategies by means of which to treat skepticism. Nonetheless their self-positioning and mode of address to Muslims are sometimes so driven by judgment as to require us to ask how is one to access the keen attention to the psychodynamics of everyday life and striving in these writings without condoning this tone? (N. Khan 2009)

Maulana Yusuf Ludhianvi and the World as Illusion

Maulana Muhammad Yusuf Ludhianvi was a well-known, some would say notorious, Deobandi scholar, jurist, author, and political leader in Pakistan. He taught at the well-reputed madrasa Jamia Uloom ul-Islamia in Banori Town in Karachi. He wrote a question-and-answer column in the national Urdu daily *Jang* for over a decade. He was a leading figure in the Aalmi Majlis Tahaffuz Khatm-e Nubuwwat (International Committee for the Protection of the Finality of Prophethood), an International body, of which President Zia-ul Haq was a supporter, which targeted the activities of the Ahmaddiya movement. Later in life he also became well known for his anti-Shi'a polemics and activities. On May 18, 2000, he was ambushed and killed by persons unknown, in Karachi, a possible victim of the two-decade-long Shi'a-Sunni conflict in Pakistan. His death coincided with efforts by President Pervez Musharraf to introduce certain procedural changes to the controversial Blasphemy Law (Section 295-C) within the Pakistan Penal Code, which would have limited the ease of application of the law. The crowds that gathered nationwide to mourn the death of Maulana Yusuf Ludhianvi protested these changes in his name, preventing the government from moving forward on the amendments.

In a marketplace replete with contemporary and historical books by famous religious scholars and knowledgeable laypeople, Ludhianvi's *Ikhtilaf-e Ummat aur Sirat-e Mustaqeem* (Differences within the Community and the Right Path), written in 1995, is well known and popular and has gone through several reprints. The book is an attempt to expose the errors of argumentation of Muslims other than Deobandis, presumably to secure the authority of the Deobandi maslak. The introduction holds particular interest for me since it is framed by Ludhianvi's response to an earnest Pakistani who wrote him from the Middle East seeking clarification on a range of theological issues. It suggests how Ludhianvi grasped the impulse to strive that took shape within everyday life and this book was an address to it. Moreover, the placement of the Pakistani man's letter at the beginning of the book and Ludhianvi's response to it hints that their purpose was to have readers undertake rigorous self-examination to ensure that they had the proper orientation toward the rest of the book.

The letter writer informs Ludhianvi that he lives in the Middle East with his brothers, cousins, and uncles. Every member of his family prays regularly. In their free time they engage in religious discussions and debate among themselves about the relative superiority of their individual maslak. Although the family is tight knit, each member is adamant that his own alim is superior and provides the best guidance toward being good Muslims. Since the family members see themselves perpetuating the very schisms present in their native country, they have collectively decided to submit to Ludhianvi's guidance on the rightful path to God. The letter writer, who presents himself as the impartial one in his family entrusted to verify the truth, begs Ludhianvi to provide answers on several questions, which include the differences among the Shi'a and Sunni, Hanafi and Wahhabi, Deobandi and Barelwi, and Maulana Abul ala Maududi himself, who was put in a category of his own.

In his response to the letter writer, Ludhianvi briefly but courteously praises the man on his family's pious strivings. However, he moves quickly to urge them to turn away from debate and disputation, to concentrate instead on the practical aspects of piety. He cites a hadis attributed to the Prophet, in which the Prophet says that the nation that has moved away from rightful instruction to self-deception is given the gift of quarrel. Ludhianvi's implication is that it is not a good omen that the family has turned to debate on its own volition. Perhaps their debates and argumentation are an indication of their self-deception? Furthermore, Ludhianvi continues, debate and disputation sap one's resolution for undertaking obligatory religious duties. The nature of competitive exchange is to set aside cajoling, explaining patiently, and waiting to be understood, qualities central to being a good Muslim, in favor of the urge to slay one's opponents to win an argument. Moreover, a person not fully acquainted with the Shari'a, such as one who is not an alim, could not possibly protect it, particularly from his own misrepresentations. Ludhianvi advised the letter writer to tell his family members that, if they have faith in their individual alim guides, they should not compare their paths of striving. Each, guided by his own alim, should busy himself or herself in reading the Qur'an, doing zikr (recitation of God's name), tasbih (praising God), and durud (praising the Prophet).

Yusuf Ludhianvi could have stopped there. Instead, he introduces the caveat that one could respect ulama other than one's own alim providing these persons were recognizably rightfully guided. This caveat gives him an opening into a discussion of the markers of rightful guidance. Religious difference as such is not a problem for Ludhianvi. However, he distinguishes between those differences that developed naturally within the history of Islam and in the Prophet's era and those that were artificially imposed upon the Muslim community. The first type, which he calls ijtihadi ikhtilaf (difference in interpretation), is natural and unavoidable. It is manifest among the different schools of law in Islam. Such differences were also apparent in the Prophet's own time. The Prophet did not reprimand anyone for undertaking different practices. He understood that if some choose to follow his outward behavior ('amal), others might choose to discern his intentions (mansha). Ludhianvi claims that the oft-cited hadis in which the Prophet says that differences in his umma (Muslim moral community) were the blessing of God applied exclusively to such type of differences.

The second type of differences Ludhianvi refers to as nazariyati ikhtilaf (ideological differences). The Prophet anticipated these differences as well, specifically in the hadis in which he was reported to have said that his umma would fragment into seventy-three firqas (sects) of which only one would be rightly guided. He was also reported to have said that except for the rightly guided one, all others would espouse such desires and delusions that would spread like contagion, likening it to the poison of a rabid dog that poisoned the constitution of the bitten person. In Ludhianvi's words:

> The Prophet (Peace be upon Him) also detailed the disease arising from the invention of bid'a [unlawful innovation] and gumrahi [deviation], which is that of following wrongful desires. This disease does not simply mutilate a person's heart and mind. Rather, it is like the disease that spreads through a man's constitution when he is bitten by a rabid dog, as a result of which a decent enough man descends to the behavior of a

nonhuman. In a similar manner, that person who has been bitten by the rabid dog of wrongful ideology, the poison of self-opinion spreads through his every vein and fiber and, except for his favored ideology, the entire world appears to him as an illusion (1995: 19, my translation).

This splenetic description of harm that awaits Muslims who overreach is a warning certainly, but it is also an astute observation of a certain condition of being in the world, in which the world appears as an illusion. But it isn't as if the world assails one as such. It is because one assails the world with the wrong desires and inclinations. In other words, the capacity to be alienated from the world lies within oneself and one's strivings.

It is in this description of those made rabid by the sense of superiority of their own religious maslak that one finds Ludhianvi's picture of mullaism. He explains that a person so deluded experiences the world as entirely fictional. Interestingly, he does not concede radical alterity to this condition, as in the accounts of mullaism to be found in horror stories, cartoons, or jokes recounted in chapter 5. In the face of widespread uncertainty about the exact coordinates of this inner mulla, Ludhianvi asserts the reality of mullaism within oneself and one's responsibility for treating it.

At the same time Ludhianvi holds out the promise that one could overcome skepticism. In his assurances to the letter writer he says that once the truths that he pronounces are entrenched in the letter writer's mind, then no doubts would remain over which was the correct path according to the Prophetic tradition. Perhaps Ludhianvi was constrained to promise relief from skepticism once one was clear on the truthful pathway to the divine. He was as much a theologian and disputant as he was a spiritual guide, and when asked to elaborate the differences among Muslims, he was compelled to. It is noteworthy that only after his bold introduction does he set out the minutiae of differences setting apart Deobandis from other groups. One can almost see the young Pakistani Muslim turn eagerly to these scholarly disquisitions on sectarian difference to educate himself on how to tell truth apart from falsehood, to erase doubt once and for all from his mind. However, it seems to me that the placement of Ludhianvi's reply to the letter-writer suggests that he requires the questioner to probe further whether he was in the camp of *ijtihadi ikhtilaf* or *nazariyati ikhtilaf*, that is, to acknowledge his true condition to himself, before reading on.

Mufti Abdul Wahid and the Dissolution of the Social

In search of mosque-related fatwa in the Dar-ul Ifta of Jamia Madania madrasa in Karim Town, Lahore, I found a file titled 'Aqida o Bid'a (Belief and Innovation) with two fatwa by Dr. Mufti Abdul Wahid, the well-known mufti (jurist) of the madrasa. I consider these fatwa to be very important in providing a sense of the manner in which exchanges between the ulama and lay Muslims are conducted, as well as for the ulama's close attention to the scene of aspiration as expressed through religious discussion and debate in everyday life.

Earlier in his life, Mufti Wahid had been a doctor in the army, but had subsequently completed the rigorous madrasa training to become a mufti. He quickly established his reputation for writing incisive fatwa relating to economic issues. These two particular fatwa, however, relate to a public incident of blasphemy against the Prophet. Two people of the same community wrote separately to Dr. Wahid to report the incident and ask his advice on what punishment to levy against the blaspheming wrongdoer. In his reply to the first inquiry Dr. Wahid performed as a typical mufti, giving technical religious advice on how the potential blasphemer should repair his ways. But in his second reply one sees how Dr. Wahid came to an assessment of the shredded nature of social life and the necessity to submit striving to the imperatives of neighborliness and cooperation. The first fatwa went as follows:

> What does the mufti have to say about the following? Some people were engaged in religious discussion. By chance a person passed by. He also joined in the discussion and during the conversation he strayed from the main topic and uttered the following words: "The Prophet did not take his due [amanat] from the kuffar [disbelievers]. Instead he selected Hazrat Ali to collect his dues while he fled from Mecca for fear of the kuffar and hid himself in a cave for three days." Upon hearing these words the people present there became very agitated. And once news of this spread, people started to burn. Consequently, somebody drew the attention of the mujrim [sinner/criminal] to this matter upon which he presented the following explanation in his own defense: "I did not say these words intentionally [niyatan]. If I had said these words intentionally then even my repentance [tauba] would not be accepted no matter how many times I do it." He also repeatedly said, "If by saying these words, even without intention, there is some shari'i punishment which is to be imposed on me,

then I am happy to admit my crime, that is, to accept the punishment imposed on me." He added that: "I have committed this crime unintentionally. Nevertheless I have requested forgiveness from Allah for my sin." Under these circumstances please favor us with your fatwa regarding the following:

1. Has the abovementioned person perpetrated disrespect of the Prophet or not?
2. Is his desired request for forgiveness acceptable or not?
3. If his request for forgiveness is not acceptable by the Shari'a, then what should be his shari'i punishment for the abovementioned crime?
4. Supposing he refuses to accept the shari'i punishment, then what are the orders of the Shari'a regarding this?

Iqbal Farooqi, Bakhar (my translation)

In his response to the first fatwa Dr. Wahid explained precisely why the man's words were highly disrespectful of the Prophet, providing a clear sequence of ritual procedures for seeking repentance (tauba). In the meantime Dr. Wahid received a second istifta (request for a fatwa):

What do the ulama and mufti have to say about the following problem: In my uncle's shop in which my younger brother and cousin were engaged in religious discussion and in the presence of my father and my uncle, a man who is also a bona fide hakim [doctor] uttered some "hurtful" words. (Naql-e Kufr, Kufr na Bashir): "The Prophet himself did not take his due [amanat] from the kuffar. Instead he made Hazrat Ali responsible for collecting his due while he hid in a cave for three days out of fear of the kuffar." Upon hearing the abovementioned hurtful words my uncle told him to watch his tongue. The big mouth [darida-dahan] quickly left the shop when he saw how angry the young men present had gotten. The day after this the public was very angry and drew the attention of a man who negotiates reconciliation to the big mouth. The latter assured him that: 1. "I did not say these words intentionally. They slipped out of my mouth unintentionally." He confessed, "If I had said these words with intention then my repentance will also not be accepted." 2. "I was filled with remorse after we said those words unintentionally and I have asked Allah for forgiveness and I am willing to accept a shari'i punishment." Under the abovementioned circumstances, please let us know in the light of Qur'an and hadis:

1. Is the excuse of the abovementioned big mouth acceptable?
2. Has the abovementioned big mouth perpetrated disrespect of the Prophet?
3. If the abovementioned incident of bigmouthed-ness was done with intention, then what are the shari'i orders regarding its perpetrator?
4. Without intention of being a perpetrator and claiming to have asked Allah for forgiveness, does any sin remain his responsibility or not? If he is deserving of shari'i punishment, what is it?
5. If the big mouth does not accept the shari'i punishment in practice, and merely goes about saying that his neck is before the Shari'a, then what is the order?

Hafiz Mohammad Shafi, District Kanjon (my translation)

Upon receiving this request, Dr. Wahid paused to reflect on the circumstances that could have prompted such a wrongdoing in the first place. While he went on to provide the correct maslak-based response to the inquiry, which was a repetition of what he said before, nonetheless, the picture of lay Muslims engaging in religious disputations vexed him. Consequently he wrote an addendum to his reply:

I had written the above reply to the istafta but it was delayed for some reasons. Meanwhile, another istafta on the same event was received. Again I was saddened that one event has been made into such a big problem without any reason. In this era full of *fitna* [civil discord, even war], it is very essential that one proceed wisely so that people's iman [faith] and Islam are maintained. First, it is wrong for ordinary people to engage in religious debate because inevitably such inappropriate words and other faults emerge. It is sufficient for ordinary people to attend the gathering of Ahl-e Haqq ulama [rightful religious scholars] to listen to religious topics, or to find out about authentic religious books from them and to study these books individually or in groups. They should not review anything on their own or they will definitely land in error.

The second thing is this that if this person had committed a mistake, then one should have adopted a behavior of good will [khair-khwahi] and sympathy [hamdardi] toward him and it should not be the kind of sympathy that destroys the person's faith but the kind that saves it. Instead these people have begun to call him names and to beat him although the mistake was really theirs for starting a religious debate in the first place and that too in a public site, thus, giving others the opportunity to take part in the debate. If this person did commit disrespect, these people are the reason for his disrespect and are responsible for it. Therefore, just as repentance is necessary for him, repentance is also necessary for them. In fact, they should repent a lot.

The demand of sincerity [toward him] is that when he says that I have repented and I am sorry for what I have done, then it was enough that he repent in front of those who heard these improper words. You people have made this into a problem of the neighborhood and the cause of disagreement within the congregation, and you gave that person an opportunity to be bold.

In my opinion the following should be done to solve the problem. The man should be called in front of certain knowing and responsible people and told, "You have claimed to have repented. Then say in the presence of these people that 'I did not say these words out of the intention to be disrespectful. Nonetheless, I ask Allah for forgiveness for my words and I solemnly declare that I will save myself from any words which bear even a tiny bit of disrespect to the Prophet. To be on the safe side I will recite again the kalma [confession of faith] with a truthful heart."

Once the person has said the kalma, then, at a later date and appropriate time, make a public announcement of this that "since that person has repented, we should forget the matter." It should also be announced that from now on nobody should dare to say such things. If the matter can be settled by these means, instead of punishment and "boycott," then it is very good. For, if there is punishment, who is going to do the punishing? And if there is "boycott," you can well see that some people are very supporting of it, which is also suspicious. Allah knows best. (my translation)

Earlier we saw how Ludhianvi presented disputations as enticing Muslims into committing more and more sins to the point that their view of the world was jaundiced. Ludhianvi shows how such forms of striving within everyday life enacted the mulla. And the condition of skepticism that he paints is the inability of people to recognize that the problem perceived to be in the world originated with themselves. Dr. Wahid's attentiveness is less to the description of this condition, which he also hints was the possible consequence of such religious discussions. He attends to its wider consequences for the fabric of the social. He advises people to refrain from such discussions simply for idle pleasure. Not only would such discussions create the opportunity for wrongful statements to be uttered, they would also serve as the spark for uncharitable behavior on part of those who overheard such statements. It could foster their desire for revenge and punishment. And with his final words, "And if there is 'boycott,' you can well see that some people are very supporting of it, which is also suspicious," Dr. Wahid tries to draw people's attention to their own acts and desires, to recognize the excesses that these produced. An acceptance of one's finitude takes the form of upholding the social by subjecting one's motivations and desires to closer scrutiny.

Maulana Ashraf Ali Thanawi's Techniques for Living with Skepticism

Maulana Ashraf Ali Thanawi was the very same alim who disputed Sayyid Ahmed Khan in Aligarh in the 1920s and served as an intellectual predecessor of sorts of Muhammad Iqbal. Although he is fully located within colonial India (he died in 1943), his reputation extends into Pakistan where his books are very popular and in wide circulation in households, libraries, bookstores, and madrasas. The one that was strongly recommended to me was Shariat o Tariqat (1971), in which Thanawi attempted to put Sufi spiritual exercises under the rubric of the Shari'a. While the entire book may be taken to be an incisive investigation of the dynamics of everyday life and everyday pursuits of spirituality, the tenth chapter on riya (hypocrisy, ostentation, dissimulation) interests me insofar it attends to the same conduct, that of excessive religiousity within lay striving, that concerned both Ludhianvi and Dr. Wahid.

In this section of the book Thanawi details all the different ways in which general, even nonreligious speech has the capacity to deliver hurts and blows to others. He provides an exhaustive litany of the excesses of speech. His sense is that many of these excesses, such as gossip and rumor, may not be excised from the social body or even from the individual. Rather, one's efforts have to be directed at reducing their appearance, lessening their impact, and alleviating the burden of sin. He recommends spiritual exercises, incantations, and prayers, to slow the tongue to cause it to reflect before it speaks. But he ends his commentary on the excesses of speech by making the counterintuitive suggestion that, should the tongue develop no self-awareness, then different parts of the body ought to take turns in excessively flattering the tongue so that it might stop out of sheer embarassment

(1971: 211). Here I find Maulana Ashraf Ali Thanawi to give expression to something very akin to Nietzsche's notion of the self as a multiplicity or Iqbal's of the body as a society in itself. Furthermore, these conceptualizations well resonate with my analysis of my teacher Farooq's sense of himself as a series of selves.

Thanawi continues his counterintuitive suggestions with reference to religious pretensions. He mocks overt shows of piety by recounting all the ways in which a Muslim attempts to appear pious, that is, through a bent head to indicate humbleness, dry lips to indicate deprivation, torn clothes to indicate a lack of interest in material goods, and loud sighs to indicate a state of suffering. While he believes that the tongues of such hypocrites may be kept busy through chanting specific formulas and recitations, their bodies required a different set of exercises. If after detailed self-examination it appears to aspirants that their body will do as it wishes to draw people's attention to itself, Thanawi urges them to let the body continue as it is. In time people's attention will wane and one's pious demonstrations will be transfigured from riya to 'adat (habit), from 'adat to 'ibadat (worship), and from 'ibadat to ikhlas (sincerity of character) (214).

Thanawi's writings are in effect explorations of the persistent presence of skepticism within everyday acts of piety and religiosity, as opposed to, say, Ludhianvi's image of an overcoming of skepticism. If the tendency of skepticism is to put into question one's relation to oneself and others, thus making naught of striving, a modulated repetition of religious practices in the face of skepticism could change striving into second nature. Thanawi's writings suggest that skepticism is unavoidable, a constant goad on the side of anyone who attempts to make himself or herself a good Muslim. If Mumtaz Mufti in the previous chapter speaks of the pain of living with an inner mulla, Thanawi in complete seriousness presents playful strategies by which one can outsmart one's mulla, making it serve the cause of striving.

Mumtaz Mufti Encounters Pakistan

In 1961, Javid Iqbal, Muhammad Iqbal's son, bemoaned Iqbal's fate in Pakistan for being caught between the ideological battles of the Left and the Right. The Progressives of the 1950s who dominated the literary scene did not know what to make of Iqbal, as he was inassimilable within the aesthetics of social realism (Faruqi 2005). The ulama and the state between the years of 1949 and 1993, on the other hand, treated Iqbal's words almost as dogma in their efforts at expelling the Ahmadiyya from Islam. Such ongoing tussles over Iqbal led Shamsur Rahman Faruqi, a prominent Urdu critic and poet of India, to make the sharp but undoubtedly fair observation that no one was reading Iqbal for his poetry (2005). Paradoxically, Faruqi claims that while Iqbal's political and philosophical writings were dated and simplistic, his poetry stood to be appreciated for itself. Faruqi knew that Iqbal's original appellation was *hakim ul-umma* (physician of the people), telling his readers as much in his essay, and providing evidence that Iqbal wished never to be seen solely as a poet. He abhorred the idea of art for art's sake. In the same issue of the *Annual of Urdu Studies* in which Faruqi's essay is published, Christina Oesterheld (2005) provides instances of how contemporary satirists of Pakistan weave their words together with Iqbal's, using his more famous verses, specifically those likely to be known by many, to provide critical appraisals of Pakistani political and societal conditions. This leads her to make the claim that Urdu literature is a site of alternative visions and dissent in Pakistan.

These two contemporary positions on Iqbal's writings, one dismissing his writings other than the poetry and the other claiming Iqbal's availability for political dissent, raise the possibility that there is yet work to be done in securing Iqbal's influence upon contemporary Muslim thought. And if Iqbal does lend himself to political dissent, what makes this dissent worth its name? In other words, what is it a dissent to and what does it hope to accomplish? In the final section of this chapter, I make a small contribution to these questions by showing a doubling effect between Iqbal and Mumtaz Mufti, and ending with the speculation that the diagnosis of the condition of skepticism may be what Iqbal gives to literature as a mode of dissent to the present in Pakistan.

Mumtaz Mufti (who died in 1995) was one among a handful of Urdu authors, including Qudrutallah Shahab, Muhammad Hasan Rizvi Askari, Banu Qudsia, and Ashfaque Ahmed, who, after long careers writing experimentally in a distinctly secular mode, turned to exploring Islamic themes in their later writings (Metcalf 1993b).[3] The book *Talash* (Search) is a collection of Mufti's essays posthumously published by his son in 1999. In *Talash*, one is invited to a light conversation (*halki phulki baten*), as if weighty matters, such as that of one's religiosity, should only be broached lightly, the lightness of touch being crucial to thinking anew. Yet it is a strange invitation to a chat. It is unkind to many. It heckles. It shrieks. It retreats into solipsism and, on occasion, silences are marked by an abrupt shift in topic. Topically, it is almost impossible to know what any of the chapters, arbitrarily drawn and further subdivided, are meant to treat. One might begin with the enigmatic title of "The Rose," meander through a mournful account of the loss of our inner child, and end by speaking about the Qur'an being a scientific rather than a religious text (1999: chapter 10).

If one is to take the invitation to a chat seriously, as I propose we do, then the burden is on us to engage the text in a conversational mode, to insert ourselves in the pauses and breaks within Mufti's speech, to be open to the possibility of the radical contingency of a conversation and the surprising places it might land us. And it is this quality of his writings that emboldens me to insert Pakistan's constitutional exercises into spaces opened up by Mufti, to extend his diagnosis of the claustrophobic atmosphere that envelopes striving as a criticism of those state practices that foster skepticism.

I find Mufti to extend the mandate of the constitution by asking the question, "Who is a Muslim?" in the form of "What is the meaning of Muslim [Musalman ka matlab kya hai?]?" Mufti slips his question into every possible occasion. He relates a story of asking a bookseller for such a book that would tell him in simple language what was the meaning of Muslim. When the shopkeeper asks him if he is a non-Muslim (ghair Musalman), he declares very seriously, "By the grace of Allah, I am a Musalman." When the exasperated shopkeeper inquires if Mufti is pulling his leg, Mufti explains that, although he was born a Muslim, he is a Muslim munh zabani, in name only, and he has yet to figure out what Muslim means (27).

This encounter is repeated many times throughout the book as Mufti poses this question to friends, religious scholars, teachers, politicians, and others around him, and is greeted with incredulity each time. Mufti ultimately finds that he has no takers for his question. Not only do people receive his question as if he is naive, they receive it suspiciously as if wary of the dissension it may produce. They do not express curiosity about Mufti's experiment. They mostly express concern that Mufti perseveres in his perverse questioning given the inflammatory nature of the present moment. And in that half-second wariness we have a sense of a milieu in which any unexpected attention to religious issues has the potential to escalate into violence.

As Mufti doggedly continues asking his question, a note of despair enters his voice. He is misunderstood, his motives are suspect, and he stands to be laughed at or berated. Mostly he is assailed by a sense of the belatedness in asking this question, in that it came to him too late in his life. He has been complicit for too long with the hegemony of the elder generation. When he meets young people who appear to him to be dead, he is assailed by his complicity in bringing about this death.

Disappointment pervades Mufti because in asking the question too late it no longer makes any sense. Although he is in fact bequeathing the question to Uxi, his son, so Uxi may in turn ask it, it is as if another question has already been asked and lodged itself securely in the minds and makeup of those around him. One immediately grasps the pervasiveness of this other question in the disconsolate words of Mufti's friend: "When have I ever claimed to be a *sahih* (authentic)Musalman when I myself don't know who is a Musalman" (40)? And it is this later question of "Who is a Muslim?" that Mufti takes to constitute a break in striving.

In asking his own question despairingly and belatedly Mufti seems to me to be in conversation with the constitutional exercises I tracked earlier, in chapter 2, which, if we recall, also arrived at the question "Who is a Muslim?" as fundamental to upholding aspiration. Furthermore, in sensing that this other question has closed off his contemporaries to themselves and those around them Mufti hints at the skeptical turn of the constitution. Mufti senses that posing the question skeptically has led Muslims away from the proper acknowledgment of strangeness within them.

In *Talash*, I find Mufti to effectively put Pakistan's present under the sign of crisis by suggesting that it is incapable, if not unworthy, of being inherited by the young. I take this to be his way of showing how the constitution has failed to recruit the young into its ranks. Mufti iterates the ways in which the youth have been failed by the older generation. In particular, he repeatedly pronounces the fact of their disenfranchisement from participation in adult conversation through the figure of the child who appears in the tortured relationship between the father and the son, and in the rupture between the younger and the older generations. For instance, he unfurls a tirade against Islamic books that preach respect of religious elders. These books are awash in respect. Yet, Mufti wonders if respect is not a wall between two people. Consider, he said, the relationship between a father and a son. They are bound by respect. Consequently, if one sees two men sitting side by side in silence, then one can take it for granted that they are father and son. When he asks the young why they have so much hostility toward the figure of the father, he is told: "The entire responsibility for this [hostility] lies with the elders. They have not trained us properly. Elders have considered us contemptible. They have never let us speak. Instead they cast the net of fear in our hearts" (29). He ends this tirade with the following line: "For centuries the elders have been ruling the young."

The above words are not a simple accusation aimed at Mufti, of his complicity with his generation in denying voice to the young for Mufti has tried hard to foster youth. He speaks of his own relationship to his son Uxi. When Uxi was little, his mother died. Mufti, a refugee in a new country, had no one who could help him to care for the child. So the child became his companion. He speaks of how Uxi would accompany him to the school where he taught, and would stand by the doorstep while Mufti gave his lessons. Uxi would go with him to the store. Uxi would eat and sleep with him. When Uxi got a little older, Mufti was transferred to Karachi. There they alighted upon Mufti's nephew Kaiser, who taught them the art of vagrancy. For two years they roamed markets together for days on end, drank endless cups of tea, and ate what they could find from stalls, ending up each night at the cinema halls. Mufti prided himself on being a liberated father, for no one looking at them would have been able to tell that he was an elder.

When Uxi turned twenty, writes Mufti, he asked his father to set him free: "For twenty years I have been leading my life according to your ideas. Please give me permission to spend the rest of my life according to my own ideas" (50). This request hits Mufti very hard because he feels as though he had never been the friend to his son that he had imagined. However, his son returns shortly to him. When asked why he has forsaken the company of his peers, Uxi replies that he has been ruined by Mufti and no longer belonged to his era. He has been made into an old man. This leads to Mufti's realization of the truth of the young, that it is necessary for them to live their own era, that exile from it is painful and destructive for them, and that elders, intentionally or not, participate in exiling them.

Although he goes on to ruefully acknowledge the ineffability of the young, Mufti accepts the necessity for them to live by their own terms, or to simply live. Yet what is life for Mufti? Life is wonderment. However, this sense is not born of the "happy culture" of the West, by which Mufti means the culture of hippies, in revolt against its society, with its promotion of beggarly lifestyles, free love and sexual experimentation (55). Mufti is repelled by such freedom. Nor is it born of the enthrallment with a particular religious path. Mufti speaks of a young man associated with the Tablighi Jama'at who comes to visit him. Mufti describes him as moribund: "His eyes were closed. The shadow of death was upon his every part" (60). Upon sight of such deathliness, Mufti is possessed by the desire to cry, such that he too could go blind so that he does not have to bear witness to the devastation the older generation has wrought upon the younger.[4]

For Mufti, the Qur'an shares the same sense of wonderment as the young. It does not ask that it be read by a reasoning mind or rapturous soul, or that it be treated as transparent or opaque, although all of these are legitimate in their place. It asks that it be approached with wonderment and an appreciation of its own sense of wonderment, or rather God's sense of wonderment toward his creation (73). It appears to Mufti that the Qur'an has an inner child. If the young bring a certain sense of wonderment to the world, similarly the Qur'an embodies youthfulness through its openness to the world. One can return to the Qur'an again and again, era after era, and still be struck by its contemporary tone.

Although Mufti draws a parallel between the Qur'an and science, seeing wonderment at work in both, he differentiates wonderment intermixed with the scholarly skepticism of Western modern science from the wonderment of the Qur'an. Mufti devotes considerable effort to draw out the contours of scholarly skepticism. It begins all inquiry with doubt (82). It dishonestly denies the place of intuition in all inquiry (84). It demands explanation and the resolution of all doubts. The Qur'an does not advocate that one begin one's inquiry from such a jaundiced outlook. "Instead, it bids, that you look, you observe, you try to understand, and you try again and again. If you don't understand, ask those who may know. If you still don't understand, don't establish an opinion . . . that is, suspend opinion" (85).

Given Mufti's entrenched location in Pakistan and his insistence upon keeping Pakistan in the horizon of his writings, I argue that he enacts several positions resonant with Iqbal's delineation of Muslim aspiration and diagnosis of spiritual exhaustion. First, one need not travel to have experiences and insights. Such things may be achieved through a change in orientation and mode of participation in what is already given.[5] Thus, in Talash, we see Mufti draw out the pervasive condition of skepticism simply by asking those around him, what is the meaning of "Muslim"? Second, the perception of a blockage to his question in Talash leads Mufti to diagnose skepticism by means of asking a very Iqbalian question, which is, does his present sustain life? And he attempts to answer this question by exploring how this present mistreats the life of the young. Third, Mufti attempts a redress of the condition of skepticism through the enactment of finitude. In his varied expressions of disappointment and despair at the wrong done to the young and various attempts to allow them their own modes of life, we find an attempt at finitude within a context in which people repress knowledge of their capacity for skepticism. Finally, given how easily Mufti comes to have spiritual experiences out of the ordinary within *Labbaik*, he suggests that travels in another order of reality is available to Pakistani Muslims (Metcalf 1993b). This position doubles that of Iqbal's on miracles when he writes that miracles are necessary and useful to everyday life. In *Talash* such travels are to the heart of strangeness with oneself and within the childlike realm of the Qur'an. And in moving from the strangeness within to the world of the Qur'an, Mufti appears to parallel the movement between the individual and creation in Iqbal's picture of striving. In these entwined ways I see Mufti not only deploying an Iqbalian diagnostic of the present but also enacting the self-corrective tendency within Muslim aspiration to enable striving.

My Own Disappointment

Several months into my fieldwork in Lahore, my roommate, another scholar from an U.S. institution, decided to shorten her stay in Pakistan because it was not as productive as she had hoped. In the midst of telling me of her plans to leave early, she stopped to take in my look of shock and in an impulsive gesture she asked me to leave with her. "It makes no sense for you to study Muslim religiosity in this place," she said. "People are not really religious. Many haven't even read the Qur'an. I wager that I know more about Islam than they do." I must confess that I was sorely tempted. In my months in Lahore I had uncovered a dizzying variety of religious conflicts and violence centered on neighborhood mosques. My conversations with Pakistani intellectuals and state officials were not leading me anywhere either, as most seemed determined to cast a blind eye to such conflict, seeing it as lowly infighting among the lower reaches of their society.

Although leaving Pakistan was never a serious option, I made a conscious decision to stay. While my roommate's remarks raised the question of what her picture of knowing Islam was, I wanted to learn what it meant to know Islam in Pakistan and why this knowing was so easily brushed aside. At the same time as I was overwhelmed by the intensity of fights within religious life in Pakistan, I was also drawn to what I was hearing and learning. The theological issues, the nuances of religious praxis, the thickness of textual references, the literary allusions, the sensorial details, the bureaucratic inter-lacement, the political and legal overlay, even the psychological portraits of individuals and communities that I was being provided both staggered and attracted me because they suggested a milieu of great turbulence and intellectual and spiritual experimentation. At times I felt as if the Prophet's era was entwined with this one. At other times that era seemed distant from the present, a period of solitary search amidst a bewildering variety of choices, all of which were likely erroneous.

I was taken by the Urdu author Mumtaz Mufti's image in *Talash*, of people in Pakistan being Muslim simply by breathing. Although he was not alone in asserting the materiality of being Muslim in Pakistan, his image forcefully conveyed the sense that the condition of being Muslim simply endured within this muddled situation. This condition did not endure as the true reality under the layers of unreality upon it. Rather, it flourished, to the extent one can call it flourishing, through one's being in this place and participating in the opportunities that it presented. At one point, the young editor of a particularly strident religious weekly, which was committed to polemics and exposures of its adversaries, told me that what Pakistan produces in plentiful was *dini jazba* (religious passion). I asked if he was speaking of those in his maslak. "No, just look around, it drips from everyone." I cannot speak for "everyone," for I found many who were wary of associating Pakistan only with Islam. However, I certainly found a passionate quality of engagement, even pleasure, in religious duties, whether they were undertaken as obligatory or in excess of obligation (this was itself a matter of much discussion and conflict), among a significant number of my informants.

I realized of course that what was before me carried the signature of its colonial past and the disorder of the postcolony. But in time I came to be interested in the lure of the emergent that led the Lahori Muslims of my acquaintance to do more than what was obligatory, exert themselves in new directions, throw themselves into conversations that had the quality of quicksand, attempt different arrangements, seek ways back to a different time or excoriate others in their myriad efforts. Not all of these were necessarily noteworthy, nor free of a certain menace. Thus, the overall effort of this book has been to capture this quality of restlessness of religious striving that I encountered in this milieu, which was informed both by disappointment with the present and by the pleasure taken in feeling bound to Islam. I have attempted to the extent possible to be attentive to Pakistan's colonial legacy, the workings of the postcolonial state, major historical actors and events, and the specificity of everyday life to which libraries, mosques, families, and the public culture of Lahore gave access in providing an account of what I have called Muslim aspiration, entwined with skepticism.

The Argument of the Book

My argument, in brief, has been that the creation of Pakistan inaugurated the aspiration to strive to be Muslim. This aspiration did not concern itself with final ends. Thus while the emphasis of striving was on self-perfectibility, it never emphasized perfection. Although undoubtedly Pakistan has seen leaders, movements, and parties with notions of what kind of society, state, or self Pakistan should forge, the particular tendency that I track through the philosophy of Iqbal to Pakistan's early constitution makers and its implementation in this place maintained the necessity of an open future to enable striving and experimentations on the self. I take the construction and maintenance of mosques in neighborhoods of Lahore to be sites of such experimentation, with struggles over these mosques expressive of aspiration and its possible undoing. Other scenes of aspiration appear in the theological arguments within the weave of everyday life and the assiduous attempts at piety that may involve bold moves to seek out extraordinary guidance within a milieu beset by ambiguities over religious authority. I even incorporate state efforts to develop a position on the Ahmadi question as a possible scene of aspiration, forcing us to accept the broadest scope and possibly distasteful nature of aspiration that may not be commensurable with the values of liberal democracy but, as Asad Ahmed (2010) shows us, are nonetheless fully expressive within the tenets of liberal law.

In tracking the forces that threaten to undo aspiration, I explore how the state's constitutional and legislative treatment of Ahmadis both upheld an Iqbal-inflected aspiration and produced the conditions of possibility for a proliferation of skepticism in relation to others within everyday life in Lahore. This effort by the state finds resonance and amplification within public culture in Lahore, suggesting that while everyday life and public culture of Pakistan are not fully determined by the state, the three are not necessarily at odds.

This conterminous relationship among different levels of Pakistani state and society make all the more interesting the question of what or who provides an evaluation of the state of striving and possible blockages to it within this milieu. While I posit a Nietzschean Iqbal to see what capacities for critical analysis Iqbal provides for the present, I also explore Iqbal's inheritance by the ulama and the literati, who produce evaluative statements on the state of spiritual health of lay Muslims within everyday life, as vibrant instances of a spiritual diagnostics that serves striving. At the same time I leave my understanding of spiritual diagnostics open to incorporate other evaluative statements from different, wider reaches of Pakistani society. I also leave open the possibility that spiritual diagnostics may constitute something like a political commentary on Pakistan, even a dissent to its present.

Muslim Becoming

I have attempted to parse the aspect of Muslim becoming in several ways. The commitment of Muslim aspiration, the inaugural tendency of Pakistan, to continual striving is a primary marker of becoming. Among other instances of becoming that have appeared in this book is the aspect of time to become, to diverge from the trajectory projected or anticipated of it. Or, individuals to become other than themselves, for instance in the course of arguments or struggles to be better Muslims. All becoming does not affirm or augment striving, as, for example, in the shading into Shi'ism or the sudden eruption of a mulla within a person.

A persistent quality of becoming within Pakistan was that it delivers up surprises, unsettling established scholarly notions about Pakistan and social theory in general. Among these surprises is the significance of uncivil politics, such as theological disputations and mosque-related struggles, as the scene of Muslim aspiration. In Iqbal's relation to Pakistan, there is the surprise of implications beyond the textbook relationship between a visionary and his vision. My readings of Iqbal prompt us to see that, while Iqbal's influence was quite widespread within Pakistan, it was not always for the nation's good and the working out of his thinking might have depleted its capaciousness. Yet the open-ended nature of Iqbal's thinking lends itself to be tried out again, of imagining even the possibility of tolerance beyond apostasy. This reading of Iqbal also brought me to Bergson and Nietzsche, important philosophers of time.

Of the state's relationship to Islam, I make the argument of a contrarian that there was a consistency in its myriad, many say, insincere efforts to establish its authority over Islam. This consistency lay in upholding, often in a desultory fashion, the striving and experimentation of its polity and often to the detriment of other sections of the polity. On the state's relationship to everyday life, I showed how everyday life came to be in the margins of the state as the latter's bureaucratic rules and procedures undergird the daily administration of mosques. While central government may remain out of reach for most Pakistanis, the state's presence was palpable as ever anticipated within the ambit of mosque-related struggles. At the same time, everyday life retained its independence insofar as it espoused concerns that were intrinsic to its own rhythms, and produced formulations on what it meant to be a Muslim that were well in excess of official ideology and nationalism. They reached into the future of what the Muslim could yet be.

On the contentious topic of the ulama, loathed, feared, and parodied at every level, who have nonetheless held on to state power by various means, I have argued that there hasn't been sufficient attention paid to the ways in which they retain their vitality for Pakistan through their diagnostic attentiveness to everyday life in its complexity. On the nature of political critique, I suggest that we ought to be more attentive to literature, specifically the diagnostic note within the literary, as the privileged mode of political critique in Pakistan. One critiques Pakistan by making sense of whether it sits right by one's constitution or not.

Becoming Present

I realize that I will be asked what bearing my analysis has on the present moment in Pakistan. Since I last visited, there have been many political developments. Benazir Bhutto returned to Pakistan and was assassinated. After much casting about, including imposing emergency rule upon Pakistan, President Pervez Musharraf resigned and temporarily bowed out of politics. Asif Zardari, Bhutto's spouse, won the elections and became the new president of Pakistan. Baitullah Masud and the Pakistan Taliban started an offensive with a demand for a state under Shari'a law in the North West Frontier Province. The government at first acceded to these demands and later launched its counteroffensive against this movement. The country is at present paralyzed by a civil war that refuses to be contained in this area and has begun to spill out into the major cities in Pakistan. Looking into the future of Pakistan, three scenarios present themselves. One is the establishment of the internationally desired democratic system of government. The second is a political meltdown. The third is a partial return to the state of turmoil and restlessness that prevailed earlier but which was not a condition of war and imminent disaster. To me it appears that the first scenario carries the whiff of revolution and redemption. The second manifests a mode of apocalyptic thinking that sometimes characterizes social theory (Agamben 1998). The third is the one most likely and at this point likely hoped for by Pakistanis.

The contribution my analysis in this book can make is to ask what would it take to face the challenging present and future of Pakistan but not submit to the discourse of decline about and within Pakistan. It would require acknowledging the fact of striving within everyday life and developing the conceptual tools to study the possibilities that it articulates and the conditions of skepticism, uncertainty, even violent closures that it can give rise to.

Perhaps I can make clearer the work of which I am thinking through the unlikely juxtaposition of two vignettes. A few months ago, just prior to the emergent situation in the North West Frontier Province, a Pakistani student, who once studied in the Lahore University of Management Sciences, a premier educational institution in Pakistan whose students were active in protests against Musharraf's government, wrote to tell me how excited she was by recent developments in the country. By this she was referring to the recent decision of the Zardari government to back down from its refusal to let the chief justice of the Supreme Court return to the position from which Musharaff had removed him. She was excited because it indicated that the rule of law was once again in place and if allowed to run on its own steam could bring positive change to Pakistan.

At around the same time I was speaking to a Pakistani man, the manager of a grocery store in my neighborhood, who also expressed excitement about recent developments in Pakistan. When asked what developments he had in mind, he said that it was the Zardari government's decision to allow the Shari'a to be implemented in the North West Frontier Province. This, he said, was finally the opportunity to establish an Islamic state in Pakistan, an opportunity that had never been given to its Muslims.

It is all too easy to scoff at these short-lived expressions of excitement. They seem to be expressive of such entrenched fantasies of the national elite whose lives are by and large untouched by the daily workings of the law, and the lower middle class who will likely never move to such an Islamic state within Pakistan, informed as much by marked differences in ethnicity as by a shared religiosity. Yet, if one casts one's mind back to my arguments in this book, one will see that to hold out hope in the workings of the law to solve Pakistan's problems has been an obdurate expression of striving, making the law a fecund site for experimentation over what it is to be a Muslim.

At the same time, counterimaginations have also flourished since the foundation of Pakistan. The Munir Report of 1954 effectively produced a picture of an Islamic state for Pakistan before waving it aside. In Maulana Abul ala Maududi's writings on what he called "The Qadiani Problem," that is, the Ahmadi question, one finds the Ahmadis accused of conspiracies, among which is the desire to establish a state of their own within Pakistan (2000). This too was the imagination of the Islamic state within Pakistan, displaced onto the desires of others.

Thus these individuals, the student and the grocer, were giving specific expressions to striving in Pakistan that have long histories. But they would likely be dismissive of each other. What would it take to acknowledge the element of striving in each other's expressions, which is not necessarily to support it or allow it to be in its own place, but to see these expressions as belonging to Pakistan? I see this mode of inhabiting Pakistan as one of allowing Muslims opportunities to reinhabit their tradition, to make it newly perfect, and, through the interventions of Muhammad Iqbal, opening it up for travels in the virtual. I also see this promise as teaching about living with doubts and skepticism and learning to acknowledge their presence and devastations in our midst.

CHAPTER ONE   *Scenes of Muslim Aspiration*

1. Faisal Devji makes a similar point in "Muslim Nationalism: Founding Identity in Colonial India" (1993). See also Eaton 2000 for an interesting survey of the difference in symbolism between temple and mosque desecrations.

2. Many more mosques were sacralized in the ripple effects of that event, as witnessed by subsequent efforts of the Pakistani courts to erect secure defenses of mosques by arguing that they constituted the threshold to heaven (N. Khan 2008).

3. While this practice of mosque committees has not been historically dated, in the context of colonial India it is significant that it was only after protracted legal battles with the colonial state that the Sikh community was able to dislodge traditional leaders from their *gurdwaras* (literally gateways to the guru; Sikh places of worship) replacing them with gurdwara committees to ensure that the wider Sikh community could exercise a coordinated administration of its places of worship (Gilmartin 1988). However, in the absence of a single structure of authority presiding over lay Muslims, in Pakistan and elsewhere, such mosque committees were local centers of power for which the idea of coordinated administration across mosques was anathema. For instance, any outreach by the Auqaf Department, the provincial department in charge of managing religious properties, was perceived as undue interference by my mosque-based interlocutors. My acquaintances within the Auqaf Department led me to understand that the department stayed out of mosque-related administration as they were not revenue-generating, as were shrines with their daily visitors numbering in the thousands.

4. The waqf is a technical instrument within Islamic law by means of which property can be endowed in perpetuity, preventing its fragmentation or alienation. This was a significant means by which the Muslim gentry ensured the integrity of their property holdings in the face of Islamic inheritance law, which tended to be more inclined to breaking up property to ensure fair inheritance. Moreover, as George Kozlowski (1985) has argued, this was a means by which the Indian Muslim gentry

accommodated themselves to changing political realities, such as the establishment of the colonial state after 1857. While some mosques were still formed by means of waqf, particularly in the rural areas, most land for mosques in cities was acquired, legally or illegally, from the state, since few people owned large holdings of land that they could readily alienate for religious purposes.

5. It was only very late into my fieldwork that I realized that there was a standing policy of getting mosques approved by the district commissioner's office prior to construction. The approval process required all state institutions concerned (district commissioner's office, Lahore Development Authority, Metropolitan Corporation Ltd., Auqaf, local police) to sign off on the petition and plans for a mosque seeking to be approved. Most of the mosques I knew about had not gone this route. Moreover, the petitions for mosque construction at the district commissioner's office were very few and did not reflect the active projects of mosque construction around the city. The fact that so many government institutions had to confer legitimacy upon mosques only implied that mosque oversight was ad hoc.

6. A quote from R. Nath (1994) summarizes the basic architectural constituents of a mosque: "'Mosque' is an aggregate of so many inspirations which it derived from divergent sources. It adopted and absorbed various elements drawn from ancient cultures of the Orient, and it is through a creative evolutionary process that such features as mihrab [niche on the wall in a mosque indicating the direction of Mecca], minbar [pulpit in a mosque, used for the delivery of the the Friday sermon], nave [the central square hall of a mosque], iwan [a chamber that is roofed or vaulted and open on one side facing on to the courtyard of a mosque], dome, arch, and minar [tower from which the call to prayer is delivered] have become its constituents" (one could add, in various combinations) (preface). In addition to Nath 1994, overviews of medieval and modern mosque architecture may be found in Wheatley 2000, Hillenbrand 1985, Fethi 1985, Pereira 1994, Frishman and Khan 2002, Prochazka 1986, and Ardalan 1983. For a more metaphysical and philosophical exploration of Islamic art and aesthetics, see Nasr 1987. The mosques I describe in this chapter varied greatly in architectural style, departing significantly from the grand sultanate or Moghul mosque style of the Indian subcontinent; the Badshahi Masjid, for example, has an onion-shaped dome above the central prayer hall and is flanked by two tall minarets but conforms, through the inclusion of some basic architectural elements, to mosques in functional use in the subcontinent. See Prochazka 1986 for floor plans of sultanate and Moghul mosque architecture, and Hughes n.d. for those of ordinary mosques in India and Central Asia. Masjid Noor conformed to a generic style of mosque commonly found in the older, poorer neighborhoods of Lahore that date prior to Partition or immediately after it. Its most startling feature was that a corner of the mosque protruded into the lane that surrounded it. It was this protrusion that indicated that this mosque was built outside of the state's imagination of the grid-like distribution of urban space, that is, that it was effectively an "encroachment."

7. This group was of nineteenth-century origin, an offshoot of the Deobandi maslak, whose primary purpose was to carry out missionary work among lapsed Muslims. See Masud 2000 for further background on this movement.

8. I have found Veena Das's description of rumors, or rather what happens to language under conditions of political turbulence or moral panic (1998, 2006), to be very productive for thinking of what happens to speech under conditions of qabza.

9. This plays on the myth of the martial race and their code of honor, a colonial construction (Fox 1985).

10. The Lahore Development Authority, like many bureaucratic institutions in Pakistan, does not maintain a central database. Patwaris, such as young Shahed Iqbal, are responsible for the files on each development scheme, and appear with them whenever these files are called up.

11. This practice was left over from the days of martial law when this quota usually went to the martial law administrator (Siddiqa 2007).

CHAPTER TWO   *A Possible Genealogy of Aspiration*

1. These interrelations have been noted but very fitfully studied, the result of either a lack of familiarity with Bergson's and Nietzsche's thought or a fear that it may make Iqbal's thought seem derivative, when in truth one receives very novel insights into both thinkers by means of Iqbal's readings of them. Vice versa, the specificity and scope of Iqbal's philosophical ambitions are more evident by placing his words alongside theirs in a relationship of critical appreciation.

2. As Javed Majeed notes, Iqbal is treated almost as a "talisman" in Pakistan and accorded the status of a prophet of the emergence of Muslims within modernity (2009: xxiii).

3. See Jan 1998 for a flavor of contemporary public discussions on Iqbal in Pakistan not dissimilar to the situation Javed Iqbal described for the 1960s, in which he claimed that the left and the right had divided up Iqbal between them.

4. As Javed Majeed writes: "In a speech delivered in Tehran on the occasion of the First International Conference on Iqbal, Mar 10–12, 1986, the then president of Iran, Sayyid Ali Khamenei, stated that the Islamic Republic of Iran is 'the embodiment of Iqbal's dream.' He added that 'our people have translated into action his doctrine of self,' and 'we are following the path shown to us by Iqbal' " (2009: xxiii). In addition, Iqbal is held in great importance among Muslims and non-Muslims in India, where a substantial portion of the Muslims of the subcontinent still reside.

5. See Connolly 2008 for a demonstration of resonance as a means to interrelate two objects of study, in his case, Christianity and capitalism in the United States.

6. The shadow of the "Hindu" upon Muslim thought and practice in colonial India and present-day Pakistan has yet to be sensitively studied. For the colonial period Faisal Devji (2009) provides a subtle but preliminary examination of the ways in which

Iqbal treated the figure of the Hindu in his poetry. Refusing to see "Hindu" or "Muslim" as categories of political representation, he presented them as two elements held together by what Iqbal called "invisible relations" that defied representation. For postcolonial Pakistan, Aamir Mufti (2004) draws out the presence of India and the Partition of 1947 in Faiz Ahmed Faiz's lyric poetry, particularly in the ways in which Faiz affects a poetics of the division of the self. One gets a powerful sense of the Muslim as a feared figure, the object of hatred, in the recent essay by Deepak Mehta (2010) on Hindu-Muslim hate discourse in Bombay in the 1920s, which is reiterated in contemporary political discourse of the Shiv Sena in Bombay. See Das 2010 for a close examination of how Hindu-Muslim difference and the work of translation are folded into everyday discourse in a poor working-class neighborhood in present-day Delhi.

7. The three eras of Islamic history most often telescoped in these two poems were those of pre-Islamic paganism, the period of Muslim rule in India amidst polytheists, and the era of modernity. Iqbal often writes as if the middle period provided Muslims, specifically Indian Muslims, with a keener appreciation than other Muslims of what the Prophet Muhammad had to struggle against in the earliest days of Islam. Similarly, it was the middle period that provided the figurations by which to apprehend and critique modernity as an era productive of new idolatries.

8. While I will indicate Iqbal's and Pakistan's changing relationship to the Prophet in this book, I list here a few general works on the veneration of the Prophet within Islam. See, for example, Carlyle 2007, the famous vitalist account of Muhammad for nineteenth-century England; Schimmel 1985 for a detailed exposition on contemporary forms of veneration of Muhammad; Brown 1996 for a historical overview of the nineteenth- and twentieth-century intellectual and theological struggles in Egypt and Pakistan to establish the meaning and scope of prophetic authority within Islam; and Waugh 1983 for a detailed examination of the various representations of the Prophet Muhammad in Iqbal's writings.

9. *The Reconstruction of Religious Thought in Islam* includes six lectures that Iqbal delivered in the late 1920s that were published in one volume in 1930. As they share similar concepts, lines of analysis, and scholarly references I have treated the work as a unit.

10. See Woodfield 1973 and Mayr 1992 for useful overviews of current understandings of teleology, religious, cultural, and scientific, although their focus is largely on the influence of metaphysical understandings of teleology upon science, specifically Darwinian biology.

11. In Woodfield's helpful formulation, it was a matter of finding the balance between purposive teleology, located in the self-striving of the species, and the teleology of final causes and ends (1973).

12. While attending one of the Round Table meetings in London, Iqbal traveled to Paris to meet an aged Bergson, to whom he showed the relevant passages from the Qur'an and hadis on divinity as time (Schimmel 1989).

13. Gilles Deleuze's *Bergsonism* (1990) and *Cinema I* (1986) have revitalized the field of Bergson studies. See Grosz 2004 for a detailed account of Bergson's position on evolution in comparison to Charles Darwin's. Scott Lash (2006) provides a brief account of the uses and abuses of vitalist philosophy in twentieth-century European politics, while Markus Daechsul (2006) does so for a Muslim politician of the same period as Iqbal, Inayatullah Khan Al-Mashriqi.

14. See Massumi's introduction to *Parables for the Virtual: Movement, Affect, Sensation* (2002) for a useful discussion on the difference between "potential" and the "possible." In brief, the term "possible" captures a pathway already determined although as yet unactualized, while "potential" speaks to the as-yet-undetermined flux out of which anything may emerge.

15. Although interested and influenced by Sufism (Hyder 2005), Iqbal could not entirely accept the idea of the annihilation of the self in the divine (Schimmel 1989, Majeed 2007, Devji 2009). Instead, he recast the Sufi perspective in the following manner: "In the higher Sufism of Islam, intuitive experience is not the finite ego effacing its own identity by some sort of absorption into the Infinite Ego; it is rather the Infinite passing into the loving embrace of the finite" (1996: 98).

16. The Nietzschean underpinnings of this formulation of striving, insofar as Iqbal sometimes spoke of striving to produce the perfect man, has been commented upon by numerous scholars (Malik 1971, Hassan 1977, Schimmel 1989, Jalal 2010). I will address Iqbal's relation to Nietzsche in chapter 6.

17. Insofar as Muhammad Iqbal and Gilles Deleuze share a deep engagement with Henri Bergson, it may be possible to liken the unique individual that Iqbal speaks of to the concept of the singularity within Deleuze. See Delueze and Guattari 1987 and Deleuze 1990. Can one then think of God's field of potential, those that exist within oneself as potential selves, as presubjective singularities? I try to pursue this line of thought in N. Khan 2006.

18. In "Asceticism and Eroticism in Gandhi, Thoreau and Nietzsche," Bhrigupati Singh draws the lineaments of such thinking in the works of Gandhi, Thoreau, and Nietzsche, all of whom were intellectually related or relatable to Iqbal. Therefore, it is useful to consider his description as holding true for Iqbal: "The kind of method in evidence here, as distinct from a mainstream of philosophy, is non-dialectical. The salience of this qualification will become clearer over time . . . as a requirement to engage Thoreau and Nietzsche, crucial to whose respective methods is a *bipolar* tendency, where two opposed propositions coexist and remain equally valid. . . . Differences between the key figures of this essay, Gandhi, Thoreau and Nietzsche will not necessarily appear as contradictions or negations. Rather, these are variable coordinates and poles, occasionally antagonistic, at other times mutually animating, sometimes gesturing simply to a difference in degree or in kind. As these differences are further sharpened, they will not be resolved in a 'higher' synthesis that overcomes the opposition. . . . Instead of a synthesis, we seek to map a *continuum* of variables, differences of degrees and of kind, along which experimentation takes place, that keeps us, and these figures, both joined and separate" (2010: 4–5).

19. While I borrow the term "intercalation" from Connolly 2008, Faisal Devji provides a nice description of this mode of interrelating different regions of time and space within Iqbal's writings: "The book Iqbal imagined writing was meant not to represent Muslim thought as something external, but rather to make it available to the West as thought in a purely internal sense. It was this translation of difference into thought that made the whole world kin, and it did so by depriving difference of all its alien particularity, historical and ethnographic, so that it might be apprehended without the mediation of the Hegelian universal. Thought in Iqbal's sense moves beyond an order of representation to one, let us say, of conversations since it takes the form of kinship. Indeed for Iqbal the university itself was a collection of subjects engaged in an infinite conversation—this being the only way in which it could have meaning for ethical life" (2009: 249–50).

20. As my effort is to make clear Iqbal's thinking in relation to thinkers of his time, I do not do sufficient justice to these thinkers in their own rights. For an account of Sir Sayyid Ahmed Khan's life see McDonough 1970 and Lelyveld 1996. See Aziz Ahmed for the intellectual climate of which Sir Sayyid was a part (1967). Daniel Brown provides an account of the widespread influence of Sir Sayyid's thought on the issue of prophetic authority (1996). Faisal Devji's 1993 unpublished dissertation is unparalleled in mapping the intellectual agon that Sir Sayyid and those like him created. For an account of Maulana Ashraf Ali Thanawi's life, see Metcalf 1997 and Zaman 2008. Metcalf's history of the Dar-ul Uloom, Deoband within the context of colonial India and other reformist movements helps locate Thanawi within his time (1987b). Muhammad Qasim Zaman (2008) and Seyyid Vali Nasr (2000) provide useful insights on how Thanawi's legacy endures in Pakistan.

21. See Talal Asad's "The Construction of Religion as an Anthropological Category" in his *Genealogies of Religion* (1993) for the emergence of "natural religion."

22. Although I would speculate that Iqbal would fault Sir Sayyid for an overly mechanistic picture of nature, insofar as it was informed by laws: "The same is true of the law of nature, upon which this universe is made. The former is the verbal promise, while the law of nature is procedural (operational) promise. Much of this law of nature God has told us and some of it man has not discovered much. . . . But whatever is discovered is undoubtedly the operational promise of God, the infringement of which is equal to the infringement of verbal promise and cannot happen" (Sayyid Ahmed Khan in Ahmed and von Grunebaum 2004: 29).

23. More specifically, *hakim* refers to a doctor of *tibb* (Islamic school of medicine).

24. See also Maududi's *Sick Nations of the Modern Age*. As B. Singh (2010) notes, the theme of sickness produced by modern civilization runs through the writings of Gandhi, Thoreau, and Nietzsche as well. However, each thinker diagnoses and attempts to treat sickness differently and the difference is crucial.

25. This text was translated into English in Pakistan by Muhammad Hasan Rizvi Askari, a famous Urdu literary critic and short story writer, whose attachment to Islam led him to disavow his earlier secularist orientation. See A. Mufti 2008 for an interesting analysis of Askari's religious self-positioning.

26. This quotation is from Sayyid Ahmed Khan's "Principles of Exegesis."

27. Ultimately Iqbal had this to say in relation to the *ulama*: "Their leading idea was social order, and there is no doubt that they were partly right, because organization does to a certain extent counteract the forces of decay. But they did not see, and our modern ulema do not see, that the ultimate fate of a people does not depend so much on organization as on the worth and power of individual men" (1986: 146). In other words, while the ulama were right to insist upon order, discipline and piety to protect the Muslim community from fragmentation, and to insist upon the transcendence and inscrutability of the divine realm to protect it from secularization, they were not able to acknowledge the force of striving and mutual attraction that continually brought together the two realms that they sought to separately protect.

28. Iqbal certainly did not affirm everyone. His dislike for Platonic thought and Ghazzali's skepticism was clear and he didn't appear to draw on those modes of thinking. See Majeed (2009 for Iqbal's Hellenisim.

29. There is currently a revival of interest in Muhammad Asad in Pakistan, as evidenced by the republication of his works by the Truth Society. See Abbas 2010 for a description of Imran Khan's reconversion to Islam through the mediation of texts by Muhammad Asad. Other influential books by Muhammad Asad of related interest but beyond the scope of this chapter include *The Road to Mecca* (1980) and *The Principles of State and Government in Islam* (1981).

30. Seyyid Vali Nasr (1994, 1996) provides a detailed account of Maududi's intellectual formation and political activism, in addition to giving us the history of his political party Jama'at-e Islami, which is currently active in politics in Pakistan, India, and Bangladesh. The writings on and by Abul ala Maududi are quite extensive. See Ahmad 1967, Adams 1983, I. Ahmed 1987, and Brown 1996.

CHAPTER THREE *Inheriting Iqbal*

1. See Binder 1960 for an overview of the ulama who supported the Pakistan movement, in which Maulana Shabbir Ahmad Usmani was very prominent.

2. See A. Mufti 2007 for a detailed exposition of his claim that Muslim politics in colonial India bears the legacy of the Jewish question in modern Europe.

3. See Asad A. Ahmed (2009, 2010) for a different reading of the Munir Report and the legal judgments discussed in this chapter. In his view this report is the product of a particular liberal working of the law for which all theological issues are translated into concepts intrinsic to such law to be adjudicated. Moreover, he makes the claim that the transformation of Ahmadis from Muslims to apostates could only have been undertaken under the rubric of this law, in other words, the state did not need some imagined form of Islamic law. His reading of the Munir Report and similar judgments departs from mine insofar as I am not as concerned to excavate the structure and logic of the law in which these shifting positions toward the Ahmadi are recorded. I am more interested in how the law imagines and attempts to effect change within the horizon of everyday life in which Ahmadis live alongside Muslims. Moreover, I consider the Munir Report and related judgments to be public documents because they travel outside of the register of the law to become part of the lay Pakistani imagination of formative texts that constitute their history and society.

4. I rely on Izutsu 2002 for my understanding of *kufr* as disbelief in a negative sense, the opposite of *iman* (belief), with kafir (pl. kuffar) referring to one who disbelieves. Also see Friedmann 2003b for a classification of unbelievers within Islam.

5. However, it should not surprise us that the ulama did not have a single definition of who or what is a Muslim, that is, "irreducible minimum conditions which a person must satisfy to be entitled to be called a Muslim and that the definition was to be on the principle on which a term in grammar is defined," as demanded by the Munir Report. There is no agreement of opinions on who is a Muslim; instead it is an agreement to a form of life (see Das 1998, N. Khan 2009).

6. This excerpt from the Pakistan Penal Code (Act XLV of 1860), as amended, can be found at www.pakistani.org/pakistan/legislation/1860/actXLVof1860.html#f110.

7. See Coombe 1998 for an anthropological account of how intellectual property law inflects everyday life and notions of cultural production in the United States. Also see Stewart 1991 for how Western law has historically attempted to contain crimes relating to the forgery of literary texts.

8. Because the discussion on toleration is vast and beyond the scope and interest of this book, and the term itself would be colloquially called "loaded," I will just list the texts I used in framing my knowledge of the issue: Heyd 1996 gives a broad philosophical overview of the tension between refraining from judgment in the face of wrongful beliefs and practices and intervention in reconstituting the subjects of these beliefs and practices; Friedmann 2003b and Sachedina 2001 provide an overview of how the issue of tolerance has been posed within Islamic studies in relation to Islam, Muslim states, and societies; Hayden 2002 discusses the way that the concept of tolerance has been used in contemporary anthropology to emphasize the grittiness of lives lived together rather than their harmonious coexistence.

CHAPTER FOUR *The Singularity of Aspiration*

1. Let me just say at the outset that I was not surprised at the claimed existence of jinns. I had been told of alternative worlds to the human one and of the material and spiritual negotiations that humans entered into with the inhabitants of these worlds. What shocked me was that I had understood Farooq sahib's family to accept only 'ibadat (worship) as the legitimate way to approach God, having heard only their derision of other intercessionary modes in the two years I had known them. Yet here I was, on the last leg of my research, learning that they had once had jinns in their possession.

2. Even the Mutazilates, early Muslim materialists, dared not discount the existence of jinns, although on the few occasions they spoke of them they referred to jinns as uncivilized tribes inhabiting the world (El-Zein 1996). Sayyid Ahmed Khan considered jinns a natural phenomenon for which rational explanation could be sought; jinns were of the order of the supernatural that he attempted to excise.

3. Rosalind Morris (2000) and Emilio Spadola (2008) have suggested that people may seek out jinns not only for the powers traditionally associated with them but also for new, uninvestigated capacities, such as that of communication and transmission within the realm of politics and politicians. In other words, this new use of the jinn is an instance of how a tradition is recast in line with emergent needs and new technological and political realities.

4. As a young boy Adeeb had seen the Prophet Muhammad twice in his dreams. According to the tenets of dream interpretation within Islam, one cannot be deluded about seeing the Prophet in one's dreams because Iblis/Satan cannot take the Prophet's form. Adeeb's piety was both a source of pride and tension within the family, as we will see. It was also the reason why the jinns associated with him were seen to be particularly efficacious.

5. To highlight the unusual nature of Maryam's relationship with the jinns, it is necessary to sketch a field of the documented states of possession in the literature on jinns and other spirits in Muslim societies. The reader should be warned that this is a very rough sketch. Some commentators speak of possession as one of any number of somatic illnesses or psychic effects of mysterious origins, and of the person possessed as a "victim" (Siegel 1969, Bowen 1993). For instance, under the description of demonical possession in Jaffur Shurreef's *Qanoon-e Islam*, a nineteenth-century text, the author writes that the symptoms of this state are as follows: "Some are struck dumb; others shake their heads; others grow mad and walk about naked; they feel no inclination to pursue their usual avocations; but lie down and are inactive" (1832: 218). However, it was believed that this state is temporary, eased by the interventions of healer-magicians ('amils), or in the last resort by medical experts (Pandolfo 2000). On the other hand, one may be permanently possessed, as in the case of Tuhami in Vincent Crapanzano's ethnography by that name (1980). He was enslaved by a female jinn by the name of Aisha Qandisha and could not easily shake off his state of enslavement. In these instances we have a picture of possession that comes from outside the self and over which the self appears to exert little control. The state of possession may be better described as the dispossession of one's self. In the case of possessed healer-magicians, the state of possession is much more of their own doing. Such persons may have jinns or related spirits in their possession and it is a matter

of undertaking the correct discipline and ritual activity to presence this jinn. Although one would not strictly call this state one of possession as described by Shurreef, possessed healer-magicians do leave themselves vulnerable to the jinn's intrusion into their body or mind or they may even encourage such an intrusion to facilitate communication and negotiations with the spirit in question (Shurreef 1832, Siegel 1969, Bowen 1993). In this picture the self maintains some control over the scene of possession. There are instances in which the healer-magician may utilize a child to summon or communicate with the spiritual being. However, the child is only seen as a conduit for the jinns being thoroughly guided in this process by the healer-magician. In other words, the subjectivity of the child is never brought into focus although of course the child must meet the objective criteria for being a medium and be known to be effective as one. With these few, granted impoverished, pictures of possession, let me turn to Maryam's relation to the jinns. She could not be called possessed either in Shurreef's or in Crapanzano's sense. In other words, the control over possession did not lie outside of her. Nor was she a trained healer-magician able to control the scene of possession. Rather, unguided by any healer-magician, she summoned the jinn on her own volition and participated in or commented on his sociality as a matter of course. In the literature on jinns, there is a category of spirit called qarin or qarina which is the evil double of the individual, born with that person and staying with him or her throughout that person's life (see Zwemer 1939). I have also heard references to children having hamzards (familiars) who do not appear innately evil as in the case of the qarin or qarina but, as we know in the case of Maryam, the jinns were given to her family and therefore cannot be grouped under these other categories. Later in the chapter, I speculate what manner of relation Maryam bore to the jinns and what it said about Maryam, her family, and her milieu, but for now I simply want to make a note of the unusualness of the arrangement before us.

6. In the following story quoted by El-Zein (1996) we have reference to a sahaba jinn: Shibli said: "Some people left for Mecca. They lost their way and felt that they were about to die, so they put on their shrouds and lay down waiting for death to come. Then a jinni came from the trees and said: 'I am one of the jinn who listened to the Prophet. I heard him saying: "The believer is like a brother to the believer. He is his eye and his guide and never forsake him." This is the water and this is the way.' Then he guided them to the water and showed them the way" (313).

7. While I have changed the names of all my subjects in this book, I have left the original name of the favored jinn. This is because I want to draw attention to the significance of the name Sulayman to the history of jinns. In the Qur'an, Sulayman is mentioned as the prophet and the king to whom God gave the power to discourse with animals and jinns, whose powers Sulayman in turn harnessed to construct the Temple named after him. In Sura Saba it is elaborated that the jinns continued to build the Temple after King Sulayman died and only realized that he was dead when the staff upon which his body had been leaned crumbled, having being eaten by termites, and

the body fell over. In *Muhammad and the Golden Bough* (1996), Jaroslav Stetkevych writes that the mythopoetic registers of the Qur'an have been neglected within the field of Islamic studies. One could make a similar argument for the mythopoetic registers of everyday life within Muslim societies. As a corrective, it may be speculated how Sulayman the jinn introduced a mythic moment in the Islamic tradition in which man, beasts and jinns lived in close communication and cooperation within a present in which prophets, kings, and caliphs are activated to express difference and dissonance among men. Veena Das has made the interesting argument that children take "frequent recourse to the mythic" in making sense of their often violently changing social reality (1989: 288). This leads me to speculate further upon the (unintended?) agency of Maryam in mediating King Sulayman's claim upon this violent present, as a different modality of living with difference.

8. Although the Ahl-e Hadis family in Momin Town that I discussed in chapter 1 routinely disparaged their neighbors' reliance upon 'amils, they were themselves very close to a self-professed Ahl-e Hadis 'amil who went by the name of Baba. Although he traveled widely, visiting people afflicted by illnesses and spells at their own homes, an Ahl-e Hadis mosque was known to be his favorite place of worship and for the dispensation of advice and medicine.

9. In contrast to these continuous efforts at pious emulation characterizing the Sunni masalik, the 1954 Constituent Assembly members discussed in chapter 3 were not intent on such emulation. Rather, through their citation of the Prophet's era and example, they were attempting to produce a resonance between their moment and the Prophet's own, investing the present with the drama and authority of earlier events. Earlier I showed how ambivalent Iqbal was toward Muslim efforts at self-transfiguration explicitly modeled upon the Prophet's own trajectory. There is a suggestion in Iqbal's writings that, given all the wrongful ways of relating to the Prophet, one must strive to model oneself upon the Prophet but to do so in silence so as not to contribute to discord and fragmentation. Moreover, his poetry suggests that it was not the earlier era of jahiliyya (ignorance) that gave poignancy to the present, but rather the historical experience of being Muslim in India that enhanced one's understanding of the Prophet's era and struggle. One begins to see how difficult it is to secure any one mode, given these varied modes of relating to the Prophet. See Waugh 1983, Schimmel 1985, and Brown 1996 for reviews of the different representations and relations to the Prophet.

10. See Das 1970 and Alavi 1972 for detailed accounts of Punjabi kinship. Note that this family was a mixed Indian *muhajir* (refugee)-Punjabi family.

11. South Asian Sunnis of the Deobandi and Barelwi paths do *taqlid* (imitation) of fiqh-e Hanafiya, one of the four major schools of Islamic jurisprudence. However the Ahl-e Hadis support only the Qur'an and the hadis as legitimate textual sources for guidance and advocate an esoteric blend of all four schools in the making of legal opinions. See J. Anderson 1959, Schacht 1964, and Coulson 1969 for an introduction to the four fields of Islamic jurisprudence in the modern world; see Metcalf 1982,

Sanyal 1996, Brown 1996 and Fyzee 1999 for the specificities of conflicts over fiqh-e Hanafiya among Sunnis in South Asia.

12. It is said that jinns are creatures of "smokeless fire," that is, they do not have a fixed form. However, if they show themselves in one particular form to humans, they remain in that form as long as those very same humans' eyes are fixed upon them. The only way they can change forms is if they can trick the humans into looking at a copy of them, which then frees them to take another form or to escape into formlessness (El-Zein 1996). This suggests something of the coercive force humans may exert upon jinns, fixing them to a form when they may wish to be other. In this instance, however, the jinns left Farooq sahib's family after the men were forced to dance the traditional *bhangra* dance at a cousin's wedding. The jinns condemned this as immoral behavior, which they did not wish to condone by remaining with the family. See Rothenberg 1998 for another instance of how jinns provide a barometer of everyday morality.

13. Married South Asian women do not normally refer to their husbands by name. However, in this family Rahima would often refer to her husband formally, as Farooq sahib. Moreover, whenever her mother referred to her husband she almost spat out the term "he," suggesting revulsion. This mode of address, combined with the stories Rahima told me of the breakup of her parents' marriage, informs my claim that the mother did not call her husband by a name or formal title because she despised him.

14. Informally a witch, but more specifically the ghost of a woman who has died during childbirth, a very inauspicious and likely vengeful figure.

15. The Ahl-e Hadis 'amil, Baba, with whom I had a brief acquaintanceship, related how he had to track down magicians of note to get their *ijaza* (permission) to use Qur'anic verses for talismanic purposes. Some of the verses were associated with jinn power and he had to undertake chilla (forty days of retreat to undertake austerities) to conquer their forces, to bring them under his possession. He had to carry out many more prayers than the five obligatory ones to continue to maintain his powers over both verses and jinns, which took up most of his days. Nonetheless, despite all his work to possess jinns he was much more comfortable utilizing *muakkals* (a minor form of jinns) to carry out his wishes because he feared jinns and their inherent capacity for evil.

16. The ability of the world to withdraw from one, to stand apart, is among Stanley Cavell's descriptions of the condition of skepticism he sees haunting everyday life (1982, 1988). In this instance, it was Farooq sahib who took a step away from the world, reducing its vivacity for him. In some respects, this gesture aligns with the Islamic injunction that one treat this world as a temporary way station on the path to God. At the same time, Islam condemns asceticism (excessive withdrawal from the world) as strongly as it does excessive attachment to it. Striking this balance is most difficult because it entails keeping up the illusory nature of everyday life, while participating in it. Farooq sahib's turn toward Maryam for guidance was for him, perhaps, an attempt to strike this balance. Taking another place to be more real than this one made everyday life illusory. Yet by making the words from another place have bearing upon his behavior, he also continued his participation within everyday life.

17. See Lambek 1980 for an account of how spirits who possess women strike up friendships or relationships with their spouses, relationships that endure even after the spirit leaves the woman's mind and body, or even in the instances in which the spouses leave the possessed women.

CHAPTER FIVE Skepticism in Public Culture

1. For more on the flourishing popular culture of stereotypes in South Asia, see Mills, Clauss, and Diamond 2003. See Titus 1998 for a detailed account of ethnic stereotypes in Pakistan and the extent to which they capture meaningful differences among communities. Writing about stereotypes in colonial India, Faisal Devji (2009) speculates that these may have been more productive than pernicious because they facilitated relatedness across communal divides, most notably between Hindus and Muslims. Laura Ring (2006) makes a similar argument about ethnic communities living together in new urban settlements in Karachi, Pakistan. However, stereotypes can also appear in rumors, constituting rumors as unfinished stories whose ends are secured by violence; see Das 2006 for this argument.

2. Other terms used by the Pakistani elite to refer to the maulwi and the mulla are beardo or fundo, the first a reference to the wearing of beards and the second a short-hand for the word, fundamentalist.

3. In her helpful overview of writings on the hajj, Barbara Metcalf (1993b) singles out Mumtaz Mufti's Labbaik as an example of a modern genre of writing on the hajj in which the individual, in particular his subjective experiences and spiritual journey, is the subject of exploration.

4. Mumtaz Mufti presented his relationship to Qudratullah Shahab as one of friendship and spiritual guidance. And, as we see in this narrative, he sought out Shahab's advice at different moments over the course of his pilgrimage when he struggled to achieve what he felt must be the pilgrim's focused state of spirituality. Barbara Metcalf (1993b) writes that the blending of personal and spiritual relationships was not uncommon in the history of South Asian Islam. But this relationship was also politically problematic, a fact that Metcalf does not remark upon. Shahab was a high-ranking civil servant in Ayub Khan's administration, with personal relations to the military leader. A respected writer and intellectual, his association with Ayub Khan, who imposed some of the most repressive controls on the media, casts a shadow on his reputation. Mufti falls under the same shadow, because Shahab secured him a government job in broadcasting during the same period, one that Mufti kept till his retirement. However, this relationship—a blend of friendship, spiritual guidance, and possibly nepotism—made Mufti a more interesting diagnostician of his

times than others who maintained a higher moral ground. In the case of the latter, it may be hard to be surprised by what shocked or dismayed them, whereas shock, dismay, or, in Mufti's case, disappointment are all the more pointed because there is an element of accommodation with the powers that be.

5. Metcalf writes that whereas writings on the hajj have tended to be factual accounts to familiarize Muslims with the journey ahead of them, recent writings tend to be more in the nature of dramas, novels, or autobiographies (1990). Yet in a closer analysis of Mufti's pilgrimage narrative in a later piece, Metcalf (1993b) notes that his account lacked dramatic pacing and character development, making it distinct from the modern novel or autobiography. The narrative meanders, simply noting what Mufti senses and feels without allowing these details to accumulate in any meaningful fashion to illuminate Mufti's possibly changing personhood. Mufti provides no background details about himself. He simply presents himself as a "nominal Muslim." There are no transformative moments to suggest a conversion experience. What there is instead is "a deep sense that reality is not limited to what is materially visible or subject to control" (ibid.: 152), an order of reality that assails Mufti in Pakistan and Mecca.

Within the context of Pakistan, "magical events" of the kind that Mufti noted as happening to him may be read as Sufistic experiences. This was how they were explained to me by many lay Muslims and the few ulama who had read and favored Mufti's book. However, some adepts of the Sabri Chisti Sufi order, in conversation with me, denied that Mufti could be said to have had spiritual experiences of the kind associated with Sufism. They saw such claims as undermining the discipline and exercises it took to have genuine encounters with the divine. Rather they saw Mufti's as a one-off experience, a sudden capture of the spiritual energy God continuously directed at humans. "Anyone can have such an experience. To have genuine experiences you have to tune yourself like a radio to receive God's grace." While this statement would seem to reduce the significance of Mufti's experiences, I felt that it releases the experiences from the easy explanation of Sufism, giving me to think that what he was encountering was an order of reality secreted by the ordinary, with surprises and strangeness built into it. This leads me to agree with Metcalf that Mufti went on hajj to seek his roots, which was a paradoxical move since one usually goes on hajj to leave one's nation-bound belonging behind. What he found in Mecca was a landscape of affects distinct to itself, which comprised intense spiritual longing, distrust, skepticism, and physical discomfort, all of which had to be traversed to constitute this as a hajj experience. It also allowed him to see that his own milieu was a landscape of affects of its own that one traversed uncertain of what pockets of doubt one could fall into.

6. When I heard jokes from actual mullas, they tended to emphasize, in a sympathetic fashion, mulla naiveté about the modern world. Consider the following: A young mulla, recently married, was asked by his new wife to buy her a bra. He went off to the relevant shop in the market and asked for a bra for his wife. The shopkeeper

inquired what size bra the mulla wished to buy. Perplexed by how to approximate the size of his wife's breasts, the mulla offered the shopkeeper his cap. This very inappropriate equation of a woman's breasts to a pious head covering was both a sign of the mulla's simplicity and his eagerness to trade in his distinctive marker for recognition from modern society.

7. I draw on Sigmund Freud's classic *Jokes and Their Relation to the Unconscious* (1991) in analyzing the jokes I heard. In it Freud argues that jokes, complexly constituted in a manner similar to dreams, aim at aggression or exposure. He put jokes on religious issues firmly in the latter category: "The joke . . . is pointing to a problem and is making use of the uncertainty of one of our commonest concepts. . . . What they are attacking is not a person or an institution but the certainty of our knowledge itself, one of our speculative possessions" (161). While care has to be taken in using Freud's speculations, as they depend on a complex architecture of concepts and psychical processes, I quote him simply to flag that he takes note of an element of jokes that interests me, which is that they have the capacity to undermine certainty of knowledge or to give expression to such uncertainty.

8. Stewart (1982) provides a very useful list of features within horror stories specific to the American context. Among those I recognize in the stories I heard are the ability of the story to amplify the original events, the emphasis on the hidden sign or hand, and the role of the audience as victim. I was particularly interested in the sense of the uncanny that infused the tales I came across. Freud (2003) argues that it is not the unfamiliar that produces the sensation of the uncanny but rather the return of the familiar. Cavell, in his reading of Freud in "The Uncanniness of the Ordinary" (1988), agrees with Freud that it is the return of the familiar, but he claims that it is not in the form of a childhood repression as Freud claims. His reading of *The Sandman* leads him to argue that it is the sharpened focus on the ordinary that horrifies by its sheer ordinariness.

9. In "Cartoons and Monuments" (1990), Anderson writes that as a late art form, the cartoon is ideal for a formal analysis in which every line, the play of light and darkness, and use of imagery all signify. Consequently, cartoons bear the signature of their creators much more visibly than the joke or story and, if they are political cartoons, may be analysed using the biography and historical period of their creators. Anderson, in his analysis of two Indonesian political cartoonists, writes of one that he depicts "vulnerabilities and complicities," such that "gossip has become form" (171). I also find noteworthy Anderson's observation that in the cartons he studied, there are never any foreigners, despite the frequent presence of foreigners in Indonesia. The explanation he provides is that "the foreigner makes no difference. Including them in the world of cartoons would not change its character, but merely extend it farther into space" (192). His observations serve as useful contrast to the cartoons I examine, in which there was an erasure of ordinary vulnerabilities and complicities, and a focus entirely on the national or international stage on which foreigners were usually depicted.

1. See Kaufman 1974 for an early careful working out of these concepts. This early analysis of Nietzsche effectively rescues him from the association with Nazism that Nietzsche's sister, an active supporter of Hitler and his official legatee, had fostered. Deleuze's work on Nietzsche (1983) has also helped mitigate his reputation as an extremist thinker.

2. See Grosz 2004 for a comparison of Bergson's and Nietzsche's understanding of evolution against Charles Darwin's.

3. For further background on Urdu literature see Zaidi 1993, Qureshi (1996, and the introduction by Muhammad Umar Memon to the edited collection of Urdu short stories titled *The Color of Nothingness* (1998).

4. The Tablighi Jama'at is a very influential movement dating from the early twentieth century, in which many in Pakistan from diverse class backgrounds participate. Adeeb was closely associated with it. See Masud 2000 for an overview. What about this young boy would strike Mufti as a visage of death? Is this simply an automatic reaction of the secular elite to an overtly pious visage?

5. In this I see Mufti to be a marked contrast to Faiz Ahmed Faiz, an eminent Pakistani poet, whose reputation is perhaps second only to Iqbal in Pakistan. In "A Lyric History of India" (2004) Mufti describes Faiz's position as one of self-exile, because, as Mufti claims, Faiz was emboldened to critique Pakistan while residing in Pakistan, from a self-imposed outsider position. His critique was of the nature of what Mufti calls "postcolonial secularism." In contrast, Mufti's position was that of an insider. In chapter 5 I described his insider location by showing Mufti's problematic relationship to Qudratullah Shahab, his friend and travel companion during his pilgrimage to Mecca. Here I note that Mufti's insider position was marked by his self-conscious location within the imaginary of Muslim Pakistan.

Abbas, Sadia. 2010. "Itineraries of Conversion: Judaic Paths to a Muslim Pakistan." In *Beyond Crisis: Re-evaluating Pakistan*, edited by N. Khan.

Abu-Lughod, Janet. 1987. "The Islamic City: Historic Myth, Islamic Essence and Contemporary Relevance." *International Journal of Middle Eastern Studies* 19: 155–76.

Adams, Charles. 1983. "Mawdudi and the Islamic State." In *Voices of Resurgent Islam*, edited by J. Esposito.

Aga Khan Award for Architecture. 1983. *Architecture and Community: Building in the Islamic World Today*. New York: Aperture.

Agamben, Giorgio. 2000. *Potentialities: Essays in Philosophy*. Stanford: Stanford University Press.

Ahern, Daniel. 1995. *Nietzsche as Cultural Physician*. University Park: Pennsylvania State University Press.

Ahmad, Aziz. 1967. *Islamic Modernism in India and Pakistan, 1857–1964*. London: Institute of International Affairs.

——. 1978. "Activism of the Ulama in Pakistan." In *Scholars, Saints, and Sufis: Muslim Religious Institutions in the Middle East since 1500*, edited by N. Keddie.

Ahmad, Aziz, and Gustave von Grunebaum, eds. 2004. *Muslim Self-Statement in India and Pakistan, 1857–1968*. Lahore: Suhail Academy.

Ahmad, Irfan. 2009. "Genealogy of the Islamic State: Reflections on Maududi's Political Thought and Islamism." *Journal of the Royal Anthropological Institute* (n.s.): S145–S162.

Ahmad, Qeyamuddin. 1966. *The Wahhabi Movement in India*. New Delhi: Munshiram Manoharlal Publishers.

Ahmed, Akbar S. 1988. "The Mulla of Waziristan: Leadership and Islam in a Pakistani District." In *Shari'at and Ambiguity in South Asian Islam*, edited by K. Ewing.

Ahmed, Asad A. 2006. "Adjudicating Muslims: Law, Religion and the State in Colonial India and Post-colonial Pakistan." Ph.D. dissertation, University of Chicago.

———. 2009. "Advocating a Secular Pakistan: The Munir Report of 1954." In *Islam in South Asia in Practice*, edited by B. Metcalf.

———. 2010. "From Muslim to Apostates: The Legal Construction of Muslim Identity and Ahmadi Difference." In *Beyond Crisis: Re-evaluating Pakistan*, edited by N. Khan.

Ahmed, Ishtiaq. 1987. *The Concept of an Islamic State: An Analysis of the Ideological Controversy in Pakistan*. New York: St. Martins Press.

Ahmed, Mumtaz. 1998. "Revivalism, Islamization, Sectarianism and Violence in Pakistan." In *Pakistan 1997*, edited by C. Baxter and C. Kennedy.

Aijaz, Zakir. 1989. *Muslim Children—How to Bring Up?* Karachi: International Islamic Publishers.

Al-Azmeh, Aziz. 1993. *Islams and Modernities*. London: Verso Books.

Al-Ghazali. 1980. *Deliverance from Error. An annotated translation of al-Munqidh min al Dalal and other works of Al-Ghazali*. Translated by Richard Joseph McCarthy. Louisville, KY: Fons Vitae.

———. 1992. *Al-Ghazali on the Ninety-Nine Beautiful Names of God*. Translated by David Burell. New York: Islamic Texts Society.

———. 2000. *The Faith and Practice of Al-Ghazali*. Translated by W. Montgomery Watt. Oxford: Oneworld Publications.

Al-Kaysi, Marwan Ibrahim. 1986. *Morals and Manners in Islam: The Guide to Islamic Adab*. Leicester, U.K.: Islamic Foundation.

Alavi, Hamza. 1972. "Kinship in West Punjab Villages." *Contributions to Indian Sociology* 6 (1): 1–27.

———. 1986. "Ethnicity, Muslim Society, and the Pakistan Ideology." In *Islamic Reassertion in Pakistan: The Application of Islamic Laws in a Modern State*, edited by A. Weiss.

———. 1988. "Pakistan and Islam: Ethnicity and Ideology." In *State and Ideology in the Middle East and Pakistan*, edited by F. Halliday and H. Alavi.

Ali, Mukhtar Ahmad. 2002. *Sectarian Conflict in Pakistan: A Case Study of Jhang*. Colombo: Regional Centre for Strategic Studies.

Althusser, Louis. 1995. "Ideology and Ideological State Apparatuses (Notes towards an Investigation)." In *Mapping Ideology*, edited by S. Žižek.

Ambedkar, B. R. 1940. *Pakistan or the Partition of India*. Bombay: Thackers Publishers.

Amin, Mohammad. 1989. *Islamization of Laws in Pakistan*. Lahore: Sang-e-Meel Publishers.

Anderson, Benedict. 1990. *Language and Power: Exploring Political Cultures in Indonesia*. Ithaca: Cornell University Press.

Anderson, J. N. D. 1959. *Islamic Law in the Modern World*. New York: New York University Press.

Antze, Paul, and Michael Lambek. 1996. *Tense Past: Cultural Essays in Trauma and Memory*. New York: Routledge.

Appadurai, Arjun. 1998. "Dead Certainty: Ethnic Violence in the Era of Globalization." *Development and Change* 29: 905–25.

——. 2003. "Archive and Aspiration." In *Information Is Alive*, edited by J. Brouwer and A. Mulder.

——. 2004. "The Capacity to Aspire." In *Cultural and Public Action*, edited by V. Rao and M. Walton.

Appadurai, Arjun, and Carol Breckenridge. 1988. "Why Public Culture?" *Public Culture Bulletin* 1, no. 1: 5–9.

Ardalan, Nader. 1983. "On Mosque Architecture." In *Architecture and Community: Building in the Islamic World Today*, edited by Aga Khan Award for Architecture.

Arjomand, Said Amir. 1996. "The Crisis of the Imamate and the Institution of Occultation in Twelver Shi'ism: A Sociohistorical Perspective." *International Journal of Middle East Studies* 28, no. 4: 491–515.

Armstrong, Karen. 1993. *Muhammad: A Biography of the Prophet*. New York: Harper Collins Books.

Asad, Muhammad. 1947. *Islam at the Crossroads*. Dalhousie, India: Arafat Publications.

——. 1980. *The Road to Mecca*. Gibraltar: Dar al-Andalus.

——. 1981. *The Principles of State and Government in Islam*. Gibraltar: Dar al-Andalus.

Asad, Talal. 1986. *The Idea of an Anthropology of Islam*. Washington, DC: Center for Contemporary Arab Studies.

——. 1993. *Genealogies of Religion*. Baltimore: Johns Hopkins University Press.

——. 2003. *Formations of the Secular: Christianity, Islam, Modernity*. Stanford: Stanford University Press.

Ashima, Hatsuki, and Armando Salvatore. 2009. "Doubt, Faith and Knowledge: The Reconfiguration of the Intellectual Field in Post-Nasserist Cairo." *Journal of the Royal Anthropological Institute*, n.s.: S41–S56.

Atiyeh, George, ed. 1995. *The Book in the Islamic World: The Written Word and Communication in the Middle East*. Albany: State University of New York Press.

Barber, Karin. 2008. *The Anthropology of Texts, Persons and Publics*. Cambridge: Cambridge University Press.

Bartells, E., and I. de Jong. 2007. "Civil Society on the Move: Four Mosque Organisations in Amsterdam Slotervaart." *Journal for Muslim Minority Affairs* 27, no. 3: 455–72.

Bausani, Alessandro. 1954. "The Concept of Time in the Religious Philosophy of Muhammad Iqbal." *Die Welt des Islams* n.s. 3, nos. 3–4: 158–86.

Baxstrom, Richard. 2008. *Houses in Motion: The Experience of Place and the Problem of Belief in Urban Malaysia*. Stanford: Stanford University Press, 1954.

Baxter, Craig, and Charles Kennedy, eds. 1998. *Pakistan 1997*. New York: Westview Press.

Bergson, Henri. 1965. *The Creative Mind: An Introduction to Metaphysics*. New York: Philosophical Library.

——. 1977. *Two Sources of Religion and Morality*. Notre Dame: University of Notre Dame Press.

——. 1996. *Matter and Memory*. New York: Zone Books.

———. 1998. *Creative Evolution*. New York: Dover Publications.

Binder, Leonard. 1960. *Religion and Politics in Pakistan*. Berkeley: University of California Press.

Bleicher, Josef. 2006. "Bildung." *Theory, Culture, Society* 23: 264–65.

Blom Hansen, Thomas, and Finn Stepputat, eds. 2001. *States of Imagination: Ethnographic Explorations of the Postcolonial State*. Durham: Duke University Press.

Borges, Jorge Luis. 1999. "The Library of Babel." In *Collected Fictions*. New York: Penguin Books.

Bose, Sugata, and Kris Manjapra. 2010. *Cosmopolitan Thought Zones: South Asia and the Global Circulation of Ideas*. New York: Palgrave Macmillan.

Bowen, John R. 1993. *Muslims through Discourse: Religion and Ritual in Gayo Society*. Princeton: Princeton University Press.

Brouwer, Joke, and Arjen Mulder, eds. 2003. *Information Is Alive*. Rotterdam, V2 Publishing/Nai Publishers.

Brown, Daniel. 1996. *Rethinking Tradition in Modern Islamic Thought*. Cambridge: Cambridge University Press.

Buehler, Arthur. 1998. *Sufi Heirs of the Prophet: The Indian Naqshbandiya and the Rise of the Mediating Sufi Shaykh*. Columbia: University of South Carolina Press.

Bulliet, Richard. 1995. *Islam: The View from the Edge*. New York: Columbia University Press.

Burkhardt, Titus. 1996. *An Introduction to Sufi Doctrine*. Lahore: S. Muhammad Ashraf.

Carlyle, Thomas. 2007. *On Heroes, Hero-Worship and the Heroic in History*. Teddington, UK: Echo Library.

Cantacuzino, Sherban, ed. 1985. *Architecture in Continuity: Building in the Islamic World Today*. New York: Aperture.

Cavell, Stanley. 1982. *The Claim of Reason: Wittgenstein, Skepticism, Morality, and Tragedy*. London: Clarendon Press.

———. 1988. *In Quest of the Ordinary: Lines of Skepticism and Romanticism*. Chicago: University of Chicago Press.

———. 1989. "Declining Decline: Wittgenstein as a Philosopher of Culture." In *This New Yet Unapproachable America: Lectures after Emerson after Wittgenstein*. Chicago: University of Chicago.

———. 1990. "The Argument of the Ordinary: Scenes of Instruction in Wittgenstein and in Kripke." In *Conditions Handsome and Unhandsome: The Constitution of Emersonian Perfectionism*. Chicago: University of Chicago Press.

———. 1996. *A Pitch of Philosophy: Autobiographical Exercises*. Cambridge: Harvard University Press.

———. 2003. *Emerson's Transcendental Etudes*. Stanford: Stanford University Press.

———. 2004. *Cities of Words: Pedagogical Letters in the Register of the Moral Life*. Cambridge: Harvard University Press.

———. 2005. *Philosophy the Day after Tomorrow*. Cambridge: Harvard University Press.

Chaghatai, Muhammad I., ed. 2006. *Muhammad Asad: Europe's Gift to Islam.* Vols. 1 and 2. Lahore: Truth Society and Sang-e-Meel Publications.

Chakrabarty, Dipesh. 2007. *Provincializing Europe: Postcolonial Thought and Historical Difference.* Princeton: Princeton University Press.

Chatterjee, Partha. 1993. *The Nation and Its Fragments.* Princeton: Princeton University Press.

——. 1994. "Secularism and Toleration." *Economic and Political Weekly,* July 9, 1768–77.

——. 1998. *Nationalist Thought and the Colonial World: A Derivative Discourse?* Minneapolis: University of Minnesota Press.

——. 2006. *Politics of the Governed: Reflections on Popular Politics in Most of the World.* New York: Columbia University Press.

Chatterjee, Roma, and Deepak Mehta. 2007. *Living with Violence: An Anthropology of Events and Everyday Life.* New Delhi: Routledge.

Choudhury, G. W., ed. 1967. *Documents and Speeches on the Constitution of Pakistan.* Dhaka: Green Book House.

Clark, Janine A. 2004. *Islam, Charity and Activism: Middle Class Networks and Social Welfare in Egypt, Jordan and Yemen.* Bloomington: Indiana University Press.

Cohen, Stephen Philip. 2006. *The Idea of Pakistan.* New Delhi: Oxford University Press.

Cohn, Bernard S. 1996. "Law and the Colonial State." In *Colonialism and Its Forms of Knowledge.* Princeton: Princeton University Press.

Cole, Juan. 1988. *Roots of North Indian Shi'ism in Iran and Iraq: Religion and State in Awadh, 1722–1859.* Berkeley: University of California Press.

Connolly, William E. 1999. *Why I Am Not a Secularist.* Minneapolis: University of Minnesota Press.

——. 2002. *Neuropolitics: Thinking, Culture, Speed.* Minneapolis: University of Minnesota Press.

——. 2005. *Pluralism.* Durham: Duke University Press.

——. 2008. *Capitalism and Christianity, American Style.* Durham: Duke University Press.

Conway, Daniel W. 1995. *Nietzsche and the Political.* London: Routledge.

Cook, David. 2008. *Martyrdom in Islam.* Cambridge: Cambridge University Press.

Coombe, Rosemary. 1998. *The Cultural Life of Intellectual Properties: Authorship, Appropriation and the Law.* Durham: Duke University Press.

Cotran, Eugene C., and Chibli Mallat, eds. 1996. *Yearbook of Islamic and Middle Eastern Law 1994.* Vol. 1. Leiden: Brill Academic Publishers.

Coulson, Noel J. 1969. *Conflicts and Tensions in Islamic Jurisprudence.* Chicago: University of Chicago Press.

Crapanzano, Vincent. 1980. *Tuhami: Portrait of a Moroccan.* Chicago: University of Chicago Press.

——. 2003. *Imaginative Horizons: An Essay in Literary-Philosophical Anthropology.* Chicago: University of Chicago.

Daechsel, Markus. 2006. "Scientism and Its Discontents: The Indo-Muslim 'Fascism' of Inayatullah Khan Al-Mashriqi." *Modern Intellectual History* 3, no. 3: 443–72.

Daniel, E. Valentine. 1996. *Charred Lullabies: Chapters in Anthropology of Violence.* Princeton: Princeton University Press.

Das, Veena. 1970. "Masks and Faces: An Essay on Punjabi Kinship." *Contributions to Indian Sociology* 10, no. 1: 1–30.

———. 1989. "Voices of Children." *Daedalus* (Fall): 263–94.

———. 1998. "Wittgenstein and Anthropology." *Annual Review of Anthropology* 27: 171–95.

———. 2006. *Life and Words: Violence and the Descent into the Ordinary.* Berkeley: University of California Press.

———. 2010. "Moral and Spiritual Striving in the Everyday: To Be a Muslim in Contemporary India." In *Ethical Life in South Asia*, edited by A. Pandian and D. Ali.

Das, Veena, and Deborah Poole, eds. 2004. *Anthropology in the Margins of the State.* Santa Fe: School of American Research Press.

Datta, Pradip Kumar. 1999. *Carving Blocs: Communal Ideology in Early Twentieth Century Bengal.* Delhi: Oxford University Press.

Deeb, Lara. 2006. *An Enchanted Modern: Gender and Public Piety in Shi'i Lebanon.* Princeton: Princeton University Press.

De Certeau, Michel. 1984. *The Practice of Everyday Life.* Berkeley: University of California Press.

Deleuze, Gilles. 1983. *Nietzsche and Philosophy.* New York: Columbia University Press.

———. 1986. *Cinema 1: The Movement-Image.* Minneapolis: University of Minnesota Press.

———. 1990a. *Bergsonism.* New York: Zone Books.

———. 1990b. *The Logic of Sense.* New York: Columbia University Press.

———. 1991. *Masochism: Coldness and Cruelty and Venus in Fur.* New York: Zone Books.

———. 1997. *Essays Critical and Clinical.* Minneapolis: University of Minnesota Press.

Deleuze, Gilles, and Felix Guattari. 1986. *Kafka: Towards a Minor Literature.* Minneapolis: University of Minnesota Press.

———. 1987. *A Thousand Plateaus: Capitalism and Schizophrenia.* Minneapolis: University of Minnesota Press.

———. 1996. *What Is Philosophy?* New York: Columbia University Press.

Deleuze, Gilles, and Claire Parnet. 2002. *Dialogues II.* New York: Columbia University Press.

Denny, Frederick M. 1980. "The Qur'anic Vocabulary of Repentance: Orientations and Attitudes." *Journal of the American Academy of Religion* 47, no. 4: 649–64.

Devji, Faisal. 1991. "Gender and the Politics of Space: The Movement for Women's Reform in Muslim India, 1857–1900." *South Asia.* 14, no. 1: 141–53.

———. 1993. "Muslim Nationalism: Founding Identity in Colonial India." Ph.D. dissertation, University of Chicago.

———. 2001. Introduction. *Cultural Dynamics* 13, no. 3: 259–61.

———. 2001. "Imitatio Muhammadi: Khomeini and the Mystery of Citizenship." *Cultural Dynamics* 13, no. 3: 363–71.

———. 2005a. *Landscapes of the Jihad: Militancy, Morality, Modernity.* Ithaca: Cornell University Press.

——. 2005b. "A Practice of Prejudice: Gandhi's Politics of Friendship." In *Subaltern Studies* 12. edited by S. Mayaram, M. Pandian, and A. Skaria.

——. 2007. "Apologetic Modernity." *Modern Intellectual History* 4, no. 1: 61–76.

——. 2008. *The Terrorist in Search of Humanity: Militant Islam and Global Politics.* New York: Columbia University Press.

——. 2009. "Illiberal Islam." In *Enchantments of Modernity: Empire, Nation, Globalization,* edited by S. Dube.

De Vries, Hent. 2006. "Introduction." In *Political Theologies: Public Religions in a Post-Secular World.* edited by H. de Vries and L. Sullivan.

De Vries, Hent, and Lawrence Sullivan, eds. 2006. *Political Theologies: Public Religions in a Post-Secular World.* New York: Fordham University Press.

Diagne, Souleyman B. 2004. "Islam and Philosophy: Lessons from an Encounter." *Diogenes* 51, no. 2: 123–28.

——. n.d. "Islam and Open Society: Fidelity and Movement in the Philosophy of Muhammad Iqbal." Manuscript.

Dirks, Nicholas, ed. 1998. *In Near Ruins: Cultural Theory at the End of the Century.* Minneapolis: University of Minnesota Press.

——. 2001. *Castes of Mind: Colonialism and the Making of Modern India.* Princeton: Princeton University Press.

Donohue, John J., and John L. Esposito, eds. 2007. *Islam in Transition: Muslim Perspectives.* New York: Oxford University Press.

Dresch, Paul, and Bernard Haykel. 1995. "Stereotypes and Political Styles: Islamists and Tribesfolk in Yemen." *International Journal of Middle East Studies* 27: 405–31.

Dube, Saurabh, ed. 2009. *Enchantments of Modernity: Empire, Nation, Globalization.* Delhi: Routledge India.

Dumm, Thomas L. 1999. *A Politics of the Ordinary.* New York: New York University Press.

Dwyer, Rachel, and Divia Patel. 2002. *Cinema India: The Visual Culture of Hindi Film.* Piscataway, N.J.: Rutgers University Press.

Eaton, Richard. 2000. "Temple Desecration and Indo-Muslim States." In *Essays on Islam and Indian History.* New Delhi: Oxford University Press.

Eickelman, Dale. 1995. "Mass Higher Education and the Religious Imagination in Contemporary Arab Societies." In *The Book in the Islamic World: The Written Word and Communication in the Middle East,* edited by G. Atiyeh. Albany: State University of New York Press.

Eickelman, Dale, and James Piscatori, eds. 1990. *Muslim Travellers: Pilgrimage, Migration, and the Religious Imagination* . Berkeley: University of California Press.

Eickelman, Dale, and James Piscatori, 1996. *Muslim Politics.* Princeton: Princeton University Press.

Eickelman, Dale and Jon W. Anderson, eds. 2003. *New Media in the Muslim World: The Emerging Public Sphere.* Bloomington: University of Indiana Press.

El-Moudden, Abderrahmane. 1990. "The Ambivalence of *Rihla*: Community Integration and Self-Definition in Moroccan Travel Accounts, 1300–1800." In *Muslim Travellers*, edited by D. Eickelman and J. Piscatori.

El-Zein, Amira. 1996. "The Evolution of the Concept of the Jinn from Pre-Islam to Islam." Ph.D. dissertation, Georgetown University.

Encyclopedia of Islam. 2003. CD-ROM. Leiden: Brill Publishers.

Ernst, Carl W. 1995. *Words of Ecstasy in Sufism*. Albany: State University of New York Press.

Esposito, John, ed. 1983. *Voices of Resurgent Islam*. New York: Oxford University Press.

Ewing, Katherine P. 1983. "The Politics of Sufism: Redefining the Saints of Islam." *Journal of Asian Studies* 42, no. 2: 251–68.

——, ed. 1988. *Shariat and Ambiguity in South Asian Islam*. Berkeley: University of California Press.

——. 1990a. "The Dream of Spiritual Initiation and the Organization of Self-Representations among Pakistani Sufis." *American Ethnologist* 17, no. 1: 56–74.

——. 1990b. "The Illusion of Wholeness: Culture, Self, and the Experience of Inconsistency." *Ethos* 18, no. 3: 251–78.

——. 1997. *Arguing Sainthood: Modernity, Psychoanalysis, and Islam*. Durham: Duke University Press.

——. 2003. "The Sufi and the Mullah: Islam and Local Culture in Pakistan." In *Pakistan in the Millennium*, edited by C. Kennedy, K. McNeil, C. Ernst, and D. Gilmartin.

Faruqi, Shamsur Rehman. 2005. "How to Read Iqbal." *Annual of Urdu Studies* 5: 1–33.

Faubion, James. 2001. *The Shadows and Lights of Waco: Millennialism Today*. Princeton: Princeton University Press.

Feldman, Herbert. 1972. *From Crisis to Crisis*. London. Oxford University Press.

Fernea, Elizabeth W., ed. 1995. *Children in the Muslim Middle East*. Austin: University of Texas Press.

Fethi, Hasan. 1985. "The Mosque Today." In *Architecture in Continuity: Building in the Islamic World Today*, edited by S. Cantacuzino.

Fischer, Michael M. J., and Mehdi Abedi. 1990. *Debating Muslims: Cultural Dialogues in Postmodernity and Tradition*. Madison: University of Wisconsin Press.

Folkenflik, Robert, ed. 1993. *The Culture of Autobiography: Constructions of Self-Representations*. Stanford: Stanford University Press.

Foucault, Michel. 1988. *The History of Sexuality: The Care of the Self*. New York: Vintage Books.

Fox, Richard. 1985. *Lions of Punjab: Culture in the Making*. Berkeley: University of California Press.

Freitag, Sandra. 1989. *Collective Action and Community: Public Arenas and the Emergence of Communalism in North India*. Berkeley: University of California Press.

——. 1991. Introduction. Special Issue: "Aspect of the 'Public' in Colonial South Asia." *South Asia* 14, no. 1: 1–13.

Freud, Sigmund. 1991. *Jokes and Their Relation to the Unconscious*. London: Penguin Books.

———. 2003. *The Uncanny*. London: Penguin Books.

Friedmann, Yohannes. 2003a. *Prophecy Continuous: Aspects of Ahmadi Religious Thought and Its Medieval Background*. Berkeley: University of California Press.

———. 2003b. *Tolerance and Coercion in Islam: Interfaith Relations in the Muslim Tradition*. Cambridge: Cambridge University Press.

Frishman, Martin, and Hasan-uddin Khan, eds. 2002. *The Mosque: History, Architectural Development and Regional Diversity*. London: Thames and Hudson.

Fyzee, Asaf A. A. 1999. *Outlines of Muhammadan Law*. New Delhi: Oxford University Press.

Gandhi, Leela. 2006. *Affective Communities: Anticolonial Thought, Fin-de-Siècle Radicalism, and the Politics of Friendship*. Durham: Duke University Press.

Geertz, Clifford. 2000. "Thick Description: Towards an Interpretive Theory of Culture." In *The Interpretation of Cultures*. New York: Basic Books.

Gilmartin, David. 1979. "Religious Leadership and the Pakistan Movement in the Punjab." *Modern Asian Studies* 13, no. 3: 485–517.

———. 1988. *Empire and Islam: Punjab and the Making of Pakistan*. Delhi: Oxford University Press.

———. 1991. "Democracy, Nationalism and the Public: A Speculation in Colonial Muslim Politics." Special Issue: "Aspect of the 'Public' in Colonial South Asia." *South Asia* 14, no. 1: 123–40.

———. 1998. "Partition, Pakistan and South Asian History: In Search of a Narrative." *Journal of Asian Studies* 57, no. 4: 1068–95.

Glover, William J. 2008. *Making Lahore Modern: Constructing and Imagining a Colonial City*. Minneapolis: University of Minnesota Press.

Golder, Ben, and Peter Fitzpatrick. 2009. *Foucault's Law*. London: Routledge Cavendish.

Goswami, Manu. 2004. *Producing India: From Colonial Economy to National Space*. Chicago: University of Chicago Press.

Government of Pakistan. 1949. *The Constituent Assembly of Pakistan Debates*. Vol. 5. Karachi: Government of Pakistan Printing Press.

———. 1953. *The Constituent Assembly of Pakistan Debates*. Vol. 15, part 1. Karachi: Government of Pakistan Printing Press.

———. 1954. *Report of the Court of Inquiry constituted under Punjab Act II of 1954 to enquire into the Punjab Disturbances of 1953*. Lahore: Superintendent, Government Printing.

———. 1956. *The Constitution of the Islamic Republic of Pakistan*. Islamabad: Ministry of Law.

———. 1973. *The Constitution of the Islamic Republic of Pakistan*. Islamabad: National Assembly of Pakistan Press.

———. 1982. "Every Challenge of Anti-Islam Forces will be Defeated, All Realms of National Life to be Reformed, Terrorists to be Given Exemplary Punishment," 4th

Session of Federal Council, Inaugural Address, President General Mohammad Zia-ul-Haq. 09 October. Islamabad: Ministry of Information and Broadcasting.

——. 1998. *Pakistan Chronology*. Islamabad: Printing Corporation of Pakistan Press.

Graber, Olag. 2002. "The Role of the Mosque in Islamic Society Today." In *The Mosque: History, Architectural Development and Regional Diversity*, edited by M. Frishman and H. Khan.

Green, Nile. 2003. "The Religious and Cultural Roles of Dreams and Visions in Islam." *Journal of the Royal Asiatic Society* 13, no. 3: 287–313.

Grosz, Elizabeth. 2004. *The Nick of Time: Politics, Evolution, and the Untimely*. Durham: Duke University Press.

Gupta, Akhil. 2002. "Reliving Childhood? The Temporality of Childhood and Narratives of Reincarnation." *Ethnos* 67, no. 1: 33–56.

Guyer, Jane I. 1996. "Traditions of Invention in Equatorial Africa." *African Studies Review* 39, no. 3: 1–28.

——. n.d. "On Poetry and Positivism: 'The Quickening of the Unknown.' " Manuscript.

Hadot, Pierre. 1995. *Philosophy as a Way of Life: Spiritual Exercises from Socrates to Foucault*. Hoboken: Wiley-Blackwell Press.

Halevi, Leor. 2007. *Muhammad's Grave: Death Rites and the Making of Islamic Society*. New York: Columbia University Press.

Hallaq, Wael B., and Donald P. Little, eds. 1991. *Islamic Studies Presented to Charles J. Adams*. Leiden: Brill Academic Publishers.

Halliday, Fred, and Hamza Alavi, eds. 1988. *State and Ideology in the Middle East and Pakistan*. New York: Monthly Review Press.

Haq, Syed M. 1982. *Ideological Basis of Pakistan in Historical Perspective, 711–1940*. Karachi: Pakistan Historical Society and Hamdard Foundation.

Harding, Susan Friend. 1991. "Representing Fundamentalism: The Problem of the Repugnant Cultural Other." *Social Research* 58, no. 2: 373–93.

——. 2001. *The Book of Jerry Falwell: Fundamentalist Language and Politics*. Princeton: Princeton University Press.

Hardy, Peter. 1998. *The Muslims of British India*. New Delhi: Foundation Books.

Hasan, Mushirul. 1994. *Nationalism and Communal Politics in India, 1885–1930*. New Delhi: Manohar Publishers.

Hassan, Riaz. 1985. "Islamization: An Analysis of Religious, Political and Social Change in Pakistan." *Middle Eastern Studies* 21, no. 3: 263–84.

Hassan, Riffat. 1977. *The Sword and the Sceptre: A Collection of Writings on Iqbal, Dealing Mainly with His Life and Poetical Works*. Lahore: Iqbal Academy Pakistan.

Hayden, Robert. 2002. "Antagonistic Tolerance: Competitive Sharing of Religious Sites in South Asia and the Balkans." *Current Anthropology* 43, no. 2: 205–31.

Hefner, Robert. 2000. *Civil Islam*. Princeton: Princeton University Press.

Heyd, David, ed. 1996. *Toleration: An Elusive Virtue*. Princeton: Princeton University Press.

Hillenbrand, Robert. 1985. "The Mosque in the Medieval Islamic World." In *Architecture in Continuity: Building in the Islamic World Today*, edited by S. Cantacuzino.

Hirschkind, Charles. 2006. *The Ethical Soundscape: Cassette Sermons and Islamic Counterpublics*. New York: Columbia University Press.

Hodgson, Marshall G. H. 1977. *The Venture of Islam*. Vols. 1–3. Chicago: University of Chicago Press.

Hoebel, E. Adamson. 1965. "Fundamental Cultural Postulates and Judicial Lawmaking in Pakistan." "Ethnography and Law," special issue of *American Anthropologist* 6, no. 2: 43–56.

The Holy Quran. Medina: King Fahd Holy Qur-an Printing Complex.

Hoodbhoy, Pervez A., and A. H. Nayyar. 1985. "Rewriting the History of Pakistan." In *Islam, Politics and the State: The Pakistan Experience*, edited by M. A. Khan.

Hourani, Albert. 1983. *Arabic Thought in the Liberal Age*. Cambridge: Cambridge University Press.

Hughes, Patrick T. 1885, reprint n.d. *A Dictionary of Islam: A Cyclopaedia of the Doctrines, Rites, Ceremonies, and Customs together with the Technical and Theological Terms of the Muhammadan Religion*. Lahore: Kazi Publications.

Hull, Matthew. 2010. "Uncivil Politics and the Appropriation of Planning in Islamabad." In *Beyond Crisis: Re-evaluating Pakistan*, edited by N. Khan.

Hyder, Syed A. 2001. "Iqbal and Karbala: Re-reading the Episteme of Martyrdom for a Poetics of Appropriation." *Cultural Dynamics* 13, no. 1: 339–62.

Iqbal, Afzal. 1986. *Islamisation of Pakistan*. Lahore: Vanguard Books.

Iqbal, Javid. 1959. *The Ideology of Pakistan and Its Implementation*. Lahore: S. Ghulam Ali and Sons.

——. 1972. *The Ideology of Pakistan*. Lahore: Ferozsons.

Iqbal, Muhammad. 1961. *Stray Reflections: A Note-book of Allama Iqbal*. Lahore: S. Ghulam Ali and Sons.

——. 1966. *Javid Nama*. Translated by Arthur J. Arberry. London: George Allen and Unwin.

——. 1973. *Speeches and Statements of Iqbal*. Edited by A. R. Tariq. Lahore: S. Ghulam Ali and Sons.

——. 1974. *Islam and Ahmadism*. Lucknow: Academy of Islamic Research and Publications.

——. 1977. *Islam as an Ethical and a Political Ideal*. Lahore: Islamic Book Service.

——. 1978. *Secrets of the Self: A Philosophical Poem*. Translated by Reynold Nicholson. Delhi: Arnold-Heinemann.

——. 1986. *The Reconstruction of Religious Thought in Islam*. Lahore: Sang-i-Meel Publications.

——. 1990. *Kuliyat-e Iqbal*. Lahore: Iqbal Academy.

——. 1994. *Shikwa o Jawab-e Shikwa*. Translated by Kushwant Singh. Delhi: Oxford University Press.

———. 1999. *Poems from Iqbal.* Translated by Victor B. Kiernam. Karachi: Oxford University Press.

———.2006. *Allama Iqbal, Selected Poetry: Text, Translation and Transliteration.* Translated by K. C. Kanda. Delhi: New Dawn Press Book.

Ismail, Salwa. 2000. "The Popular Movement Dimensions of Contemporary Militant Islamism: Socio-Spatial Determinants in the Cairo Urban Setting." *Comparative Studies in Society and History* 42, no. 2: 363–93.

Izutsu, Toshihiko. 1980a. *The Concept of Belief in Islamic Theology.* New York: Arno Press.

———. 1980b. *God and Man in the Koran.* Manchester, U.K.: Ayer Company Publishers.

———. 2002. *The Ethico-Religious Concepts in the Quran.* Montreal: McGill-Queen's University Press.

Jackson, Sherman A. 2002. *On the Boundaries of Theological Tolerance in Islam: Abu Hamid al-Ghazali's Faysal al-Tafriqa.* Karachi: Oxford University Press.

Jaffrelot, Christopher. 2002. *Pakistan: Nationalism without a Nation?* New Delhi: Munshiram Manoharlal Publishers.

Jalal, Ayesha. 1981. "Alternatives to Partition: Muslim Politics between the Wars." *Modern Asian Studies* 15, no. 3: 415–54.

———. 1991. *The State of Martial Rule: The Origins of Pakistan's Political Economy of Defence.* Lahore: Vanguard Books.

———. 1994. *The Sole Spokesman: Jinnah, the Muslim League, and the Demand for Pakistan.* Cambridge: Cambridge University Press.

———. 1995. "Conjuring Pakistan: History as Official Imagining." *International Journal of Middle East Studies* 27, no. 1: 73–89.

———. 2000. *Self and Sovereignty: Individual and Community in South Asian Islam since 1850.* Lahore: Sang-e-Meel Publications.

———. 2008. *Partisans of Allah: Jihad in South Asia.* Cambridge: Harvard University Press.

———. 2010. "Iqbal on Nietzsche." In *Cosmopolitan Thought Zones: South Asia and the Global Circulation of Ideas,* edited by S. Bose and K. Manjapra.

James, Allison, and Alan Prout, eds. 1997. *Constructing and Reconstructing Childhood: Contemporary Issues in the Sociological Study of Childhood.* London: Falmer Press.

Jan, Najeeb. 2010. "The Metacolonial State: Pakistan, the Deoband Ulama and the Biopolitics of Islam." Ph.D. dissertation, University of Michigan.

Jan, Tariq, ed. 1998. *Pakistan between Secularism and Islam: Ideology, Issues and Conflict.* Islamabad: Institute of Policy Studies.

Jones, Kenneth W. 1999. *Socio-Religious Reform Movements in British India.* New Delhi: Foundation Books.

Jones, Kenneth W., ed. 1992. *Religious Controversy in British India: Dialogues in South Asian Languages.* Albany: State University of New York Press.

Karim, Fazlul. 1960. *Al-Hadis (Books 1–4): An English Translation of Mishkat ul-Masabih.* New Delhi: Islamic Book Service.

Katz, Marion Holmes. 2002. *Body of Text: The Emergence of the Sunni Law of Ritual Purity.* Albany: State University of New York Press.

Kaufman, Walter. 1974. *Nietzsche: Philosopher, Psychologist, Antichrist*. Princeton: Princeton University Press.

Kaviraj, Sudipta. 1998. *The Unhappy Consciousness: Bankimchandra Chattopadhyay and the Formation of Nationalist Discourse in India*. Delhi: Oxford University Press.

Keddie, Nikkie, ed. 1978. *Scholars, Saints, and Sufis: Muslim Religious Institutions in the Middle East since 1500*. Berkeley: University of California Press.

Kennedy, Charles H. 1989. "Towards the Definition of a Muslim in an Islamic State: The Case of the Ahmediyya in Pakistan." In *Religion and Ethnic Minority Politics in South Asia*, edited by D. Vajpeya and Y. Malik.

——. 1990. "Islamization and Legal Reform in Pakistan, 1979–1989." *Pacific Affairs* 63, no. 1: 62–77.

——. 1992. "Repugnancy to Islam—Who Decides? Islam and Legal Reform in Pakistan." *International and Comparative Law Quarterly* 41: 769–87.

Kennedy, Charles, and Craig Baxter, eds. 2000. *Pakistan 2000*. New York: Lexington Books.

Kennedy, Charles, Kathleen McNeil, Carl Ernst, and David Gilmartin, eds. 2003. *Pakistan in the Millennium*. New York: Oxford University Press.

Khan, Ajmal. 1993. *Islami Mu'ashare men Masjid ka Maqam* [The Position of Mosques in Islamic Society]. Lahore: Maktaba Ishaat-e Islam.

Khan, A. Sattar. 1999. "The Role of the Ulama and Mashaikh in the Pakistan Movement." *The Journal of the Research Society of Pakistan* 36, no. 2: 21–32.

Khan, Hamid. 2004. *Constitutional and Political History of Pakistan*. New York: Oxford University Press.

Khan, Hasan-uddin, and Renata Holod, eds. 1997. *The Mosque and the Modern World: Architects, Patrons and Designs since the 1950s*. London: Thames and Hudson.

Khan, Mohammad Asghar, ed. 1985. *Islam, Politics and the State: The Pakistan Experience*. London: Zed Books.

Khan, Naveeda. 2003. "Grounding Sectarianism: Islamic Ideology and Muslim Everyday Life in Lahore, Pakistan." Ph.D. dissertation, Columbia University.

——. 2005. "Trespasses of the State: Ministering to Theological Dilemmas through the Copyright/Trademark." In *Bare Acts*, Sarai Reader 5, edited by L. Liang.

——. 2006. "Of Children and Jinns: An Inquiry into an Unexpected Friendship in Uncertain Times." *Cultural Anthropology*. Vol. 21, no. 1 (May): 234–64.

——. 2008. "The Martyrdom of Mosques: Imagery and Iconoclasm in Modern Pakistan." In *Enchantments of Modernity: Empire, Nation, Globalization*, edited by S. Dube.

——. 2009. "Maulana Yusuf Ludhianvi on the Limits of Legitimate Religious Differences." In *Islam in South Asia in Practice*, edited by B. Metcalf.

——, ed. 2010. *Beyond Crisis: Re-evaluating Pakistan*. Delhi: Routledge India.

Khan, Sayyid Ahmed. 1970. *The Causes of the Indian Revolt*. Karachi: Oxford University Press.

——. 2004. "Principles of Exegesis." In *Muslim Self-Statement in India and Pakistan 1857–1968*, edited by A. Ahmad and G. von Grunebaum.

——. 2006. *Selected Essays by Sir Sayyid Ahmad Khan*. Lahore: Sang-e-Meel Publications.

——. 2007. "Islam: The Religion of Reason and Nature." In *Islam in Transition: Muslim Perspectives*, edited by J. J. Donohue and J. L. Esposito.

——. n.d. "An Article on Jihad, Published in the Editorial Columns of the *Pioneer* of the 23rd November, 1871." Appendix 7 of *Review on Dr. Hunter's Indian Musalmans: Are They Bound in Conscience to Rebel against the Queen?* Lahore: Premier Book House.

——. n.d. *Review on Dr. Hunter's Indian Musalmans: Are They Bound in Conscience to Rebel against the Queen?* Lahore: Premier Book House.

Khan, Yasmin. 2008. *The Great Partition: The Making of India and Pakistan*. New Haven: Yale University Press.

Koselleck, Reinhart. 2004. *Futures Past: On the Semantics of Historical Time*. Cambridge: MIT Press.

Kozlowski, Gregory. 1985. *Muslim Endowments and Society in British India*. Cambridge: Cambridge University Press.

Krenkow, F. 1912. "The Appearance of the Prophet in Dreams." *Journal of the Royal Asiatic Society*, 77–79.

Kugle, Scott. 2001. "Framed, Blamed and Renamed: The Recasting of Islamic Jurisprudence in Colonial South Asia." *Modern Asian Studies* 35(2): 257–313.

——. 2007. *Sufis and Saints' Bodies: Mysticism, Corporeality and Sacred Power in Islam*. Chapel Hill: University of North Carolina Press.

Kurin, Richard. 1984. "Personhood, Morality and the Exemplary Life: Popular Conceptions of Muslims in Paradise." In *Moral Conduct and Authority: The Place of Adab in South Asian Islam*, edited by B. Metcalf.

——. 1988. "The Culture of Ethnicity in Pakistan." In *Shari'at and Ambiguity in South Asian Islam*, edited by K. Ewing.

Lambek, Michael. 1980. "Spirits and Spouses: Possession as a System of Communication among the Malagasy Speakers of Mayotte." *American Ethnologist* 7, no. 2: 318–31.

Landua, Jacob. 1990. *The Politics of Pan-Islam: Ideology and Organization*. Oxford: Clarendon Press.

Lapidus, Ira. 1976. "Adulthood in Islam." *Daedalus* 105: 93–107.

Lash, Scott. 2006. "Life (Vitalism)." *Theory, Culture, Society* 23: 323–29.

Latour, Bruno. 1993. *We Have Never Been Modern*. Cambridge: Harvard University Press.

Lau, Martin. 1996. "Islam and Fundamental Rights in Pakistan: The Case of Zaheer-ud-din v. The State and its Impact on the Fundamental Right to Freedom of Religion." In *Yearbook of Islamic and Middle Eastern Law 1994*, vol. 1, edited by E. C. Cotran and C. Mallat.

——. 2005. *The Role of Islam in the Legal System of Pakistan*. Leiden: Martinus Nijhoff Publishers.

Lavan, Spencer. 1974. *The Ahmadiyah Movement: A History and Perspective*. New Delhi: Manohar Book Service.

Lazarus-Yafeh, Hava, Mark Cohen, Sasson Somekh, and Sidney H. Griffith. 1999. *The Majlis: Interreligious Encounters in Medieval Islam*. Wiesbaden: Harrassowitz for Libraries.

Lefebvre, Alain. 1999. *Kinship, Honour and Money in Rural Pakistan: Subsistence Economy and the Effects of Internal Migration*. London: Curzon Press.

Lelyveld, David. 1996. *Aligarh's First Generation: Muslim Solidarity in British India*. New Delhi: Oxford University Press.

Lewis, Bernard. 2003. *What Went Wrong? The Clash between Islam and Modernity in the Middle East*. New York: Harper Perennial.

Liang, Lawrence, ed.2005. *Bare Acts*. Sarai Reader 5. New Delhi: Sarai Programme.

Livan, Emmanuel. 1990. *Radical Islam: Medieval Theology and Modern Politics*. New Haven: Yale University Press.

Loughlin, Martin, and Neil Walker, eds. 2007. *The Paradox of Constitutionalism: Constituent Power and Constitutional Form*. New York: Oxford University Press.

Low, Donald A. 1991. *The Political Inheritance of Pakistan*. New York: St. Martin's Press.

Ludhianvi, Maulana Yusuf. 1995. *Ikhtilaf-e Umma aur Sirat-e Mustaqim* [Differences within the community and the right path]. Karachi: Maktaba Ludhianvi.

Mahmood, Saba. 2004. *Politics of Piety: The Islamic Revival and the Feminist Subject*. Princeton: Princeton University Press.

Mahmud, Khalid. 1988. *The Authenticity of Hadith*. Lahore: Dar-ul-Ma'arif.

Majeed, Javed. 2008. *Muhammad Iqbal: Islam, Aesthetics and Postcolonialism*. New Delhi: Routledge.

Makdisi, George. 1981. *The Rise of Colleges: Institution of Learning in Islam and the West*. Edinburgh: Edinburgh University Press.

Makdisi, Ussama S. 2000. *The Culture of Sectarianism: Community, History and Violence in Nineteenth Century Ottoman Lebanon*. Berkeley: University of California Press.

Malik, Charles. 1972. *God and Man in Contemporary Islam*. Beirut: American University Press.

Malik, Hafeez. 1970. "Sir Sayyid Ahmad Khan's Contributions to the Development of Muslim Nationalism in India." *Modern Asian Studies* 4, no. 2: 129–47.

——, ed. 1971. *Iqbal: Poet-Philosopher of Pakistan*. New York: Columbia University Press.

——. 2001. *Pakistan: Founders' Aspirations and Today's Realities*. New York: Oxford University Press.

Malik, Jamal. 1990. "The Luminous Nurani: Charisma and Political Mobilization among the Barelwis in Pakistan." *Social Analysis* 28: 38–50.

——. 1996. *Colonization of Islam: Dissolution of Traditional Institutions in Pakistan*. New Delhi: Munshiram Manoharlal Publishers.

Maluka, Zulfikar K. 1995. *The Myth of Constitutionalism in Pakistan*. Karachi: Oxford University Press.

Marrati, Paola. 2006. "Mysticism and the Foundation of the Open Society: Bergsonian Politics." In *Political Theologies: Public Religions in a Post-Secular World*, edited by H. de Vries and L. Sullivan.

Marsden, Magnus. 2005. *Living Islam: Muslim Religious Experience in Pakistan's North-West Frontier*. Cambridge: Cambridge University Press.

——. 2009. "A Tour Not So Grand: Mobile Muslims in Northern Pakistan." *Journal of the Royal Anthropological Association* n.s.:S57-S75.

Maruf, Mohammad. 1983. "Iqbal's Concept of God: An Appraisal." *Religious Studies* 19, no. 3: 375–83.

Massumi, Brian. 2002. *Parables for the Virtual: Movement, Affect, Sensation*. Durham: Duke University Press.

Masud, Muhammad Khalid. 1975. *Iqbal's Reconstruction of Ijtihad*. Lahore: Iqbal Academy Pakistan.

——. 1990. "The Obligation to Migrate: The Doctrine of Hijra in Islamic Law." In *Muslim Travellers*, edited by D. Eickelman and J. Piscatori.

Masud, Muhammad Khalid, ed. 2000. *Travelers in Faith: Studies of the Tablighi Jama'at as a Transnational Islamic Movement for Faith Renewal*. Leiden: Brill Academic Publishers.

Masud, Muhammad K., Brinkley Messick, and David S. Powers, eds. 1996. *Islamic Legal Interpretations: Muftis and Their Fatwas*. Cambridge: Harvard University Press.

Maududi, Syed Abul ala. 1955. *Islamic Law and Constitution*. Edited by Khurshid Ahmad. Karachi: Jamaat-e-Islamic Publications.

——. 1976. *Islam and Ignorance*. Lahore: Islamic Publications.

——. 1991. *The Sick Nations of the Modern Age*. Lahore: Islamic Publications.

——. 1995. *Purdah and the Status of Woman in Islam*. Lahore: Islamic Publications.

——. 2000. *The Qadiani Problem*. Lahore: Islamic Publications.

——. 2004. "The Necessity of Divine Government for the Elimination of Oppression and Injustice" and "The Moral Foundations of the Islamic Movement." In *Muslim Self-Statement in India and Pakistan, 1857–1968*, edited by A. Ahmad and G. von Grunebaum.

Mayaram, Shail, M. S. S. Pandian and Ajay Skaria, eds. 2005. *Subaltern Studies 12: Muslims, Dalits, and the Fabrications of History*. New Delhi: Permanent Black.

Mayr, Ernst. 1992. "The Idea of Teleology." *Journal of the History of Ideas* 53, no. 1: 117–35.

Mbembe, Achille. 2001. *On the Postcolony*. Berkeley: University of California Press.

McDonough, Sheila. 1970. *The Authority of the Past: A Study of Three Muslim Modernists*. Chambersburg, PA: American Academy of Religion.

McGrath, Allen. 1996. *The Destruction of Pakistan's Democracy*. Karachi: Oxford University Press.

Mehta, Deepak. 2010. "Words That Wound: Archiving Hate in the Making of Hindu and Muslim Publics in Bombay." In *Beyond Crisis: Re-evaluating Pakistan*, edited by N. Khan.

Menon, Muhammad Umar. 1998. "Introduction." In *The Color of Nothingness: Modern Urdu Short Stories*. Karachi: Oxford University Press.

Merkl, Peter, and Ninian Smart. 1982. *Religion and Myth in the Modern World*. New York: New York University Press.

Messick, Brinkley. 1993. *The Calligraphic State: Textual Domination and History in a Muslim Society*. Berkeley: University of California Press.

Metcalf, Barbara Daly. 1982. "Religious Myth and Nationalism: The Case of Pakistan." In *Religion and Myth in the Modern World*, edited by P. Merkl and N. Smart.

——, ed. 1984. *Moral Conduct and Authority: The Place of Adab in South Asian Islam*. Berkeley: University of California Press.

——. 1987a. "Islamic Arguments in Contemporary Pakistan." In *Islam and the Political Economy of Meaning*, edited by W. Roff.

——. 1987b. *Islamic Revival in British India: Deoband, 1860–1900*. Karachi: Royal Book Company.

——. 1990. "The Pilgrimage Remembered in South Asian Accounts of the Hajj." In *Muslim Travelers*, edited by D. Eickelman and J. Piscatori.

——. 1993a. "Living Hadith in the Tablighi Jama'at." *Journal of Asian Studies* 52, no. 3: 584–648.

——. 1993b. "What Happened in Mecca: Mumtaz Mufti's 'Labbaik.'" In *The Culture of Autobiography: Constructions of Self-Representations*, edited by Folkenflik.

——, ed. 1996. *Making Muslim Space in North America and Europe*. Berkeley: University of California Press.

——. 1997. *Bihisti Zewar: Perfecting Women* (Maulana Ashraf Ali Thanawi's *Bihisti Zewar*, A Partial Translation with Commentary). Lahore: Idara-e-Islamiat.

——. 2007. "Imagining Muslim Futures: Debates over State and Society at the End of the Raj." *Historical Research* 8, no. 208: 286–98.

——. 2008. *Hussain Ahmad Madani: The Jihad for Islam and India's Freedom*. Oxford: Oneworld Publications.

——, ed. 2009. *Islam in South Asia in Practice*. Princeton: Princeton University Press.

Miller, Larry Benjamin. 1984. "Islamic Disputation Theory: A Study of the Development of Dialectic in Islam from the Tenth to the Fourteenth Centuries." Ph.D. dissertation, Princeton University.

Mills, Margaret, Peter Claus, and Sarah Diamond, eds. 2003. *South Asian Folklore: An Encyclopedia*. London: Routledge.

Minault, Gail. 1982. *The Khilafat Movement: Religious Symbolism and Political Mobilization in India*. New York: Columbia University Press.

Minnow, Martha, Michael Ryan, and Austin Sarat, eds. 1995. *Narrative, Violence and the Law: The Essays of Robert Cover*. Ann Arbor: University of Michigan Press.

Mitchell, Timothy. 1991. *Colonizing Egypt*. Berkeley: University of California Press.

——. 2000. Introduction. In *Questions of Modernity*, edited by T. Mitchell.

Mitchell, Timothy, ed. 2000. *Questions of Modernity*. Minneapolis: University of Minnesota Press.

Mittermiaer, Amira. 2007. "The Book of Visions: Dreams, Poetry and Prophecy in Contemporary Egypt." *International Journal of Middle East Studies* 39: 229–47.

Morris, Rosalind. 2000. *In the Place of Origins: Modernity and Its Mediums in Northern Thailand*. Durham: Duke University Press.

Mufti, Aamir R. 1995. "Secularism and Minority: Elements of a Critique." *Social Text* 45: 75–96.

——. 2000. "The Aura of Authenticity." *Social Text* 64: 87–103.

——. 2004. "Towards a Lyric History of India." *Boundary 2* 31, no. 2: 245–74.

——. 2007. *Enlightenment in the Colony: The Jewish Question and the Crisis of Postcolonial Culture*. Princeton: Princeton University Press.

Mufti, Mumtaz. 1975. *Labbaik* [I am present]. Lahore: Sang-e Meel Publications.

——. 1999. *Talash* [Search]. 1995. Lahore: Sang-e-Meel Publications.

Mumtaz, Kamil K. 1985. *Architecture in Pakistan*. Singapore: Concept Media.

Munn, Nancy. 1992. "The Cultural Anthropology of Time: A Critical Essay." *Annual Review of Anthropology* Vol. 21: 93–123.

Nabi Khan, Ahmad. 1991. *Development of Mosque Architecture in Pakistan*. Islamabad: Lok Virsa Publishing House.

Naim, C. M., ed. 1980. *Iqbal, Jinnah and Pakistan: The Vision and the Reality*. Syracuse: Syracuse University Press.

——. 1995. "Popular Jokes and Political History: The Case of Akbar, Birbal and Mulla Do-Piyaza." *Economic and Political Weekly* 30, no. 24: 1456–64.

——. 1999. "Iqbal, Jinnah, and Pakistan: The Vision and the Reality." In *Ambiguities of Heritage: Fictions and Polemics*. Karachi: City Press.

Nandy, Ashis. 1995. *The Savage Freud and Other Essays on Possible and Retrievable Selves*. Princeton: Princeton University Press.

Nasr, Seyyed V. R. 1994. *The Vanguard of the Islamic Revolution*. Berkeley: University of California Press.

——. 1996. *Mawdudi and the Making of Islamic Revivalism*. New York: Oxford University Press.

——. 2000a. "International Politics, Domestic Imperatives and Identity Mobilization: Sectarianism in Pakistan 1929–1988." *Comparative Politics* (January): 171–90.

——. 2000b. "The Rise of Sunni Militancy in Pakistan: The Changing Role of Islamism and the Ulama in Society and Politics." *Modern Asian Studies* 34, no. 1: 139–80.

——. 2002. "Islam, the State, and the Rise of Sectarian Militancy in Pakistan." In *Pakistan: Nationalism without a Nation?*, edited by C. Jaffrelot.

Nasr, Seyyed Hossein. 1987. *Islamic Art and Spirituality*. Albany: State University of New York Press.

Natarajan, Nalini, ed. 1996. *Handbook of Twentieth Century Literatures of India*. Westport: Greenwood Press.

Nath, R. 1994. *Mosque Architecture: From Medina to Hindustan, 622–1654 A.D.* Jaipur: Historical Research Documentation Programme.

Nelson, Matthew J. 2006. "Muslims, Markets, and the Meaning of a 'Good' Education in Pakistan." *Asian Survey* 46, no. 5: 699–720.

Netton, Ian R. 1997. *A Popular Dictionary of Islam*. Atlantic Highlands, N.J.: Humanities Press International.

Newburg, Paula R. 1995. *Judging the State: Courts and Constitutional Politics in Pakistan.* New Delhi: Cambridge University Press.

Niazi, Quasar. 1976. *Masjid ka Maqam* [The Position of the Mosque]. Islamabad: Ministry of Religious Affairs.

Nietzsche, Friedrich. 1961. *Thus Spoke Zarathustra.* New York: Penguin Classics.

——. 1968. *The Will to Power.* New York: Vintage Books.

Obarrio, Juan. 2010. "Beyond Equivalence: The Gift of Justice (Mozambique 1976, 2004)." *Anthropological Theory* 10: 163–70.

Oesterheld, Christina. 2005. "Urdu Literature in Pakistan: A Site for Alternative Visions and Dissent." *Annual of Urdu Studies* 20: 79–98.

Oesterheld, Christina, and Claus Peter Zoller, eds. 1999. *Of Clowns and Gods, Brahmins and Babus: Humor in South Asian Literature.* New Delhi: Manohar Publishers.

Osella, Filippo and Benjamin Soares, eds., 2009. "Islam, Politics and Anthropology." *Journal of the Royal Anthropological Institute* n.s.: S1–S23.

Pandian, Anand, and Daud Ali, eds. 2010. *Ethical Life in South Asia.* Bloomington: Indiana University Press.

Pandolfo, Stefania. 1998. *Impasse of the Angels: Scenes from a Moroccan Space of Memory.* Chicago: University of Chicago Press.

——. 2000. "The Thin Line of Modernity: Some Moroccan Debates on Subjectivity." In *Questions of Modernity,* edited by T. Mitchell.

——. 2007. "'The Burning': Finitude and the Politico-Theological Imagination of Illegal Migration." *Anthropological Theory* 7: 329–64.

Parkin, David, and Stephen Headley, eds. 2000. *Islamic Prayer across the Indian Ocean: Inside and Outside the Mosque.* London: Curzon Press.

Parry, Jonathan. 1980. "Ghosts, Greed and Sin: The Occupational Identity of Benares Priests." *Man* 15, no. 1: 88–111.

Pasha, Mustafa Kamal. 2001. "Savage Capitalism and Civil Society in Pakistan." In *Power and Civil Society in Pakistan,* edited by A. Weiss and S. Z. Gilani.

Pemberton, Kelley. 2002. "Islamic and Islamicizing Discourses: Ritual Performances, Didactic Texts and the Reformist Challenge in the South Asian Sufi Milieu." *Annual of Urdu Studies* 17: 55–83.

Pereira, Jose. 1994. *Islamic Sacred Architecture: A Stylistic History.* New Delhi: Books and Books.

Pirzada, Sayyid A. S. 2000. *The Politics of the Jamiat Ulema-I-Islam Pakistan, 1971–1977.* Karachi: Oxford University Press.

Pirzada, Sayyid A. S., ed. 1969. *Foundations of Pakistan.* Vols. 1 and 2. Karachi: National Publishing House.

Piscatori, James. 2005. *Imagining Pan-Islam: Religious Activism and Political Utopias.* Proceedings of the British Academy. Oxford: Oxford University Press.

Platts, John T. 1988. *A Dictionary of Urdu, Classical Hindi and English.* New Delhi: Munshiram Manoharlal Publishers.

Povinelli, Elizabeth. 2001. "Radical Worlds: The Anthropology of Incommensurability and Inconceivability." *Annual Review of Anthropology* 30: 319–39.

Powell, Avril A. 1992. "Muslim-Christian Confrontation: Dr. Wazir Khan in Nineteenth-century Agra." In *Religious Controversy in British India: Re-evaluating Pakistan*, edited by K. Jones.

———. 1993. *Muslims and Missionaries in Pre-Mutiny India*. London: Curzon Press.

Prigogene, Ilaya, and Isabelle Stengers. 1984. *Order out of Chaos*. Boston: Shambhala Press.

Pritchett, Frances. 1994. *Nets of Awareness: Urdu Poetry and Its Critics*. Berkeley: University of California Press.

Prochazka, Amjad B. 1986. *Introduction to Islamic Architecture*. Zurich: Muslim Architecture Research Program.

Qadeer, Muhammad A. 1983. *Urban Development in the Third World: Internal Dynamics of Lahore*. New York: Praeger Publishers.

———. 2006. *Pakistan: Social and Cultural Transformations in a Muslim Nation*. New York: Routledge.

Qadri, Maulana Badrul. 1999. *Masjid Allah ka Ghar* (The Mosque Is Allah's Abode). Lahore: Ziaul Quran Publishers

Qureshi, Ishtiaq H. 1972. *Ulema in Politics: A Study Relating to the Political Activities of the Ulema in the South-Asian Subcontinent from 1556 to 1947*. Karachi: Ma'aref Publishers.

Qureshi, M. Naeem. 1979. "The Ulama of British India and the Hijrat of 1920." *Modern Asian Studies* 13, no. 1: 49–59.

Qureshi, Muhammad Saddique. 1989. *The Role of the Mosque in Islam*. Lahore: Publishers United Limited.

Qureshi, Omar, 1996. "Twentieth Century Urdu Literature." In *Handbook of Twentieth-Century Literatures of India*, edited by N. Natarajan.

Rahman, A. N. M. Wahidur. 1993. "Modernist Muslims Approach to Hadith: Aligarh School." *Hamdard Islamicus* 16, no. 4: 13–26.

Rahman, Fazlur. 1970a. "Islam and the Constitutional Problem of Pakistan." *Studia Islamica* 32: 275–87.

———. 1970b. "Islamic Modernism: Its Scope, Method and Alternatives." *International Journal of Middle East Studies* 1, no. 4: 317–33.

———. 1971. "The Ideological Experience of Pakistan." *Islam and the Modern Age* 2, no. 4: 1–20.

———. 1974. "Islam and the New Constitution of Pakistan." In *Contemporary Problems of Pakistan*, edited by J. Henry Kolson.

———. 1979. *Islam*. Chicago: University of Chicago Press.

———. 1982. *Islam and Modernity: Transformation of an Intellectual Tradition*. Chicago: University of Chicago Press.

Rais, Rasul B. 2007. "Identity Politics and Minorities in Pakistan." *South Asia: Journal of South Asia Studies* 30, no. 1: 111–25.

Rao, Vijayendra, and Michael Walton, eds. 2004. *Cultural and Public Action*. Stanford: Stanford University Press.

Reinhart, Kevin. 1995. *Before Revelation: The Boundaries of Muslim Moral Thought*. Albany: State University of New York Press.

Reynolds, Pamela. 1996. *Traditional Healers and Childhood in Zimbabwe*. Athens: Ohio University Press.

Ring, Laura A. 2006. *Zenana: Everyday Peace in a Karachi Apartment Building*. Bloomington: Indiana University Press.

Robinson, Francis. 1974. *Separatism among Indian Muslims: The Politics of the United Provinces Muslims 1860–1923*. Cambridge: Cambridge University Press.

——. 1999. "Religious Change and the Self in Muslim South Asia." *South Asia: Journal of South Asia Studies* 22: 13–27.

——. 2000a. *Islam and Muslim History in South Asia*. New Delhi: Oxford University Press.

——. 2000b. "Islam and the Impact of Print in South Asia." In F. Robinson, *Islam and Muslim History in South Asia*.

——. 2000c. "Religious Change and the Self in Muslim South Asia since 1800." In F. Robinson, *Islam and Muslim History in South Asia*.

——. 2004. "Other-Worldly and This-Worldly Islam and the Islamic Revival." *Journal of the Royal Asiatic Society* 14, no. 1: 47–58.

——. 2008. "Islamic Reform and Modernities in South Asia." *Modern Asian Studies* 42, nos. 2–3: 259–81.

Robinson, Francis, ed. 1996. *The Cambridge Illustrated History of the Islamic World*. Cambridge: Cambridge University Press.

Roff, William, ed. 1987. *Islam and the Political Economy of Meaning*. Berkeley: University of California.

Rosen, Lawrence. 1984. *Bargaining for Reality: The Construction of Social Relations in a Muslim Community*. Chicago: University of Chicago Press.

——. 2002. "Never in Doubt: Salman Rushdie's Deeper Challenge to Islam." In *The Culture of Islam: Changing Aspects of Contemporary Muslim Life*. Chicago: University of Chicago Press.

Roth, Michael S., and Charles G. Salas, eds. 2001. *Disturbing Remains: Memory, History and Crisis in the Twentieth Century*. Los Angeles: Getty Research Institute.

Rothenberg, Celia E. 1998. "Spirits of Palestine: Palestinian Village Women and Stories of the Jinn." Ph.D. dissertation, University of Toronto.

Rotman, Brian. 2008. *Becoming beside Ourselves: The Alphabet, Ghosts, and Distributed Human Beings*. Durham: Duke University Press.

Rozehnal, Robert. 2006. "Faqir or Faker?: The Pakpattan Tragedy and the Politics of Sufism in Pakistan." *Religion* 36, no. 1: 29–47.

——. 2010. "Re-imagining the 'Land of the Pure': A Sufi Master Reclaims Islamic Orthodoxy and Pakistani National Identity." In *Beyond Crisis: Re-evaluating Pakistan*, edited by N. Khan.

Rubin, Uri. 1985. "The 'Constitution of Medina': Some Notes." *Studia Islamica* 62: 5–23.

Rustomji, Nerina. 2008. *The Garden and the Fire: Heaven and Hell in Islamic Culture.* New York: Columbia University Press.

Sachedina, Abdulaziz. 2001. *The Islamic Roots of Democratic Pluralism.* New York: Oxford University Press.

Salvatore, Armando, and Dale Eickelman, eds. 2006. *Public Islam and the Common Good.* Leiden: Brill Academic Publishers.

Sambar, Bilal. 2003. "Fate and Prayer in the Thought of Iqbal." *Hamdard Islamicus* 26, no. 1: 37–43.

Sandeela, Fateh M. 1978. "Sovereignty of Allah as a Political Fact." *All Pakistan Legal Decisions,* vol. xxx, 102–9.

Sanyal, Usha. 1996. *Devotional Islam and Politics in British India: Ahmad Riza Khan Barelwi and His Movement, 1870–1920.* Delhi: Oxford University Press.

Sarkar, Sumit. 1983. *Modern India: 1885–1947.* Madras: Macmillan India.

Sayeed, Khalid bin. 1979. "Mass Urban Protests as Indicators of Political Change in Pakistan." *Journal of Commonwealth and Comparative Politics* 17, no. 2: 111–35.

Schacht, Joseph. 1964. *An Introduction to Islamic Law.* Oxford: Clarendon Press.

Schielke, Samuli. 2009. "Being Good in Ramadan: Ambivalence, Fragmentation and the Moral Self in the Lives of Young Egyptians." *Journal of the Royal Anthropological Association* n.s.: S24–S40.

Schimmel, Annamarie. 1985. *And Muhammad Is His Messenger.* Chapel Hill: University of North Carolina Press.

———. 1989. *Gabriel's Wing: A Study into the Religious Ideas of Sir Muhammad Iqbal.* Lahore: Iqbal Academy.

Schmitt, Carl. 2006. *Political Theology: Four Chapters on the Concept of Sovereignty.* Chicago: University of Chicago Press.

Scott, David. 1999. *Refashioning Futures: Criticism after Postcoloniality.* Princeton: Princeton University Press.

Shahab, Qudrutullah. 2005. *Shahabnama.* Lahore: Sang-e-Meel Publishing House.

Shaikh, Farzana. 2009. *Making Sense of Pakistan.* New York: Columbia University Press.

Sharif, M. M. 1959. "Islam and Spiritual Values." *Philosophy East and West* 9, nos. 1–2: 41–43.

Shepard, William. 1987. "Islam and Ideology: Towards a Typology." *International Journal of Middle East Studies* 19, no. 3: 307–35.

Shurreef, Jaffur. 1832, reprint 1973. *Qanoon-e-Islam, or The Customs of the Mussalmans of India.* Translated by G. A. Hercklots. Lahore: Al-Irshad.

Siddiqa, Ayesha. 2007. *Military Inc.: Inside Pakistan's Military Economy.* New York: Pluto Press.

Siegel, James. 1969. *The Rope of God.* Berkeley: University of California Press.

———. 1979. *Shadow and Sound: The Historical Thought of a Sumatran People.* Chicago: University of Chicago Press.

———. 1998. *A New Criminal Type in Jakarta: Counter Revolution Today.* Durham: Duke University Press.

———. 2005. *Naming the Witch.* Stanford: Stanford University Press.

Simon, Gregory. 2009. "The Soul Freed of Cares? Islamic Prayer, Subjectivity, and the Contradictions of Moral Selfhood in Minangkabau, Indonesia." *American Ethnologist* 36, no. 2: 258–75.

Singh, Bhrigupati. 2006. "Inhabiting Civil Disobedience." In *Political Theologies: Public Religions in a Post-Secular World*, edited by H. de Vries and L. Sullivan.

———. 2010. "Asceticism and Eroticism in Gandhi, Thoreau and Nietzsche." *Borderlands* 9, no. 3: 1–34.

Singh, Khushwant. 1994. "Introduction." In M. Iqbal, *Shikwa wa Jawab-e Shikwa.*

Sinha, Mrinalini. 2006. *Specters of Mother India: The Global Restructuring of an Empire.* Durham: Duke University Press.

Sivan, Emmanuel. 1990. *Radical Islam: Medieval Theology and Modern Politics.* New Haven: Yale University Press.

Skovgaard-Patteron, Jakob. 1997. *Defining Islam for the Egyptian State: Muftis and Fatwas of the Dar Al-Ifta.* Leiden: Brill Academic Publishers.

Smith, Wilfred Cantwell. 1957. *Islam in Modern History.* 1948. New York: Mentor Books.

Spadola, Emilio. 2008. "The Scandal of Ecstasy: Communication, Sufi Rites and Social Reform in 1930s Morocco." *Contemporary Islam* 2, no. 2: 119–38.

Spengler, Oswald. 1926. *The Decline of the West: Form and Actuality.* New York: Alfred A. Knopf.

Starrett, Gregory. 1995. "The Hexis of Interpretation: Islam and the Body in the Egyptian Popular School." *American Ethnologist* 22, no. 4: 953–69.

———. 1998. *Putting Islam to Work: Education, Politics, and Religious Transformation in Egypt.* Berkeley: University of California Press.

———. 2003. "Muslim Identities and the Great Chain of Buying." In *New Media in the Muslim World: The Emerging Public Sphere*, edited by D. Eickelman and J. Anderson.

Stetkevych, Jaroslav. 1996. *Muhammad and the Golden Bough: Reconstructing Arabian Myth.* Bloomington: Indiana University Press.

Stewart, Susan. 1982. "The Epistemology of the Horror Story." *The Journal of American Folklore* 95, no. 375: 35–50.

———. 1991. *Crimes of Writing: Problems in the Containment of Representation.* Durham: Duke University Press.

Stokes, Eric. 1990. *The English Utilitarians and India.* New York: Oxford University Press.

Strathern, Marilyn. 2004. *Partial Connections.* Walnut Creek, Calif.: AltaMira Press.

Su, John J. 2001. "Epic of Failure: Disappointment as Utopian Fantasy in Midnight's Children." *Twentieth-Century Literature* 47, no. 4: 545–66.

Talbot, Ian. 2005. *Pakistan: A Modern History.* New York: Palgrave Mcmillan.

———. 2007. *Divided Cities: Partition and Its Aftermath in Lahore and Amritsar.* 1998. New York: Oxford University Press.

Taussig, Michael. 1998. "Viscerality, Faith, and Skepticism: Another Theory of Magic." In *In Near Ruins: Cultural Theory at the End of the Century*, edited by N. Dirks.

Taylor, Mark C., ed. 1998. *Critical Terms for Religious Studies*. Chicago: University of Chicago Press.

Thanawi, Maulana Ashraf Ali. n.d. *Adab-e Zindagi* (The Etiquette of Life). Karachi: Darul Ishat.

———. n.d. *Ihkam al-Masjid* (Orders Regarding the Mosque). Multan: Idara Talifaat Ashrafiya.

———. 1971. *Shariat o Tariqat*. Lahore: Idara-e-Islamiat.

———. 1976. *Answer to Modernism*. Translated by Muhammad Hasan Askari and Karrar Husain. Karachi: Maktaba Darululoom.

Titus, Paul. 1998. "Honor the Baloch, Buy the Pushtun: Stereotypes, Social Organization and History in Western Pakistan." *Modern Asian Studies* 32, no. 3: 657–87.

Troll, Christian. 2004. *Muslim Shrines in India: Their Character, History and Significance*. New York: Oxford University Press.

Vajpeya, Dhirendra, and Yogendra Malik, eds. 1989. *Religion and Ethnic Minority Politics in South Asia*. New Delhi: Munshiram Manoharlal Publishers.

Van Ess, Josef. 1972. "Skepticism in Islamic Religious Thought." In *God and Man in Contemporary Islam*, edited by C. Malik.

Verkaaik, Oskar. 2001. "The Captive State: Corruption, Intelligence Agencies, and Ethnicity in Pakistan." In *States of Imagination: Ethnographic Explorations of the Postcolonial State*, edited by T. Blom Hansen and F. Stepputat.

———. 2004. *Migrants and Militants: Fun and Urban Violence in Pakistan*. Princeton: Princeton University Press.

Viswanathan, Gauri. 1989. *Masks of Conquest: Literary Study and British Rule in India*. New York: Columbia University Press.

Von Grunebaum, Gustave. 1951. *Muhammadan Festivals*. London: Curzon Press.

Von Grunebaum, Gustave, and Roger Caillois, eds. 1996. *The Dream and Human Societies*. Berkeley: University of California Press.

Watt, William M. 1981. *Muhammad at Medina*. London: Oxford University Press.

Waugh, Earle. 1983. "Images of Muhammad in the Work of Iqbal: Tradition and Alterations." *History of Religions* 23, no. 2: 156–68.

Weiss, Anita. 2002. *Walls within Walls: Life Histories of Working Women in the Old City of Lahore*. New York: Oxford University Press.

Weiss, Anita M., ed. 1986. *Islamic Reassertion in Pakistan: The Application of Islamic Laws in a Modern State*. Syracuse: Syracuse University Press.

Weiss, Anita M., and S. Z. Gilani, eds. 2001. *Power and Civil Society in Pakistan*. New York: Oxford University Press.

Westermarck, Edward Alexander. 1926. *Ritual and Belief in Morocco*. Vols. 1 and 2. London: Macmillan.

Wheatley, Paul. 2000. *The Places Where Men Pray Together*. Chicago: University of Chicago Press.

Woodfield, Andrew. 1973. "Darwin, Teleology and Taxonomy." *Philosophy* 48: 38–49.

Zahab, Mariam A. 2002. "The Regional Dimension of Sectarian Conflicts in Pakistan." In *Pakistan: Nationalism without a Nation?*, edited by C. Jaffrelot.

Zaidi, Ali Hassan. 2006. "Muslim Reconstructions of Knowledge and the Reenchantment of Knowledge." *Theory, Culture, Society* 23, no. 5: 69–91.

Zaidi, Ali Jawad. 1993. *A History of Urdu Literature*. New Delhi: Sahitya Akademi.

Zaman, Muhammad Qasim. 1998. "Sectarianism in Pakistan: The Radicalization of Shi'i and Sunni Identities." *Modern Asian Studies* 32, no. 3: 689–716.

——. 1999. "Commentaries, Print and Patronage: Hadith and the Madrasas in Modern South Asia." *Bulletin of the School of Oriental and African Studies* 62, no. 1: 60–81.

——. 2002. *The Ulama in Contemporary Islam: Custodians of Change*. Princeton: Princeton University Press.

——. 2008. *Ashraf Ali Thanawi: Islam in Modern South Asia*. Oxford: Oneworld Publications.

Zamindar, Vazira. 2008. *The Long Partition and the Making of Modern South Asia: Refugees, Boundaries, Histories*. New York: Columbia University Press.

Zingel, Wolfgang Peter, and Stephanie Zingel-Avé Lallemant. 1985. *Pakistan in the 80s*. Lahore: Vanguard Books.

Ziring, Lawrence. 1984. "From Islamic Republic to Islamic State in Pakistan." *Asian Survey* 24, no. 9: 931–46.

——. 1997. *Pakistan in the Twentieth Century*. Karachi: Oxford University Press.

Žižek, Slavoj, ed. 1995. *Mapping Ideology*. New York: Verso.

Zwemer, Samuel M. 1939. *Studies in Popular Islam: A Collection of Papers dealing with the Superstitions and Beliefs of the Common People*. London: Sheldon Press.

aspiration (*cont.*)
  the shadow of skepticism, 148, 196;
  self–correction within, 199; state
  claims upon, 92; to state form, 8; as
  tendency, 9. *See also* diagnostics; skepticism
Assembly, Constituent, 18, 88, 93–100,
  104–5, 108, 151–52, 219 n. 9; National,
  104, 106–8, 152
attraction, 10, 75, 78, 215 n. 27
Auqaf Department, 30, 40, 209 n. 3, 210
  n. 5
Ayodhya, 21
azan (as call to prayer), 40, 49, 111–12,
  124, 129, 149, 153, 183, 210 n. 6; 219
  n. 6

Badshahi Masjid, 30, 62, 210 n. 6
Bang-e Dara (M. Iqbal), 122–23
Bangladesh, 15, 105, 215 n. 30
baradari, 149
Barelwi, 2–3, 5, 23, 28, 33–37, 42, 44, 49–
  52, 122, 132–33, 137–38, 169, 185, 219
  n. 11; as Ahl-e Sunnat wa Jama'at, 32
Basic Principles Committee of 1953, 94–
  95, 97
becoming, 8–9, 19–20, 24, 71, 77, 88,
  123, 205; individuation as, 76; jinn,
  138, 140; life as, 179; mad, 140; Muslim, 93, 118, 204; time as, 5–7, 10, 18,
  56, 175; the world as, 73
belatedness, 195
Bergson, Henri, 6, 10, 16, 18, 56–57, 72–
  74, 77–78, 140, 174–79, 181–82, 204,
  211 n. 1, 212 n. 12; in *Bergsonism*, 213
  n. 13; 224 n. 2; his cone: 70–71, 75. *See
  also individual works*
Bergsonism (Gilles Deleuze), 213 n. 13
Bhutto, Benazir, 205
Bhutto, Zulfiqar Ali, 105–8
bid'a, 3, 125, 186, 188
Bihishti Zewar (Thanawi), 81
blasphemy, 4, 50, 55, 123, 188; as law, 5,
  184

body: in theories of evolution, 70; of a
  martyr, 4; as putrid, 162; as a society
  179, 193. *See also* mulla; Prophet
  Muhammad
Boltzmanian Probability, 177
Bose, Sugata, 56
Buddhists, 107
bureaucracy, of the city, 24; bureaucrats in
  mosques, 26–27; as form, 44–45, 53;
  language of, 47; of the state, 31, 48, 93,
  204. *See also* legality; mosque

calligraphy, 131–32
caricature, 168. *See also* mulla; stereotype
cartoons, 17, 19, 147–48, 163–68, 187,
  223 n. 9
Cavell, Stanley, 11–13, 146, 220 n. 16, 223
  n. 8
Chatterjee, Roma, 36
chilla, 32, 135, 220 n. 15
Christians, 10, 39, 96, 101, 107, 110, 211
  n. 5
churail, 137
colonial India, 78; archives of, 23; useful
  education in,150; Muslim politics in, 5,
  10, 26, 56–62, 78–79, 82–86, 118, 209
  n. 1, 210 n. 4, 215 n. 2; separate electorates in, 97; its signature in the present,
  13–14, 202. *See also* Ahmad, Mirza
  Ghulam; Ahmadiyya movement; blasphemy; Hinduism; Iqbal, Muhammad;
  Khan, Sayyid Ahmed; Muhammadan
  Anglo-Oriental College; state; stereotype; Thanawi, Ashraf Ali
compositing, 124, 132
Connolly, William E., 211 n. 5, 214 n. 19
conscience: bad, 176; freedom of, 111. *See
  also* contagion; debasement; decadence
Constituent Assembly, 18, 88, 93–100,
  104–5, 108, 151–52, 219 n. 9
constitution, human, 79–80, 88, 115, 174,
  186, 205; in Islamic history, 98; of
  jinns, 127; of a mosque, 38, 41, 44
constitutional politics, 18–19, 52, 57, 87–

90, 93–97, 100, 106, 111–13, 123, 152, 182, 195–96, 203

Javid Nama (M. Iqbal), 181

Jawab-e Shikwa (M. Iqbal), 61, 65, 76, 90, 119, 145

jealousy, 3, 138

Jews, 98, 118, 215 n. 2

jinn: by means of 'amil, 125, 136, 220 n. 15; within family life, 129–30, 135, 137–38, 142, 173, 217 n. 4; as a form of life, 126–28, 141, 216 n. 1, 217 nn. 2–3, 218 n. 7; as a guide, 19, 123–24, 133–34, 139–40; as possession, 217 n. 5; as sahaba, 131, 218 n. 6. See also becoming; friendship; mythic

Jinnah, Muhammad Ali, 9, 58–59, 62

jokes, 17, 146–48, 153–54, 163, 167–69, 187, 222 n. 6, 223 n. 7, 223 n. 9

Judgment Day, 4

jurisprudence, Islamic, 85, 135, 149, 219 n. 11

justice, 94, 97, 111

Ka'aba, 159, 161

kafir. See kufr

kalam, 10, 149

kalma, 116, 191

kamil insan, 175

Karachi, 184, 197, 221 n. 1

Karbala, 34, 133

Karim, Maulana Fazlul, 141

Khan, Chaudhry Muhammad Zafarullah, 96–99, 101, 103, 152

Khan, Liaquat Ali, 89–90

Khan, Muhammad Ayub, 105, 221 n. 4

Khan, Sayyid Ahmed, 18, 57, 60, 77–81, 174, 192, 214 n. 20, 214 n. 22, 216 n. 26, 217 n. 2

Khan, Yahya, 105

khatm, 112

kinship: conversation as, 214 n. 19; to doubt, 181; Punjabi, 149, 219 n. 10. See also figuration

Kozlowski, George, 209 n. 4

kufr, 189, 216 n. 4; as kafir, 103–4, 106, 109, 110

Labbaik (Mufti), 158–61, 199, 221 nn. 3–4

Lahore, 1, 28, 37, 60, 92, 121, 132, 136, 146, 155–56; Development Authority of, 30–31, 210 n. 6, 211 n. 10; High Court of, 38, 100, 110; martial law in, 99–100; Muhammad Asad in, 84; Muhammad Iqbal in, 60–62, 65; Mumtaz Mufti in, 159–60; neighborhoods in, 11, 18–19, 21, 23, 26, 45–47, 52, 91, 124, 141, 164, 203; private institutions in, 41–42, 135, 147, 164, 188; public culture of, 14, 17, 56, 148, 158, 163, 183, 202; urban landscape of, 24–25, 138; University of Management Sciences, 206

lament, 63–64, 66–67

land: claims upon, 27, 29, 37; public, 26; of the pure, 1; grabbing of, 27, 30, 46, 163; registration of, 93; sale of, 27, 31, 38, 40; state allocation of, 45, 48. See also waqf

law: as Civil Procedure Code, 111; contra colonial law, 94; limits of, 116; of nature, 80–81, 115, 214 n. 22; as Ordinance XX, 108, 111; as site of disputation, 33; as Specific Relief Act of 1887, 110; as Societies Registration Act, 31; as state striving, 14, 92–94, 206. See also Ahmad, Mirza Ghulam; blasphemy; Constitution of Pakistan; copyright; Federal Shariat Court; Lahore; martial law; shari'a; state; Supreme Court of Pakistan; trademark; waqf

legality, 27, 30

life: as becoming, 175, 177; as movement toward individuation and perfection, 71, 179; multiplicity as reality of, 72, 75, 77; as social, 12; without teleology, 73, 178; as wonderment, 197; of words, 37. See also creativity; everyday life; reason; symptomatology; teleology

literati, 16, 19, 175, 203. See also Iqbal, Muhammad; Mufti, Mumtaz; Shahab, Qudratullah

loudspeaker, 34–35, 37, 46–47, 152

love: in religion, 2, 4, 6, 31, 64–65, 67, 119, 127, 132–33, 158, 169, 181, 197
Ludhianvi, Muhammad Yusuf, 174, 184–87, 191–93

madrasa, 17, 42–43, 46, 88, 155, 169, 184, 188, 192
Majeed, Javed, 59, 211 n. 2
Malik, Omar Hayat, 151
Manjapra, Kris, 56
mansha, 186
manuals: on children, 129; on disputation, 10; on jinns, 127, 138
markaz, 135
martial law, 1, 5, 99–100, 105, 146, 211 n. 11
martyr, 4
Massumi, Brian, 71, 213 n. 14
Masud, Baitallah, 205
Matter and Memory (Bergson), 70
Maududi, Abul Ala, 18, 57, 84, 86–88, 106, 157, 185, 214 n. 24. See also individual works; Jama'at-e Islami
maulwi, 30, 33, 37, 39, 51, 148, 153–54, 163, 168–69. See also mulla
Mbembe, Achille, 168
Mecca, 3, 22, 39, 65, 98, 158–60, 188, 210 n. 6, 222 n. 5. See also hajj
Medina, 3, 22, 28, 39, 96–98, 124, 132–33, 136. See also Prophet Muhammad
Mehta, Deepak, 36, 212 n. 6
memorandum of understanding, 43–44, 53
messiah, 69, 118. See also Iqbal, Muhammad; Prophet Muhammad
Metcalf, Barbara Daly, 221 nn. 3–4, 222 n. 5
Milad un-Nabi, 34, 49, 133
Mina, 160
miracle, 80, 82–83, 199; Pakistan as a, 22
Mirza, Sikandar, 105
Morris, Rosalind, 217 n. 3
mosque: Ahmadis in, 91–92, 110–12; ar-

chitectural elements of, 28, 32, 39, 210 n. 6; bureaucratic requirements of, 31, 93, 210 n. 5; committee of, 27, 31, 37–38, 43, 49, 92, 209 n. 3; comportment in, 22, 53; construction and conflict as striving, 10–11, 18–19, 24, 50–51, 55, 123, 201, 203–4; humiliation of, 44; as Masjid Zarar, 33; employees of, 40, 149; neighborhood based, 2, 26, 29–30, 46, 54, 124; ownership of, 23; Pakistan as, 1, 21, 171; qabza of, 23 54, 109, 123, 134, 146–47, 155, 163, 171–73, 211 n. 8; religious practices within, 28, 42, 49, 135, 139; sites of sin and corruption, 164, 168; Tablighis in, 33–34, 52, 125. See also Auqaf Department; azan; Badshahi Masjid; documents; encroachment; illegality; imam; land; legality; loudspeaker; maulwi; Mecca; Medina; memorandum of understanding; mulla; patwari; Prophet Muhammad; qabza
movements: Khilafat, 61, 65; for Pakistan, 62, 86, 105, 215 n. 1; reform or piety, 9, 214 n. 20; swadeshi, 60; Wahabi movement, 151. See also Aalmi Majlis Tahaffuz Khatm-e-Nubuwwat; Ahmadiyya movement; Tablighi Jama'at
muakkal, 220 n. 15
mu'amalat, 69
muezzin (one who calls), 35, 37, 40, 149
mufti, 149, 169, 188–89
Mufti, Aamir, 212 n. 6, 215 n. 2
Mufti, Mumtaz, 16–17, 19, 148–49, 158–62, 171, 183, 193–99, 202, 221 nn. 3–4, 222 n. 5, 224 nn. 4–5. See also individual works
Mufti, Uxi, 196–97
muhajir, 219 n. 10
Muhammad, Ghulam, 105
Muhammadan Anglo-Oriental College, 60, 79, 81
Muharram, 34, 133

Qadiani. *See* Ahmadis

The Qadiani Problem (Maududi), 207

Qadiri, Tahirul, 50

qarin/qarina, 218 n. 5

Qudsia, Banu, 194

Qu'ran, 15, 36–37, 40, 50, 60, 79, 82–85, 90, 96–97, 103, 111, 126–27, 129, 149, 152, 155–57, 186, 189, 195, 198–99, 201, 212 n. 12, 218 n. 7, 219 n. 11, 220 n. 15

Qutb, Sayyid, 86

Rabwah, 92, 106

Ramzan, 135

reason: as aql, 129; biological basis of, 80, 115, 174; as intelligence, 71, 73–76, 178; in contrast to jahalat, 50; as logic, 82; in the practice of orthodoxy, 155; and revelation, 57, 78–79, 83–84, 102; specious variety of, 119, 168

Reconstruction of Religious Thought in Islam (M. Iqbal), 62, 68–69, 72, 79, 212 n. 9

resentment, 50, 68, 119, 176

resonance, 59–60, 89, 97–98, 203, 211 n. 5, 219 n. 9. *See also* dissonance

revelation. *See* reason

The Road to Mecca (Asad), 215 n. 21

rumor, 35, 37, 51–53, 121, 192, 211 n. 8, 221 n. 1

Samdani Commission, 106

satan. *See* devil

sathi, 135

Saudi Arabia, 35, 158–59

sayyid, 131, 135

Schmitt, Carl, 11

Secrets of the Self (M. Iqbal), 180, 182

sectarianism, 36; inflections of, 23, 25; politics of, 26, 43; as geography, 52; as religious differences, 187; violence of, 28, 138, 145, 153

secularism, 39, 101, 152, 155, 194, 215 n. 25, 215 n. 27, 224 n. 4

self: annihilation of, 132, 181, 213 n. 15;

as divine, 73–74, 102; experimentation by, 62, 81, 88, 90, 94, 151; government by, 60–61; as impersonal, 78; as judging, 176–77; as newly vitalized, 68; as next self, 55, 76–77, 141, 179–80; multiplicity of, 193, 213 n. 17; as nafs, 128; as penetrable by forces, 160; as possessed, 217 n. 5; pursuits of, 11, 16, 24, 39, 57, 68, 76, 85, 87–88, 109, 117, 122, 139, 172, 175, 212 n. 11; as self-diagnostic, 16, 173; series of, 140; split within, 153–54, 212 n. 6; in state of becoming, 71, 175, 178; strangeness within, 153–54, 158, 199. *See also* personality; skepticism

Shahab, Qudratullah, 158, 162, 194, 221 n. 4, 224 n. 5

shakk-o shubha. *See* doubt

shari'a, 111, 113, 149–50, 185, 189, 192, 205–6, 209 n. 4, 216 n. 3

Shariat o Tariqat (Thanawi), 192

Shi'a, 2–4, 29–30, 34–35, 52, 133, 137, 147, 153, 156, 172, 184–85

shi'ar, 112–14

Shikwa (M. Iqbal), 61, 63, 65, 145

Sick Nations of the Modern Age (Maududi), 214 n. 24

Sipah-e Hanafiyya, 135

Sipah-e Sahaba, 135, 156

sirat, 133

shirk, 125

shrine, of saints, 3, 21, 36, 133, 209 n. 3

Shurreef, Jaffur, 217 n. 5

Singh, Bhrigupati, 11

skepticism: acknowledgement of, 175, 199, 207; as disappointment with human condition, 12–13; Ghazzali's, 215 n. 28; as opportunity, 162; as a pervasive condition, 14, 148, 154, 168, 172, 195, 203; strategies to treat, 184, 187, 191, 193–94; as a tendency within the social, 13–14, 19, 25, 54, 146, 174, 220 n. 16; scholarly, 198

Smith, W. C., 8–9, 13, 18

soul, 15–16, 66, 87, 181, 183, 198

sovereignty, in God, 95

Spadola, Emilio, 217 n. 3

speech, 63, excesses of, 192; freedom of, 5; hateful, 36–37; by politicians, 43, 62, 89, 96–97, 148, 152–54, 211 n. 4; as reported, 130; as taqrir, 2; as conversation, 195; unauthorized, 158. *See also* rumor

Spinoza, Baruch, 118

state: administration of mosques by, 1, 21, 23, 26–28, 30–31, 38, 41, 45–46, 48, 53–54, 92–93, 205, 210 n. 6; as aspirant, 19, 57, 94, 109, 131, 146, 148, 157, 172, 203–4; as Islamic, 7–9, 44, 86–89, 95–96, 99–104, 152, 205–7; police as, 28, 52; transcriptions of, 13–14, 17–18. *See also* law

stereotype, 2, 6, 64, 147–48, 150–51, 155, 165, 170, 174, 183, 221 n. 1

Stetkevych, Jaroslav, 219 n. 7

Stewart, Susan, 223 n. 8

striving. *See* aspiration

study circles: women, 155–56

Sufism, 81, 118, 132, 180, 213 n. 15, 222 n. 5

Sultan, Tipu, 117

sunna, 89–90, 132, 152

Sunni, 2, 29–30, 34–35, 42, 49, 122, 132–35, 137, 139, 153, 184–85, 219 n. 9, 219 n. 11

Supreme Court of Pakistan, 45, 93, 111, 113–14, 118, 130, 157, 182, 206

Sura Al-Jinn, 126

Sura Saba, 218 n. 7

suspicion, 3, 13, 34, 50, 154, 160, 182–83. *See also* doubt; hypocrisy; jealousy; skepticism

symptomatology, 15–16; literature as, 173–74

Tablighi Jama'at, 32–34, 40, 52, 125, 135, 141, 197, 224 n. 4

tafsir, 149

Talash (Mufti), 194–99, 202

Taliban: Pakistan, 205

taqdir, 72

tasawwuf, 81

tauba, 109, 188–89

taziya, 133

teleology, 6, 68–77, 78, 90, 176, 212 nn. 10–11

texts, within everyday life, 6, 10, 17–18, 22, 41, 112, 114, 123–24, 132, 146, 148–49, 152–53, 156, 173–74, 215 n. 25, 216 n. 3, 216 nn. 7–8. *See also* affect; documents; gesture; speech

Thanawi, Ashraf Ali, 15, 18, 57, 78, 79, 81–84, 174, 192–93, 214 n. 20. *See also* individual works; hakim

theology: as Islamic, 50, 69, 78, 149; as political, 11

Thus Spoke Zarathustra (Nietzsche), 177, 179

time: creative workings of, 7, 56, 68; as destiny, 72; durational, 57, 70–71, 76, 176, 179; from God's perspective, 75, 77, 84, 212 n. 12; held in potential, 177. *See also* Bergson, Henri; becoming; belatedness; future; Massumi, Brian

tolerance, 5, 94, 96–97, 116, 118–19, 152, 181, 204, 216 n. 8

trademark, 111–15

transcendence, 11, 75, 78, 84, 215 n. 27

transgression, religious, 28, 109, 114–15, 168

"True Lies" (Nazar), 164, 166

Two Sources of Religion and Morality (Bergson), 74, 182

übermensch, 177–78

ulama, 10, 12–13, 16–17, 19, 33, 45, 60, 80–81, 88, 99–105, 109, 129, 134, 147–54, 158–59, 163–69, 174–75, 182–93, 203, 205, 215 n. 1, 215 n. 27, 216 n. 5, 222 n. 5. *See also* alim; maulwi; mulla

umma, 112, 186, 194
uncertainty, 14, 104, 109, 154, 178, 187, 206, 223 n. 7
Usmani, Shabbir Ahmad, 95–98, 215 n. 1

virtual, 207
voice, 1, 29, 66, 117, 130, 134, 159, 197

Wahhabi, 35, 185
Wahid, Abdul, 174, 188–92
wahy, 4
waliullah, 2, 133. See also shrine, of saints
Waliullah, Shah, 80
Walled City, 38, 41
waqf, 23, 31, 210 n. 4

The Will to Power (Nietzsche), 175, 179
wonderment, 197–98

Yathrib. See Medina
youth: Ahmadi, 106; contra elders, 196; of the future, 67; as inner child, 198; Muslim, 12, 84

Zaman, Muhammad Qasim, 183
Zardari, Asif, 205–6
zikr, 28
ziyarat, 3
zombification, 168
Zoroastrianism, 65; as Magian culture, 69

Naveeda Khan is assistant professor of anthropology at Johns Hopkins University. She is the
editor of *Beyond Crisis: Reevaluating Pakistan* (2010).
Her articles have appeared in *Cultural Anthropology*,
Social Text, *Anthropological Theory*, *Theory and Event*,
CSSH, among other journals and edited volumes.
In her current research, Naveeda moves from the
study of everyday religiosity in urban Pakistan to
the perception of weather on silt islands within the
river system in Bangladesh.

Library of Congress Cataloging-in-Publication Data
Khan, Naveeda Ahmed
Muslim becoming : aspiration and skepticism in
Pakistan / Naveeda Khan.
p. cm.
Includes bibliographical references and index.
ISBN 978-0-8223-5217-4 (cloth : alk. paper)
ISBN 978-0-8223-5231-0 (pbk. : alk. paper)
1. Islam—Pakistan. 2. Muslims—Pakistan. 3. Iqbal,
Muhammad, Sir, 1877–1938. 4. Islam and state—
Pakistan. I. Title.
BP63.P2K485 2012
306.6'97095491—dc23
2011041906